Explorations in Art and Technology

Springer
London
Berlin
Heidelberg
New York
Barcelona
Hong Kong
Milan
Paris
Singapore
Tokyo

Linda Candy and Ernest Edmonds

Explorations in
Art and Technology

 Springer

Linda Candy, BA, MPhil, PhD
Ernest Edmonds, BSc, MSc, PhD, FBCS, FIEE, CEng
Creativity and Cognition Research Studios, Loughborough University,
Leicestershire, LE11 3TU, UK

Graphic Design: Emma Candy
Front Cover Image by Michael Quantrill and Dave Everitt
'Before the Peony' 1999: art work translating movement density through an interactive sensor space.

British Library Cataloguing in Publication Data
Candy, Linda
  Explorations in art and technology
  1. Art and technology 2. Human-computer interaction
  I. Title II. Edmonds, Ernest A.
  700.1'05
ISBN 1852335459

Library of Congress Cataloging-in-Publication Data
A catalog record for this book is available from the Library of Congress

ISBN 1-85233-545-9 Springer-Verlag Berlin Heidelberg New York
A member of BertelsmannSpringer Science+Business Media GmbH
http://www.springer.co.uk

Typesetting: Electronic text files prepared by authors and Gray Publishing, Tunbridge Wells, UK.
Printed and bound at The Cromwell Press, Trowbridge, Wiltshire
34/3830-543210 Printed on acid-free paper SPIN 10845452

In Memory of Roy Stringer

www.roystringer.com

Foreword

I was born in 1947, the year before American artist Charles Biederman published *Art as the Evolution of Visual Knowledge*. In that central year of the twentieth century he gave art a focal place in the new scholarship of consciousness and cognition. Now, at the dawn of a new millennium, some scientists suggest that art is one of the few activities that distinguish homo sapiens from our hominid ancestors. It would seem that art is not only a powerful and uniquely human language that helps us engage with and comprehend and communicate our universe: perhaps it is art amongst all human endeavours that defines who we are.

With the advent of the computer and in the context of the twentieth century international art and technology movement, many artists began to explore the boundaries of cybernetics, cognition and artificial intelligence. In the late 1960s and 1970s some were amongst the pioneers who defined an entirely new field of study now know as artificial life. By the end of the century we were using terms like computational paradigm to describe the proliferating knowledge base that had been uniquely enabled by digital technology.

And now, some 50 years after Biederman's pioneering publication it is possible to bring together some of the key practitioners whose work has helped define the intersection of art and technology. All have been associated in some way with the Creativity and Cognition Research Studio (C&CRS) programme at Loughborough University.

It is perhaps apt that a university that was founded in the 1960s in a small English market town should have provided the venue for one of the world's most dynamic interdisciplinary research programmes addressing this exciting area. I grow ever disenchanted by the traditional universities – those lumbering dinosaurs with their fortress faculties designed only to defend discipline against discipline whose economic rationalism both undermines and actively discourages collaboration whilst simultaneously ossifying the past at the expense of the future.

The dualism invoked by CP Snow's "two cultures" is at last being eroded. A new synthesis is emerging, slowly to be sure, but wasn't it Kuhn himself who suggested that "disciplines change when old men die"? But disciplines *are* changing: science is accommodating the qualitative and art the quantitative. We can no longer hold dear to the modernist and simplistic grand narratives of science as the logical 'left brain' expression of human endeavour and of art as the lateral 'right lobe' activity.

In their introductory chapters, Linda Candy and Ernest Edmonds provide a valuable background and introduction to the book's themes. They plot a history of art and science collaborations and trace the origins and context of the C&CRS. Much of the work of the centre has investigated the technological needs of artists and how to meet them. Several of the chapters describe projects they have undertaken. These are complemented by essays by pioneers and practitioners whose work has helped define the field and its achievements and needs.

Art and technology were associated with the period of late modernism in the twentieth century. The field suffered when it was rejected by the youthful and aggressive post-modernists who, like all children, deny their heritage. However, I am glad to see that this important historical contribution is being re-addressed and re-contextualized by a more mature generation who can now acknowledge the continuity of history and the connectivity of ideas.

These essays make an exceptional and essential publication. I am grateful to the authors whose commitment and effort over several decades has made such a book possible. It comes at an important time and will provide a valuable keystone reference. The historical contributions are especially welcome. Some of the pioneers have already returned their elements to the matrix. Soon it will no longer be possible to write about this period in the first person singular.

Paul Brown
The Sunshine Coast
February 2002

Any sufficiently advanced technology is indistinguishable from magic.
Arthur C. Clarke, 1962: Profiles of the Future

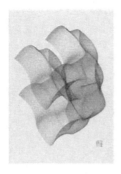  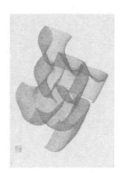

I did not want
answers that might
show up on the
monitor seemingly
by magic.
Michael Kidner, 1996

Art does not reproduce the visible:
rather, it makes visible.
Paul Klee, 1958: Inward Vision

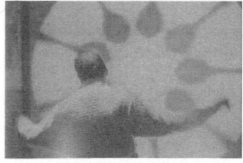

Digital technology
may enable what is
already there to
be seen.
Michael Quantrill, 1999

Preface

Imagine a scene: in a darkened room a moving image is projected onto a large screen. In front of it, several people are moving rapidly in different directions, waving their arms and simultaneously watching the screen. They might be laughing or chatting to one another or quietly observing the shapes, colours and sounds that are continually changing as if in reaction to the movements of those present. As a matter of fact that is exactly what is happening. In today's world of art and technology this is an interactive or 'participatory' art experience. Together, artists and technologists have created spaces in which infra–red sensors detect people's movements and by detecting the movements in the space, a computer generates visual images and sounds which are displayed so that everyone can see the artwork as it evolves.

Experiments in art that involve audience participation have been taking place for some time and, because they subvert conventional expectations about the nature of art, they can appear in unexpected quarters and sometimes in disguise. The Millennium Dome of the Year 2000 in London received extensive media coverage and was the butt of many jokes. Some things, however, escaped press attention. One, in particular, is an interesting reflection on our current ideas of what is art and what is play. Few of the thousands who crowded into the Play Zone realized that the games they were enjoying were originally experiments in art. The innovative art and technology projects that gave rise to the Iamascope were direct descendants of Cybernetic Serendipity, the groundbreaking computer art show of 1968.

Interest in play and games is now a common theme in art. It might take the form of a sculpture that invites touching or climbing, as well as viewing, or a community project initiated by an artist, but created by people living in the same building who record their daily experiences in text and images. There are even computer games designed by artists. The link between play and art is participation. Participation in interactive art brings with it the kind of engagement in the creative process that is normally denied the art viewing public. Interaction is central to art practice today but is not part of conventional gallery culture. The new art and technology experiences do not necessarily fit comfortably into familiar cultural contexts. Being in interactive spaces is engaging and interesting. Children and adults too can have fun with this kind of experimental art. It is one example of the new forms and the new audience relationships that are developing at the intersection of art and technology.

This book is an exploration of creative practice in art and technology. It brings together artists, technologists and researchers who have written about emerging correspondences between virtual and physical worlds, between human and machine processes, between abstract concepts and their physical realizations, between music and visualization and between film and painting. It is a story of new visions and new forms.

Digital art is not always recognized by the conventions of traditional art culture. It has a different character and form that means it is not necessarily reliant upon the usual outlets for artworks such as the public and commercial gallery system. The digital world lends itself to new modes of dissemination and, indeed, many of the practitioners are attracted to it for that very reason. The Internet, the vast system of computers that form a communicating network throughout the world, has opened up many access and delivery options for art.

The book arose from research into the intersection of art and technology through a series of artist-in-residence projects. Artists worked with technologists to develop new artworks whilst researchers gathered information in order to learn as much as possible about the creative processes involved. A practice–based action research approach was used to investigate the creative process in a real context and as it takes place. One aim was to learn how to evolve strategies for developing responsive environments for art and technology innovation. We learn that creative practice offers new challenges and inspirations for the technologist as well as the artist and that artist and technologist need to find imaginative ways forward together if they are to realize their ambitions and gain mutual benefit. Most important, successful collaboration involves developing effective and personal partnerships that sustain creativity over time.

There are significant changes in art practice taking place as a result of the potential that digital technology offers. Artists are facing considerable demands upon artistic concepts and art making skills alike. It is those very challenges that make it exciting. Digital technology can perform a number of roles in art practice: it can act as an aid to the artist by making multi-dimensional visualizations of an image; it can perform a direct role in the artwork itself by controlling movement or sound or a combination of elements; it can carry out instructions to create the contours and configuration of a work by generating instructions for laser cuttings or high quality screen-printing. Some of the artists represented in this book combine all these roles of the technology in their work. All are using the unique characteristics of digital technology to advance their art practice. This collection of experiences and viewpoints provides a picture of this changing world as it is taking place at the start of the twenty-first century.

A Note of Thanks

The contributors to this book are associated with Creativity and Cognition Research Studios either as artist-in-residents, speakers or exhibitors. We wish to thank them for their participation in those events and for their co-operation in the production of this book. We would also like to acknowledge many other people who could not make a written contribution but who, nevertheless, played significant roles in the work that gave rise to the book: thank you to Helmut Bez, Rob Doyle, Pip Greasely, Antonia Kelly, Peter Lowe, Simon Nee, Mike North, Kip Sahnsi, Sarah Tierney, Greg Turner, Paul Wormald and Bill Marshall. We would also like to mention the people active in the fields of art, technology and human-computer interaction whose support we have enjoyed over the years. The lively exchanges of views and, of course, the personal friendships that have developed, have contributed to our work in so many ways: with thanks to Ken Baynes, Steve Bell, Maggie Boden, Paul Brown, Nigel Cross, Anita Cross, Ben Shneiderman, Bronac Ferran, Gerhard Fischer, John Gero, Bryan Lawson, Kenji Mase, Marvin Minsky, Kumiyo Nakakoji, Patricia Railing, Doug Riecken, Steve Scrivener and Steve Willats. Finally, we are most grateful to Meroë Candy, Judith Mottram, Tom Hewett and Ingrid Holt whose thoughtful comments and useful tips helped us hone the ideas and the writing.

Funding support was provided from the following organizations:

Loughborough University: The School of Art and Design, Department of Computer Science and Department of Design and Technology.
The Arts Council of England
East Midlands Regional Arts, UK
National Association for Fine Art Education in collaboration with the National Arts Association: Access to Art Colleges Scheme (AA2A)
Year of the Artist (YOTA) National Lottery Scheme, UK
Higher Education Funding Council of England and Wales (HEFCE)
Engineering and Physical Sciences Research Council, UK (EPSRC)
Silicon Graphics Ltd
Drexel University USA: Department of Psychology and Department of Mathematics and Computer Science.

Linda Candy and Ernest Edmonds
February 2002

Contents

Part 1

Part 2

16.   Working with Artists: Manumaya Uniyal   161

17.   Creating Graspable Water in Three-Dimensional Space: 167
        Joan Ashworth

18.   The Artist as Digital Explorer: Dave Everitt   173

19.   Hybrid Invention: Beverley Hood   179

20.   Contemporary Totemism: Jean-Pierre Husquinet   185

21.   The Illusion and Simulation of Complex Motion: Fré Ilgen   191

22.   The Computer: An Intrusive Influence: Michael Kidner   197

23.   Switched On: Marlena Novak   205

24.   The Color Organ and Collaboration: Jack Ox   211

25.   Digital Spirituality: Anthony Padgett   219

26.   Integrating Computers as Explorers in Art Practice: 225
        Michael Quantrill

27.   Deconstructing the Norm: Juliet Robson   231

28.   Shifting Spaces: Esther Rolinson   237

29.   Going Somewhere Else: Ray Ward   243

30.   New Directions for Art and Technology: George Whale   249

31.   Defining Interaction: Linda Candy   261

        Biographical Notes   267

        Bibliography   281

        Index   283

        Colour Plates   289

Part 1

Context

It is no longer enough to speak of the convergence or reciprocity of art and science ...but to specify which art and which science, and, by what means they might fruitfully interact. Roy Ascott

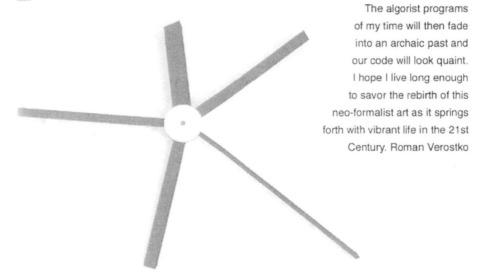

The algorist programs of my time will then fade into an archaic past and our code will look quaint. I hope I live long enough to savor the rebirth of this neo-formalist art as it springs forth with vibrant life in the 21st Century. Roman Verostko

  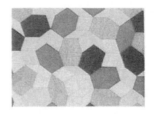

And this isn't merely a technological revolution. We are being swept forward in an accelerating cultural revolution of unprecedented scale. Harold Cohen

1   Context

In the popular mind, computers have a poor reputation when it comes to creativity. Until the invention of the World Wide Web, they were associated mainly with calculations, science, banking and word processing. However, from the early days of computers, some people have always been interested in using them to create art. In 1963 the magazine, *Computers and Automation* began its annual competition on computer art. Computer graphics were publicly exhibited as art by Georg Nees[1] at the Studio Galerie, University of Stuttgart in January, 1965. The exhibition, which was opened by Max Bense,[2] showed works produced with a graph plotter and generated by computer programs written by Nees himself. Later in the same year, A. Michael Noll and Bela Julesz[3] showed computer graphics at the Howard Wise Gallery in New York and, in November, Frieder Nake[4] exhibited his computer graphics at the Wendelin Niedlich Galerie, also in Stuttgart. He recalls that distant beginning and the personalities involved later in this chapter. For a few people, at least, a new era had really begun.

Some of the outcomes of the early explorations in computers in art were shown at the Cybernetic Serendipity exhibition held at the Institute for Contemporary Art in London in 1968 [1]. It was curated by Jasia Reichardt who also produced one of the first books on the subject, *The Computer in Art* in 1971 [2]. The 1965 exhibitions, the 1968 Cybernetic Serendipity event and Reichardt's 1971 book all demonstrated the coming together of technologists and artists in collaborations of one form or another. Sometimes it was hard to know who was the artist and who was the technologist, a distinction that was, perhaps, irrelevant in any case.

In her book, Reichardt associates concrete poetry and computer art as art movements that had no masterpieces associated with them, but nevertheless, are significant both socially and artistically:

> The salient points are that both these movements are international, that they are motivated by the use of media, technique and method, rather than an ideology, and that those participating in them come from a variety of professions, disciplines and walks of life. Not all concrete poets are in facts poets, and very few so-called computer artists are in fact what we usually mean by "artists" [2, p. 7].

A case in point is Frieder Nake, Professor of Computer Graphics, who, showed his work in one of the 1965 exhibitions.

Personal Recollections of a Distant Beginning by Frieder Nake

On an afternoon in late January 1965, Max Bense had invited the usual crowd of intellectuals, artists, and hangers-on to his Studiengalerie up in the ivory tower that housed his institute of philosophy at the University of Stuttgart. Bense was well-known, by that time, to a dedicated international group of avant-garde artists, writers, and thinkers for his critical rationalism and, in particular, his theory of information aesthetics. Shannon and Weaver's concept of information defined the background for attempts by Bense and his students to invent quantitative measures of the aesthetics of objects.

Many artists had exhibited their works, or had read their texts, in the Studiengalerie. It had become a place for all those who shared the view that generating works of art ("aesthetic objects") was as rational an activity as anything in the natural sciences. Now the announcement of this *vernissage* promised something really new, something never (or hardly ever) heard of computer-generated art.

Georg Nees, a mathematician at Siemens in Erlangen, exhibited a small set of no more than ten line drawings. A little brochure appeared for the occasion in the series *rot* (no. 19 of the series). It contained six reproductions of computer drawings accompanied by short descriptions of the algorithmic essence of each of the graphics. The brochure also carried a text in the style of a manifesto by Bense: "Projects of generative aesthetics".

A flock of artists from the Stuttgart Academy of Fine Arts, and from the city were present. Among them, if I recall correctly, Anton Stankowski, Heinz Trökes, K.R.H. Sonderborg, Herbert W. Kapitzki. Some of them became nervous, hostile, furious. Some left. If these pictures were done by use of a computer, how could they possibly be art? The idea was ridiculous! Where was the inspiration, the intuition, the creative act? What the heck could be the message of these pictures? They were nothing but black straight lines on white paper, combined into simple geometric shapes. Variations, combinatorics, randomness. Indeed, randomness had played an important role in the generative process whereby a digital computer had controlled a flat-bed drawing machine, the remarkable Zuse Z64 Graphomat, to output the graphics.

But even randomness, the artists learned, was not really random but only calculated pseudo-randomness, the type of randomness possible on a digital computer. A fake, from start to end, christened as art!

Max Bense, observing the unrest among his guests and friends, was provocative as always but, at the same time, made an attempt to dampen their protests. He quickly invented the term "artificial art" to distinguish the computer products from human pictures. A great idea, it seems to me: generative art was artificial art. Chomsky's generative grammar and Minsky's artificial intelligence were combined into a new approach to one of the most cherished human endeavors. The birth of digital art became the birth of artificial art. In 1965, in Stutttgart, a new page in the book of artificiality was turned over.

For me as a young and innocent witness of the scene, all this was exciting and puzzling. How seriously these famous people seemed to be taking something that, to me, was everyday and business as usual. Only a few kilometres away from the location of this worldwide first exhibition of computer art, at the computing center of the university, I had programmed drawings quite similar to some of George Nees'. Sets, bundles, and structures of straight lines, determined by calculated randomness and put on paper by a computer controlled drawing device – it existed all up there, at the centre, too. It had been my job as a student assistant to develop from scratch a basic program package to control the same Graphomat drawing machine that Nees had access to, but from a different computer platform. This job was finished by mid 1964. As one set of test pictures, I had chosen random line patterns of different kinds.

Now I discovered that elsewhere, others had had similar ideas. But to top this, Nees had dared to exhibit the works and claim they were fine art, albeit only artificial art. Why then shouldn't I dare do the same?

I approached Wendelin Niedlich, a bookseller, art gallery owner, and cultural institution in Stuttgart. To my surprise, he agreed to mount a show later that year. So in November of 1965, a second exhibition of computer generated art took place in Stuttgart. The set that Georg Nees had shown earlier was included as an add-on to an exhibition of a substantially larger collection of my works. Around the time I learned that, in the USA, A. Michael Noll and Bela Julesz had had a show at the Howard Wise Gallery in New York already in April that same year. Noll was awarded the first prize of the computer art contest of the journal, *Computers and Automation*, in August 1965. So 1965 marks the year of three such events.

The press, television, some art colleges, symposia got interested in what I did. A great time started for a young mathematician who had become an artist. In 1966, *Computers and Automation* honoured me with the first prize in their contest. In 1969, Georg Nees published his doctoral dissertation. It became the first ever, I believe, on computer art. Max Bense had been his advisor.

Projects in generative art played a role motivating Jasia Reichardt to assemble that now historic show, Cybernetic Serendipity, at the Institute of Contemporary Art in London, in the summer of 1968. By far not as well known is a series of symposia, exhibitions, even an international journal (*BIT International*) that were initiated and directed by the late Boris Kelemen and his colleagues at the Galleries of the City of Zagreb, Yugoslavia. Concrete and constructivist art then met emerging computer art in a socialist country. The country doesn't exist any more. How about the art?

Frieder Nake, University of Bremen, 2001

The 1965 exhibitions and Cybernetic Serendipity were not the only signs in the 1960s of the emerging importance of the computer in the arts. The interdisciplinary art, science and technology journal, *Leonardo*, was founded in 1967. Subsequently, in 1969, the Computer Arts Society was formed in London to "promote the creative use of computers in the arts". This society staged Event One and began a lively debate through its bulletin, *Page* which continued into the 1980s [3].

In 1966, Billy Kluver founded Experiments in Art and Technology-(E.A.T.), in New York [4]. He had been Assistant Professor of Electrical Engineering at the University of California at Berkeley, and was subsequently at Bell Telephone Laboratories. In the early 1960s, he collaborated with artists on works of art incorporating new technology, including Jean Tinguely, Jasper Johns, Yvonne Rainer, Robert Rauschenberg, John Cage and Andy Warhol. Garnet Hertz[5] interviewed him about E.A.T. in 1995. That interview forms the next section.

An Interview with Billy Kluver by Garnet Hertz

Garnet Hertz: In an attempt to bring technologists and artists together, Experiments in Art and Technology was formed in 1966. E.A.T., as the group was called, existed to link artists and engineers in collaborative projects. The apparently impossible gap of engineering and art was explicitly spanned for the first time. At the forefront of this movement was the electrical engineer Billy Kluver, a PhD in electrical engineering, who was equally involved in the contemporary art scene.

To get to the historical bottom of E.A.T. and the art and technology movement, I tracked down Billy Kluver in New York. Still directing E.A.T. after thirty years, he shared with me his memories, thoughts, and goals.

H: What were some of the original ideas and goals in the formation of E.A.T.?

Billy Kluver: The goal from the beginning was to provide new materials for artists in the form of technology. A shift happened because, from my own experience, I had worked in 1960 with Tinguely to do the machine that destroyed itself in the Garden of MoMA. At that time I employed – or coerced – a lot of my co-workers at Bell Labs to work on the project.

When I saw that, I realized that the engineers could help the artists; the engineers themselves could be the materials for the artists. After the event, I got besieged by a lot of artists in New York like Andy Warhol, Robert Rauschenberg, Jasper Johns-all of them. Robert Whitman and Rauschenberg put the notion together that it should be a collaboration between artists and engineers, where they were equally represented. The idea was that a one to one collaboration could produce something that neither of the two could individually foresee. And that was the basis for the whole thing, and the system developed from there.

We had to do a lot of 'propaganda' because in the 1960s the difference between art and engineering was an enormous canyon. We understood that we had to recruit engineers – that was the barrier we had to go through.

This whole thing spread within a year or two all over the United States. So, when an artist phoned in and said: "I have this problem" we had one person on the staff that would find an engineer to help them out – and that was it.

The other thing that we did from the very beginning was organize large projects. The first one of course was NINE EVENINGS in 1966, out of which

E.A.T. actually came. The main breakthrough in NINE EVENINGS was scale. Everybody in New York was there. Practically every artist in New York helped make it a go, and about 10,000 spectators saw it. Since then we have initiated 40-50 projects, the last one happening last summer in Northern Greenland. So those are the two operations of E.A.T.: matching and making projects.

H: I have a quote here... "Kluver saw many parallels between contemporary art and science, both of which were concerned basically with the investigation of life...a vision of American technological genius humanized and made wiser by the imaginative perception of artists..." Does that accurately describe your goal?

K: Well, it could be said better than that...The way I see it is that artists provide non-artists − engineers or whomever − a certain number of things which non-artists do not possess. The engineer expands his vision and gets involved with problems which are not the kind of rational problems that come up in his daily routine. And the engineer becomes committed because it becomes a fascinating technological problem that nobody else would have raised.

If the engineer gets involved with the kinds of questions that an artist would raise, then the activities of the engineer go closer towards that of humanity... Now, this is all sort of philosophical − in practice, it has to do with doing it.

H: So, is technology a transparent medium that artists should be able to use... there's not really a moral side to technology?

K: Well, no. The artists have shaped technology. They have helped make technology more human. They automatically will because they're artists. That's by definition. If they do something it automatically comes out human. There's no way you can come out and say that if art is the driving force in a technological situation then it will come out with destructive ideas. That's not possible. But what happens, of course, is that the artist widens the vision of the engineer.

H: And so artists can provide a conscience or humanizing element to the technology?

K: Yes, that's what I mean... but that's saying it too much. There might be other consciousness that comes from other sources than art. I think there is a huge consciousness inside technology that hasn't been tapped.

H: It seemed like the whole art and technology movement of the late 1960s seemed to lose some of its initial momentum in the 1970s − at least that's the impression that the postmodern texts give.

K: The texts are horrible. One of the amusing things is that they tell us we've done things we never did. But, on the question of the momentum − already in the first newsletter, we said that if we were successful we would disappear. We would disappear because there is really no function like E.A.T. that needs to exist in society if we were successful. It would be perfectly natural for an artist to be able to contact an engineer him or herself. If it was natural, why should we be involved? And that's what we have stated from the beginning – and of course, that is what has happened. The universities, the computer graphic societies, artist societies, and organizations like your own – it was inevitable.

People in New York wanted us to move in, to set up labs with all of the equipment, but we constantly refused. It was not a matter of institutionalizing. I'm very pleased that the initial attitude was like that because it meant that we could still exist. To institutionalize anything in this area is dangerous and self-destructive. It's just a matter of solving problems, and you can do that forever.

H: It makes sense that people who are critical of E.A.T. have misinterpreted it as being very institutionalized when in reality, it is quite the opposite.

K: The main thing is that we never anticipated the growth in the late sixties – and you had to take care of it – so you needed a staff. Everybody then immediately thought "Oh my God, they're making a lot of money". Actually, you can't believe all of the debts that we had. I saved E.A.T. by selling every artwork I had, not by making money. I sold things that would have made me a billionaire if I would have held on to them.

H: How do you "match" artists through E.A.T.?

K: Almost anybody who calls us, we help. I never ask to see people's paintings or anything that they do. Usually the conversation starts off with "I have a problem..." After that, I always ask the same three questions when somebody calls me about something: (1) How big is it, (2) How many people are going to see it, and (3) Is it inside or outside? If there is no answer to any one of these three questions – like "It could be as big as you want", or "It could be inside or outside" – you know that he or she has no idea of what they're doing. They haven't taken into account the reality of the project. If you can get down to the reality of the problem, you can usually solve it in a few minutes. It's amazing how simple it is to find the answer.

While matching, I always have the artist call the engineer directly. There is a lot of intimidation there in the first place. E.A.T.'s most important role is to eliminate the initial intimidation. Once the engineer and the artist get to talk together – if there is anything there – it will happen. If there isn't, it will die in ten seconds. It's happened that way for over thirty years.

H: So there's no mission of E.A.T. overtaking the art scene...

K: Overtake? It's already been overtaken. Namely that people can talk about it without being terrified. This has been what I've said since the early sixties. Nobody then could believe that an artist could talk to an engineer...For example, do you know the group called SRL?

H: Yeah, Survival Research Laboratories with Mark Pauline...

K: We talk now and then. I see them as being brilliant – just totally brilliant. He is of the next generation and he understands the business of "getting things done". And that's what it's all about – GETTING IT DONE – that's the key to all of it. Artists will often be intimidated by "Oh, it's a problem" – they think a power plug is an enemy.

H: So, what if somebody were to call you the "Godfather of Technology and Art"?

K: Well, I guess in a way it's probably true. However, Tatlin is to me the real Godfather – the constructivist artist. That group embraced technology, and embraced it in terms of art.
   Many people wanted E.A.T. to be about art and science, but I insisted it be art and technology. Art and science have really nothing to do with each other. Science is science and art is art. Technology is the material and the physicality. However, as far as that goes – other people would have to agree with you, but I think that's probably true – that I would be the Godfather of Art and Technology.

Interview date: 19 April 1995

Systems into Art

The period from the mid to late 1960s was an exciting time in experimental art. Frieder Nake demonstrates both the energy of the time and the tensions between the technologist and artist roles. Kluver even says that "nobody then could believe that an artist could talk to an engineer". This tension between technology and art remains, in a lesser form, even today. In many ways it is a persistent theme in this book. To a few people in the 1960s and to many today, however, it is seen as a creative tension driving forward the development of new art.

   Both Frieder Nake and Billy Kluver refer to the artistic tradition of Constructivism[6]. New movements in Russian art in the early part of the twentieth century provides an important context to the arrival of new technology in art. An even earlier starting point for the story of computers in art could be Malevich's essay of 1919, *On New Systems in Art* [5]. In it, he introduces the notion of making art with the help of "a law for the constructional inter-relationships of forms", by which he meant the language, or system of form, rather than representations of the visual world. Patricia Railing, in *From Science to Systems of Art* [6] shows how Malevich looked towards science to give a formal basis to his art. Developments of such notions were widespread in the twentieth century, for example, in a discussion of the influences on British Systems movement, Stephen Bann says:

It is not the recurrence of the rectangle in Van Doesburg's work which needs
to engage us, but the series of relationships between rectangles and the extent to which those relationships can be adequately formalised. [7]

Malevich's insight into science and systems came well before the advent of computers, but at a time when mathematical logicians were developing theories that proved to be very important for the invention of
the computer. This work on mathematical logic was investigating particular kinds of systems, known as formal systems These are sets of precise rules that apply to finite sets of objects rather like the rules of chess
and the chess pieces. Such systems are fundamental in computer programming. A computer is basically a logical machine that manipulates
systems of symbols. The symbols have formal rules that determine how
they relate to one another, rather as the pieces on a chess board can be
placed in very many different arrangements, but only ones in which certain rules are obeyed. When a computer manipulates such a system, it
automatically moves the pieces, keeping within the rules, and searches
for a result, such as check-mate. Another example of such a system is a
collection of shapes with defined correspondences between them, such as
a Lego^{TM} set [8]. In effect, the computer can rearrange the pieces in any
way, but only so that the rules, that determine how they fit, are followed.

The output that a computer produces, be it text, sounds, drawings or
movement, is generated by a mapping from a set of internal symbols to a
set of physical entities such as marks, sounds or actions. The internal
symbols, in turn, are determined by the operation of a formal system. For
all its ability to calculate quickly or put images on screens or paper, it is
the operation of formal systems that is at the core of what is unique
about the computer.

For artists with an interest in systems, the computer was a natural and
irresistible medium to explore. Whilst a role for logical systems in art is
both possible and interesting, the concrete realization of formal systems
in logical machines, i.e. computers, brought new possibilities into play.
The formal systems became dynamic as, in effect, they became expressed
in computer programs. Whereas before, formal systems were abstract and
manipulated by human action, now a machine existed that could perform
such manipulation automatically. It became possible, for example, to
build machines that could play chess. This meant that an important step
forward from Malevich's concept of systems in art was taken by the artists who adopted programming in the 1960s. Each of them approached
the subject from his or her personal point of view and not all of them
would use the term 'system' in relation to their art, but if they programmed, they certainly used a system in practice.

Recent Developments

In the last part of the twentieth century, there was a remarkable growth in technology and art. Many organizations have been formed and the number of artists involved with digital technology has multiplied. By the 1980s, YLEM (Artists in Science and Technology) had been formed in Palo Alto, California [9]; Electra, a large exhibition of electricity and electronics in the art of the twentieth century, was held in Paris [10]; and the artists' initiative V2 [11], in Rotterdam, made the exploration of the impact of technology on society central to its work. In 1987, Ars Electronica in Linz, Austria, began the Prix Ars Electronica. Each year, juries of international experts award highly prestigious prizes to artists working in a wide range of digital media. The Ars Electronica Centre, with its Museum of the Future, has recently opened [12]. Another important organization is ZKM (Zentrum für Kunst und Medientechnologie) in Karslruhe, Germany, which combines dedicated exhibiting space with research and library facilities, all dedicated to art and digital media [13]. The NTT-InterCommunication Centre in Tokyo is equally active in high-value and high standard exhibitions, competitions and meetings on art and technology [14]. The research in art and technology that has been undertaken at the Advanced Telecommunications Research Institute (ATR) in Kyoto is particularly notable because it is grounded in a technological world into which artists have entered as full collaborators and, in some cases, as project leaders [15].

At ATR, new technologies were developed with, and by artists, at the same time as new art forms were evolved. This investigation into art and technology was not an easy research project especially in Japan. It was not a main project but operated as a sub-project of the Media Integration and Communications Research Laboratories (MIC). The exposure to the public was enormous. In that sense, it was successful in demonstrating an innovative research direction and many other sub-projects at MIC were influenced. Naoko Tosa and Christa Sommerer and Laurent Mignonneau had to fit into the MIC projects in certain ways that they were able to demonstrate: for Tosa – non-verbal interaction with character agents; for Sommerer and Mignonneau – A-life and augmented reality (cyber space) interaction. Some installations were successful as art, but some were not. However, they demonstrated that serious technological research can be undertaken in an art–technology context.

Today, the initiatives in this area are growing every day and it is well beyond the scope of this book to survey all the important and large centres that have been established since the 1960s.

Organizations promoting digital art have arisen from a wide variety of backgrounds, including the visual arts, music, performance and film. Each of these starting points brings with it its own critical framework and orientation with respect to art and technology. The conceptual paths represented by performance and film, for example, have also embraced digital technology and offer their own perspective. In fact, computer generated films were made at Bell Laboratories from the early 1960s. Time, as employed in film and performance, as well as interaction and participation, are particularly significant in the context of the computer. These possibilities have come to the fore most strongly in the recent past now that the power of the computer is sufficient for many of the early dreams to be realized. Computers are important for art practice in many different ways and in relation to a wide range of media.

The media that are used in digital art apply to many art forms, including painting, performance, film and participation. Where the medium is static such as printing, the technology issues concerned with the output devices (e.g. printers, video projection) are well understood. However, the situation is quite complex when it comes to interactive art work. Here, we are concerned with the way that the technology behaves, as well as, for example, how it looks.

There are many pathways to the development of innovation in art and technology and the organizations mentioned above have different agendas and frameworks that influence the particular approach adopted. The experiences in art and technology exploration that underpin this book spring from a field with a multi-disciplinary character. Human–Computer Interaction (HCI) combines new developments in interactive digital technology with research into the associated human issues [16].

Our understanding of the creative process is based on studies in science and design and, more recently, in art. In order to bring practice and research together in our search for more knowledge about the creative process in art and technology, it was necessary to create an organizational context in which new developments in the field could take place and research could be undertaken in parallel.

Creativity and Cognition

The background to the development of an environment for bringing art and technology together began with ideas and initiatives raised in key meetings at the Creativity and Cognition conferences [17]. The conference series has helped to develop a community and led to the formation of the Creativity and Cognition Research Studios (C&CRS) [18] where digital artist-in-residence programmes have enabled artists and technologists to work on collaborative projects. These programmes enabled an investigation into the requirements for an environment in which digital art can be produced, using the practice-based action research approach discussed later in Chapter 3.

From Conference to Environment

The idea for the Creativity and Cognition conferences began on a small Dutch island, Terschelling, at a New Year gathering at the end of 1991. Many in the group were artists, while others studied creativity or the creative use of computers. The idea came from reflection during this gathering a series of meetings held throughout the world in the preceding four years. One was held in 1989, during a small conference on Heron Island on the Great Barrier Reef called Modeling Creativity and Knowledge-Based Creative Design [19]. Others took place in the same year at the exhibition, Constructivism versus Computer, and at the associated PRO Foundation conference, which took place in Rotterdam [20]. Some of these meetings considered questions about the modelling of creativity in the computer or the role of smart computer systems in creative work, such as design. Others looked at art or design practice and theory and the implications of the evolving computer-based technologies.

The problem that was identified in Terschelling was that the two groups, one might say the scientists and the artists, did not meet together. The computer-oriented meetings were not informed by creative practitioners and the art-based meetings were not informed by computer experts. The Creativity and Cognition series was created in order to bring all of the participants together.

The first Creativity and Cognition meeting was held in 1993 and the second in 1996 [21, 22]. Both succeeded in bringing together lively and active people from the different fields of art and science, enabling experts from one field to mix with experts from other fields. This very fact meant that many well-worn assumptions had to be abandoned or, more often, be justified anew.

With the 1999 and 2002 meetings the series has matured and is now running as Association of Computing Machinery (ACM) Special Interest Group in Computer–Human Interaction (SIGCHI) sponsored events [23]. ACM SIGCHI is the special interest group in Human–Computer Interaction, which is part of the Association for Computing Machinery, the largest international association devoted to the subject of computing. As well as meeting at the conferences, artists and technologists also came together in collaborative projects. An initial artist-in-residence programme preceded the 1996 Creativity and Cognition conference.

Creativity and Cognition Research Studios (C&CRS)

C&CRS was established in 1998 as a joint venture between the School of Art and Design and the Department of Computer Science at Loughborough University, England. The ethos of C&CRS is to make the art practice the central focus of the work and to give artists equal status with technologists. C&CRS provides an environment where artists and technologists work as collaborators in the exploration of art and technology. The main goals are:

- to create a strategy for encouraging innovation and change.
- to foster inter-disciplinary work between artists and technologists.
- to drive digital art practice in ways that are new and challenging.

The key disciplines are:

- *creative cognition*: human capability for generating and evaluating new ideas.
- *creative media*: digital technologies for enabling and encouraging creativity.
- *digital arts*: new art forms employing digital concepts and technologies.

A requirement of the C&CRS strategy is to put in place a mechanism for informing our general understanding of the technologies and creative processes involved. C&CRS facilitates new initiatives in creative digital art and, at the same time, provides a means of informing our understanding of the art practices and how to extend the technologies involved. Experts in both computer science and digital art combine to develop art and technology projects within a single organizational framework. The strategy has, at its centre, a strong requirement for multiple viewpoints both in terms of contributors to the process and in terms of what is delivered.

To gain a clearer sense of the approach, C&CRS can be compared with the PARC Artists In Residence (PAIR) programme at XeroxPARC [24]. A common goal of C&CRS and PAIR is to have a strategy in place that encourages innovation and change across the whole spectrum. However, there are significant differences in the fundamental drivers and the resulting approaches of the two programmes.

C&CRS is concerned with developing and researching innovative forms in art practice and facilitating that practice by enabling artists to work in a technical and physical environment not normally available to them. The goal is to enable new digital artwork to be developed and to study both the implications for art practice and future technologies. A key aim is to understand the requirements for support environments for creative practitioners. PAIR was used to maintain and stimulate the parent organization's culture as a fertile ground for new ideas and new forms of technological innovation. As one programme amongst many others, the primary driver was to enrich the company's scientific and product capability through a flow of new technological problems to be solved. At C&CRS, the primary aim is the co-evolution of art and technology accompanied by studies of the processes and the outcomes in order to provide a better understanding for creative practice generally.

At C&CRS, artists and technologists are developing systems for creative exploration through virtual and physical interactivity, pushing the technology and the art forward on several fronts. An understanding of the potential for supporting creativity is being pursued using the strategy of bringing in multiple knowledge contributions and generating multiple forms of output, supported by case studies of artists and technologists in collaboration.

Whatever level of computer expertise the artist might have, the issue of the influence of the use of the technological environment on creative practice is important. The characteristics of art and technology intersection and correspondence have implications for technological requirements and the environments in which new developments can take place as well as directly upon art practice. In looking at developments in the computer-based environments that increasingly support the artist we can draw upon the results of studies in many domains. In particular we will be considering what we know and what we need to find out about in relation to:

- environments for supporting the development process

- research into conditions for individual and collaborative creativity

- practitioner accounts of personal and collaborative explorations.

Notes

[1]   Georg Nees is thought to have gained the first PhD in Computer Art in 1969.
[2]   Max Bense has been credited with founding the field of Visual Semiotics.
[3]   A. Michael Noll and Bela Julesz both worked at AT&T Bell Laboratories in 1965 on visual research, communications and computer graphics.
[4]   Frieder Nake: see the biographical note.
[5]   Garnet Hetz is a Canadian artist who investigates technology and communication.
[6]   Constructivism: in its broad meaning, abstract geometric art with its origin in Russia in the early twentieth century.

References

1. Reichardt, J.: (editor) Cybernetic Serendipity: the Computer and the Arts. Studio International, London (1968)

2. Reichardt, J.: The Computer in Art. Studio Vista, London (1971)

3. Page: Bulletin on the Computer Arts Society. British Computer Society, London. (1968–1981)

4. Pontus Hultén, K.G.: The Machine, as Seen at the End of the Mechanical Age. The Museum of Modern Art, New York (1968)

5. Malevich, K. S.: On New Systems in Art. Anderson, T. (ed) Essays on Art 1915–1933. Rapp and Whiting, London (1968) 83-117

6. Railing, P.: From Science to Systems of Art. Artists' Bookworks, Forest Row, East Sussex, England (1989)

7. Bann, S.: Introduction, In Systems. Arts Council, London (1972) 5-14

8. Lego™: http://www.lego/com/

9. YLEM: http://www.ylem.org/

10. Popper, F.: Electra. Musée d'Art Moderne de la Ville de Paris, Paris (1983)

11. V2: http://www.v2.nl/index.php

12. Ars Electronica: http://www.aec.at/

13. ZKM: Zentrum für Kunst und Medientechnologie.: Hardware, Software, Artware. Cantz Verlag, Ostfildern (1997)

14. NTT-InterCommunication Centre Concept Book. NTT Publishing Company, Tokyo (1998)

15. Advanced Telecommunications Research Institute, Kyoto: http://www.mic.atr.co.jp/

16. Hewett, T.T., Baecker, R., Card, S., Carey, T., Gasen, J., Mantei, M., Perlman, G., Strong, G., and Verplank, W.: ACM SIGCHI Curricula for Human–Computer Interaction (1992)

17. Creativity and Cognition: see http://www.creativityandcognition.com

18. Creativity and Cognition Research Studios: http://creative.lboro.ac.uk/ccrs/

19. Gero, J.S. (ed): Modeling Creativity and Knowledge-Based Creative Design. University of Sydney, December (1989)

20. Constructivism versus Computer Exhibition, World Trade Centre, Rotterdam. Pro Foundation (1989)

21. Candy, L. and Edmonds, E. A.: (eds) Proceedings, 1st International Symposium on Creativity and Cognition, Loughborough University, UK (1993)

22. Candy, L. and Edmonds, E.A.: (eds) Proceedings 2nd International Symposium on Creativity and Cognition, Loughborough University (1996)

23. Candy, L. and Edmonds, E.A.: (eds) Proceedings 3rd International Symposium Creativity and Cognition, ACM Press, New York (1999)

24. Harris, C.: (ed) Art and Innovation: The Xerox PARC Artist-in-Residence Program. MIT Press, Cambridge, MA (1999)

Most artists probably need access to new technology 'doctors' or 'surgeries'...we need residencies with technical support to get projects started and then regular check ups. Joan Ashworth

I would rank people skills as paramount closely followed by technical resources and know-how. The intelligence, good will and sensitivity of the support team are vital. Peter Lowe

Whilst the conceptual developments are the key issues, the role of the technology in encouraging, enabling and inspiring them has been central. Ernest Edmonds

The ideal way is a network of resources offering a variety of opportunities, software and hardware. Beverley Hood

Developing a broad horizontal framework covering logistics like access, permissions, bookings, getting hold of the right people, basic software support and general standard software. Dave Everitt

2   Environment

The challenge in creating a strategy designed to explore the nature of the relationship between artists and scientists is to create circumstances that engender the kind of communication that leads to a successful exchange of knowledge and perspectives and to an opportunity to explore new territory. The symbiotic merging establishes a pattern of exploration, development, and innovation, as each participant responds to the other's viewpoints and areas of expertise. [1]

Intersection between art and technology in the 1960s was led by artists and computer specialists whose commitment was essential for the survival of those early ventures. It was also a time when academic equipment proved a useful resource for experimentation. From the 1980s onwards, the rapid changes in technologies presented new opportunities and demanded different approaches. Inter-disciplinary research, such as the early Xerox PARC work on user interfaces, was to have a profound effect on the take up of digital technology in the wider community. The invention of new metaphors for interaction made available in the Xerox Star, Apple Lisa and Apple Macintosh user interfaces and later, as Windows on PCs, were to open access to widespread computer use that would have been unimaginable twenty years before [2,3,4,5].

Accessible personal computing on a large scale resulted in the arrival of a new kind of participant in the digital art world. Art and design colleges began to introduce courses on digital technologies that provided artists with new media opportunities. Ironically, it could be said that the very accessibility of the new "easy to use" technology reduced the scope for innovation because there was less emphasis on learning programming languages which allowed the user to design and develop personalized systems. Software applications for image manipulation, such as Photoshop [6], gave artists tools that provided quick and easy methods for presentation of digital work. However, at the same time, they imposed a conformity of appearance that many struggled to overcome.

To be able to push the boundaries of digital art forms, it is often necessary to do the same for the technology. However, digital technology is a field over which few people have complete mastery. To overcome this problem, systematic approaches that bring together the various disciplines, practices and resource suppliers are required. This implies creating environments in which digital artwork can be developed, supported by access to appropriate human expertise as well as technological facilities and physical spaces.

The Nature of Environments

Just as a potter needs a studio with a wheel, kiln, running water and other tools, digital artists need an environment with the means to produce their works. But what kind of environment is appropriate for digital art?

Defining what makes an appropriate environment for making digital art is less easy than it might be for the potter with thousands of years of history behind him. For one thing, the digital world of today is still very new and continuously evolving. As any experienced practitioner will testify, pottery and painting are complex enough activities, taking many years to master, even for the gifted. In the digital domain of today, however, the huge variety of choices and standards, as well as the inherent difficulty of using some kinds of hardware and software, makes it particularly complex. At this time, it is hard to arrive at a stable, all-purpose environment that meets the requirements of every user.

In computing, the term environment is often used to refer to a set of software facilities for assisting the development of a digital system. Computer programmers need an editor to compose and modify the program, a compiler or interpreter to translate the program into a form that the computer can execute, and a "de-bugger" to help them search for errors in what they have done, and so on. A collection of facilities is known as a software development environment, and its precise nature critically influences the ease with which the programmer can work. Software developers argue endlessly about which environment is best and what features must, or must not, be included.

Environments in computing may incorporate hardware as well as software because, in certain cases, new hardware, or new inter-linking of existing hardware, such as robot arms, has to be achieved. This is important in relation to the artists' needs when, in particular, interactive art systems are being constructed.

As well as the computer processor and the computer screen, more conventional things, such as books and whiteboards, are important parts of the artist's working environment. Behind the screen lies the Internet, an important part of the development environment for the software designers of today. Searching the World Wide Web for help is a normal part of day-to-day practice for both artists and technologists. Even when working on a solitary activity, the Internet links them to other people, making these contacts, with various skills and knowledge, also part of the working environment.

A development environment for art and technology exploration was established at the Creativity and Cognition Research Studios with the express intention of assessing its role and identifying requirements for creativity support. The discussion that follows was informed by art and technology developments that took place over a number of years.

Co-Evolution in Environments

A fundamental requirement of an environment for creative practice is that it supports and enables the development of new forms in art and the new knowledge that is required to achieve such outcomes. The point is that creativity in art and technology requires circumstances that enhance development possibilities. The question is how do we ensure that both the art and the technology development is fostered by the environment? This question raises a number of issues about how appropriate environments are formed and we will consider them below.

In order to shape the kind of environment needed for digital art, it is necessary to begin by defining the ethos and approach required. An obvious starting point is to define the potential user requirements by addressing the artists' needs and expectations. As anyone involved in this kind of exercise knows, the apparently straightforward activity of identifying client requirements and scope of the tasks to be carried out, and then matching them with facilities and tools, is often a moving target. Nowhere is this more so than in creative digital work. The requirements gathering exercise for art-technology environments must be a highly responsive, iterative process. Only in this way is it possible to inform and shape the environment in the light of the experiences of digital art under development. This co-evolutionary process is a form of practice-based action research where the existing technology is subject to new perspectives from which technology research derives new answers. In turn, the use of new digital technology may lead to transformation of existing art forms and art practice. This approach is described further in Chapter 3.

Co-evolution requires evidence on which to base judgements and decisions. This involves the gathering of first-hand accounts of creative practice by the participants as well as records of observations of the processes involved by researchers. Based on these accounts of events and an analysis of the issues arising from them, different audiences may draw a variety of lessons. For the organizers of environments for art and technology, the issues range from software usability and fitness for purpose to physical space requirements beyond the computer laboratory.

The Technology Environment

The creation of a fully integrated system of facilities comprising equipment, devices, software and networks must be a key objective of an art and technology environment strategy. The resources available to the artists-in-residence need to include a range of expertise, accessible at short notice and a repertoire of software and hardware acquired for the specific requirements of the participants.

In the case of C&CRS, considerable preparation was carried out before artist residencies took place in order to make sure that each artist had a realistic opportunity to achieve their goals. They were also intended to help contributors learn about what is needed to make art and technology collaborations successful and, in that respect, they served the purpose well. For, although considerable effort was spent in identifying the technological infrastructure and the human skills required for each participating artist, this was never sufficient for predicting everything that would be needed in advance for all situations. It could also not anticipate unforeseen events and unexpected failures in those things we thought had been addressed. However, it was possible, by observing and monitoring closely the work in progress, to add to the knowledge needed to make art-technology collaboration a realistic prospect and, most important, to develop responsive strategies for addressing change.

In the short-term, tasks needed to be carried out in order to optimize the existing technology without incurring additional costs. At a broader level, there were important lessons to be learned about the physical and technological environments that are needed for this kind of activity and that do not necessarily come within the normal remit for computer science laboratories, art college facilities and gallery and exhibition spaces. This is new art and new technology and, in venturing into the area, new and imaginative architectures are likely to be required.

Given that an appropriate technology infrastructure is an essential basis for digital art practice, it is important to address the limitations of what is currently available. When C&CRS was first set up, the facilities and resources available at that time imposed their own constraints. A significant aspect of the response strategy was to draw upon the full resources of the university including the knowledge base of the personnel across many disciplines. Much equipment was available that had not been acquired for artistic purposes, such as virtual reality (VR) laboratories and computer aided engineering design systems. These proved useful for some digital art projects. However, most of the C&CRS artists began and finished their work in the studios where the facilities existed for use primarily in art practice. It was an important strategic decision to ensure that artists were not placed in a position of begging or borrowing from scientists and technologists with other pressing needs for the facilities. The primary reason for this was to ensure that the responsiveness to changes required by artists in the environment could be undertaken without creating conflicts in existing hardware or software configurations.

In setting up the studios, the facilities had to be heterogeneous, connected and of high quality. The computers used a variety of operating systems, including Unix, Windows NT and Apple Operating Systems. Some software could run on just one of these systems and some were cross platform. Consequently, it was sometimes necessary to move work from one type of machine to another in order to make full use of them. Naturally, everything was fully networked and connected to the Internet. The specific computers included Apple Macs, various PC models, Silicon

Graphics machines [7], including an Onyx 2 and Origin server with 600Gbytes of disc space. The Apple Mac G4, for example, is well suited to extensive image manipulation and graphics design work and the SG Onyx can handle complex 3D graphics in real time. It must be said, though, that the power of an Onyx comes at a non-financial cost, in that non-specialists can find it quite hard to use to full advantage. For that reason, the importance of human technical experts in C&CRS was helpful in some cases and vital in others.

It is also important to note that complexity and sophistication is not always desirable. Very often, artists, like mathematicians, value simplicity and elegance in what they do. Therefore, it is also important to ensure that basic facilities are included. A simple system may not have every conceivable function available within it, but for creative purposes the constraints that it imposes may be a positive stimulus to new ideas.

C&CRS technology included high quality CRT displays, a 42 inch plasma display, smaller flat panel screens, and video projection. Artists could also use a variety of printers, including a sophisticated IRIS machine [8], and connections to video and sound equipment. In retrospect, neither sound nor video was as flexible or extensive as was desirable, but otherwise the basic provision held up well when used in real practice. The software repertoire, on the other hand, was not extensive enough. Buying new packages or downloading new patches to enable the software provision to match each individual's needs was continually needed. The diversity of specific computer package skills is a continuing problem. It is clearly an advantage to capitalize on an artist's acquired skill with a particular system, but it may not be the best system and, more significantly, the technical experts may not have sufficient knowledge of it. Hence the requirement for a broad base of expertise in various software applications outside the core support that can be drawn upon as needed.

Beyond the provision of a standard range of systems and output devices, digital artists often wanted the computer to control or affect something not normally attached to it, such as a light bulb, a slide projector or, perhaps, a waving flag. Equally, they wanted the computer's behaviour to be modified by a sensor of some kind, such as a blood pressure read-out. Interactive art systems often require new input/output devices or new interfaces to otherwise well-known devices. At one level, building computer-based interactive systems like this is not a problem as computers come with the raw ability to communicate with other electronic devices. However, arranging for a computer to communicate with a new device is far from easy. It requires professional programming skills, working at quite a deep level in the computer system.

In the C&CRS environment, it was quite common to enable the construction of new interactive systems, such as a sensor space in which a person's position can be tracked by the computer. Up to now, this has only been achieved by teams that include the relevant technical experts.

This is an area in need of significant software support development. There are useful facilities to manipulate images on screens or in print, and facilities for editing and producing music. These systems allow people to work with image or sound without first having to become computer science experts. However, the building of interactive art is not well supported by standard tools and requires the expertise of programmers and hardware specialists.

Technology Opportunities and Constraints

Just as the softness of a pencil affects an artist's drawing, the nature of the digital technology used influences the product generated. The computer and its associated equipment constitutes an exceptionally broad spectrum of options and opportunities. However, by the same token, this diversity represents an exceptionally wide range of pitfalls to encounter.

The core of computing is the symbol processor that operates according to given instructions and, most important of all, can accept and process any set of instructions that can be specified. This sounds very impressive, but it brings with it a problem. The very generality of the computer makes it hard to use because it implies that there are very many options to choose from. It can do anything that we can instruct it to do, but formulating those instructions is a challenge to most people.

Instructing the Computer

In recent years, many new software applications have been invented that are relatively easy to use and that automatically generate the instructions that a computer needs. Today, millions of people use word processors, email systems and web browsers without having to even think about directly instructing computers. Unfortunately, this does not mean computer use is problem free. Creative people often require the computer to do things that are hard or almost impossible to specify, even though they are theoretically possible. This is where the main problem lies. How can we specify what we want without spending years doing it?

For the artist, there is often a specific aspect of this problem to be concerned about when creating interactive artworks where the computer controls special devices. Controlling displays, printers and other output devices requires both a detailed understanding of the device and an understanding of how the computer interacts with it. Controlling customized or new devices is often even harder.

For the digital artist, some basic technical matters can pose a problem or, alternatively, can be used as an opportunity. In printing, for example, the rate of dots per inch (dpi) is important when it comes to the printing of smooth lines as against showing *jaggies* (i.e. stair-like lines that appear where there should be smooth straight lines or curves).

At least three strategies are used by artists. The first, and most common one, is to make the selected dpi sufficient, given the size of the print, to ensure that normal viewing would not lead to the jaggies being perceived. A second approach is used by artists who see the jaggie as an integral part of inkjet printing technology. To them, it does not make aesthetic sense to try to hide it. This could be seen as an example of being true to the material. Just as a carver might choose to bring out the grain, so a digital printer might choose to show the jaggies, in order to be true to the material. A third approach to the existence of the jaggie is to only allow vertical and horizontal lines as acceptable in such a medium.

The key point to note is that the artist must be able to decide on the issue rather than have it decided by the technology. The example of jaggies is one of many. Similar thinking must go into colour, display luminance, and refresh rates. In relation to three-dimensional (3D) graphics and virtual reality systems, the things to consider multiply even further. For example, displaying information in 3D, and representing and experiencing motion in space, must all be subject to explicit decision-making on the part of the artist. For the technologist, it may seem that we need to be as close to "reality" as possible, but the artist will wish to consider the nature and "truth" of the medium. These two contrasting views may lead to very different decisions about how to use the features of digital technology.

Interactive Art

A considerable amount of the work by artists involves interaction between art systems and the viewer. There is also interest in the relationships that exist, or can be developed, between the physical world and virtual ones or between physical movement and symbolic representation. One of the C&CRS artists uses swimming to help understand the nature of the water to be modelled in computer animations. Another artist is concerned with the precise nature of the relationships her audience forms with her work. Another artist uses movement in a space as an integral part of his interactive works, so that performance and visual art are brought together. Dynamic systems of one sort or another are often at the core of the artworks produced. The digital computer system manages interactions with or representations of physical behaviour.

Implementing artworks of this kind often involves the construction or selection of sensor and control systems. These are ways in which the computer can learn about its environment and affect what happens next. In general, the applications and programming languages available to build and use these systems are much less advanced and easy to use than the software we are used to. Artists working in this area either need to work at a detailed level with programming or work in collaboration with a software developer. The problems of instructing the computer in these situations are quite unlike the current problems of using a printer, although it was not so many years ago when basic computer graphics were as hard to work with as interactive position sensor systems are now. The artists' needs are always advancing and so seem to outstrip the application developer's progress, in that, by the time a requirement has been met, the artist has formulated a new need.

Art Practice and Technology Environments

Art practice is closely influenced by the tools of the trade used by the artist. The introduction of acrylic in painting or welding in sculpture led to new forms and new kinds of artwork. By the same token, the introduction of computers and digital media has changed what artists do. Computers are very special tools, however. We do not only use them to shape or construct objects. We also use them to shape or construct ideas. Using them can help us to think more clearly or, sometimes, more imaginatively. Of course, computers drive printers and screens, are connected to any number of devices that interact with the world and, even carve objects. However, before a computer can be used to produce work, we have to somehow provide it with the necessary instructions.

Before we can fully instruct a computer to produce something, we have to formulate the idea of what is to be created with precision. This formulation of instructions is a form of creation and shaping of ideas. Because of this, computers help us to think as well as make. Hence, they can be expected to change the way that artists think about their work as well as changing the form of the work. Every artist knows that holding the pencil and drawing with it is, in reality, as much about thinking as doing. Specifying a computer program takes this aspect further by engaging the artist in determining very precisely how the work will appear or behave.

Many questions and difficulties are associated with any tool or medium, but it is particularly so with the computer. These issues formed part of what was considered during the C&CRS artist-in-residencies. The innovations that we saw were at times conceptual, at times in the form of artifacts, and at times purely technological. Much of this innovation was related to interchanges between artists and technologists as much as between artists and technology. Consequently, the impact of the technology on the creative process often depended on the relationship between artist and technologist. We see that the impact of the digital world on the artist falls into two areas: on thinking about art (development) and making art (delivery). There is also an impact on the world of technology in generating or, at least, directing technical innovation.

Digital Technology and Thinking

It is a familiar experience to most people who work with computers that, as they work and struggle to persuade the machine to do what they want, they come up with new questions and new ideas. We say that teaching is the best way to learn, and teaching such a demanding student as the computer certainly requires us to make up our minds quite precisely about what is required. However, it goes further than that.

Art practice is an evolving creative process. By the same token, art practice using digital technology is also creative. Therefore, it is not surprising to find that, whilst working with the computer, artists often come up with new ideas and approaches that have no direct derivation from what they were originally trying to do. For example, one artist used a computer system to create performances in which changing images were projected coordinated with music. This led to the invention of a set of correspondences between the music and visual forms and then to artworks that represented music purely visually. The new ideas came to him only because of his work with the computer system. Although the new artworks had nothing directly to do with digital technology they would not have been created if he had not made his digital exploration with music and visual correspondences.

Digital Technology and Making

The use of digital media for creating a work of art has certain kinds of technical issues associated with it, such as the particular visual quality of an image. To take a simple example, how many pixels per inch should be used for an image? For a high quality print we might choose 600 and use as much as 500 Mb of data to store the image. On the other hand, if the image is to be shown on a Web page, we would normally use just 72 pixels per inch and hold its size down to much less than 1 Mb.

At another level, digital media enables new forms of art making, for example, where interaction between the artwork and the audience is part of the work or part of the process of making it. With the help of digital technology, we can create new kinds of art, but how does the technology influence the art-making process?

The nature of the work is embodied not just in how it looks or what images are used, but in the way that it behaves when people interact with it. The problem of working with and defining interaction is a key one. From a practical perspective, there are many problems that most people working with interactive art systems encounter. It is not a simple task to write software to drive an interactive artwork that uses data such as position information from infra-red sensors. There are no high level tools to do this, and only by creating computer programs from scratch can interactive systems of this kind be made to work to an artist's specification. When this takes place, it is not simply a matter of an artist passing the

problem over to a technologist. Many of the detailed decisions made
during such programming have an impact on the outcomes of the interaction, and it is these very outcomes that the artist is particularly interested
in. An example from the early programming of computer drawing packages illustrates this point. When the ideas were first being developed for
using a mouse to draw with, the question of sensitivity was identified as
being significant for good interaction. For example, we can measure even
a few microseconds of letting go of a button, but how does that help us
decide on what should count as *really* releasing it? What should count as a
clear enough signal that an item has been selected? These time intervals,
built deep into the software, can be critical in defining the interactive
experience that the user has. They can also be significant in defining the
nature of the experience of an interactive artwork.

Making Electronic Marks

The Soft-board is a whiteboard connected to a computer and is designed
to support business meetings [9]. Marks made on the whiteboard using
pens of different colours are immediately represented in a computer window. A page is one workspace displayed on the monitor and a set of pages
forms a sequence. When any mark is made it is recorded as a set of points
for the current page. Both pen marks and eraser marks are recorded. At
any time a new page can be generated as a new blank canvas or inclusive
of the previous pages marks. The controls for starting and stopping the
recording and entering new pages are situated both at the whiteboard and
on the computer screen. This enables the user to complete a whole sequence with pen in hand and without having to touch the computer keyboard or mouse.

   The Soft-board does not use a computer-specific input device, such as a
graphics tablet or mouse, and therefore complete freedom of movement
is possible for the artist. This freedom allows the work to evolve in a way
that overcomes some of the constraints usually associated with electronic
media and the need to make allowances for them. One artist began his
experimental drawings using such a device. He found that it was a very
interesting method for making time-based work. The work with the Soft-
board transformed his thinking about his drawing activity into one that
involved time and movement. This change of thinking was at least as
important as the drawings produced by using the technology.

   A number of artists have deployed the Soft-board for different artistic
purposes. One set out to use it as an open-ended exploratory tool to see
what would happen in his personal drawing process. Another began by
adopting an exploratory approach also, but with a difference. By medi-
tating before each session, he aimed to remove all conscious thought
during the execution of the drawings. He wanted to see how far he was
able to achieve this and to do this he used the particular facilities of this

medium for capturing and replaying the act of drawing. The replay in real-time proved to be a particular attraction for a number of artists: this was something that they had not seen in any other medium.

Controlling the Technology

A standard question for designers of interactive computer systems inter-action design is how to determine if and how the user, rather than the computer, is in control of the interaction. Sometimes, the computer takes control, for example, in a car breaking system, but mostly users want to be in control themselves. When teams of people are involved in the interaction with the technology as, for example, in computer sup-ported meetings, the nature of the meeting will affect how the system is designed. For example, if the situation is a democratic one where every-one has an equal say, how can the interaction be mediated? Is there a leader, a moderator or a chairperson?

Artists tend to be very particular about who or what is in control. They will wish to be the author of the creative concept and its progress, if not the actual physical realization of the artifact, where it exists. In this situation, developing new kinds of digital technology can provide a problem of control and, hence, ownership. When a software developer collaborating with an artist, writes a program for an interactive artwork which only they understand, who controls the artistic decisions then? Some technologies are easier for the artist to control than others. Some artists insist on learning how to stay in control. If they cannot control the process fully, they do not go in that technological direction.

Issues of control are closely related to the level of complexity the computer has. The more different things that a computer can do, the more complex its instruction language has to be and so the harder it is to control. The harder it is to control, the more has to be learnt in order to master it. This is often the dilemma. An application program may be quite easy to use and quick to learn. It might enable many things to be done beautifully. But, almost inevitably, it will restrict what can be done by the user. Often, it will impose too many limitations for the creative mind. Faced with these dilemmas, it is too easy to conclude that technol-ogy should stay as it is and artists should restrict their ambitions in order to accommodate it. However, for new ideas and art forms to be created, it is more helpful to view the limitations in the current technology as the requirements for new technological initiatives. Taking this line, by opening up the horizons of the software developers, artists might be the driving force behind the development of the next generation of technol-ogy. Likewise, by initiating new ideas and carrying them through them-selves, artists can become the drivers of innovative digital art forms.

Moving Technology Forward

The activities of artists who seek to break new ground in art are fruitful areas for discovering innovative technology. During collaborative art and technology projects, opportunities for new developments in technology often arise. The experiences and lessons from the C&CRS artist residencies about technology provision helped the participants to define new requirements for creative technology environments. In many cases, solutions to meet the requirements were relatively easy to find, but often they raised more questions that are not so easy to answer. For example: what impact do different kinds of media and technology used in art practice have on one another? Do artists re-conceptualize one medium when they use it in relation to another? Technologists are often taken by surprise to find that their world can be looked at in unfamiliar terms.

Re-Conceptualizing Technology

The way that artists have deployed the Soft-board is an example of the creative use of a business meeting support device. It is intended to help brainstorming and the organization of ideas, particularly in meetings, by keeping an electronic record of all that is done. In effect, the meeting can be played back through a dynamic record of what was written on (and removed from) the Soft-board. When it was explored as a way of supporting drawing, or as a drawing tool, its role was quite different. Not only was it useful to be able to record and play back the drawing process in a way that was parallel to the use in meetings, it also became a way of making dynamic art – the playback of the process could become an artwork in itself. In effect, both the process of drawing as well as the result achieved, became the work of art. Such a view of the device brought revised requirements. Fine details about how it played back and how the timing and control work became vital whereas, in the original use, this was a secondary issue and small delays were acceptable limitations of the system behaviour.

Environments for Building Environments

A fundamental question that we have been considering is, what kind of environments best support the development of digital art? There is one answer to this question which, although it may sound a little strange, is, nevertheless, appropriate. In art and technology, we need to have *environments for building environments*. This approach is analogous to having a store which stocks all of the components that one might need in order to build a carpenter's workbench. The store is an environment that has all of the components that one might need, such as vices, bench tops, tool racks etc. By selecting from them and assembling the items in our

own workroom, we can build a specific environment suitable for our particular carpentry needs. The store provides an environment for building
the particular environments that its customers need.

One artist, concerned with developing environments for her particular
needs, makes works in which music and images are closely related in an
interactive system. To build such systems from scratch, every time a new
work is created, is a difficult undertaking. She has sought to find a more
general method that can be used to help make a whole class of artworks
using the same technology. See Chapter 24 for information about her
solution, the Color Organ. She uses a set of building blocks with which she
can improve the flexibility of the instrument. This is still hard to construct, as it requires skilled programming. What is needed is support for
building the Color Organ in the first place: that is, a software environment in which systems such as the Color Organ can be developed. In
other words, what is needed is an environment to support the development of environments such as the Color Organ.

Flexibility and Exploration

When we are not sure what we want or what we *might* want when we start
a task or project, we need flexible tools and methods that allow us freedom. We need to be able to change our minds and to bend the rules or
develop new rules as we go along. In this sense, we need the technology in
digital art environments to be flexible. A natural consequence of the
flexibility required in the technology was a requirement for multi-
platform work. An artist might begin with material developed on one
type of machine, e.g. a PC, but with a need to process it that could only
be satisfied on a second type, e.g. a Silicon Graphics machine. Sometimes,
even a third type was needed before completion of the task. This kind of
process requires an environment in which it is easy to switch between one
machine and another and in which an artist can move their data with
them as they move from one machine to another. Thus, it is important
to provide multi-platform, multiple format systems for creative work.

If the technology is to play any part in extending the boundaries of
human thought and actions, then a critical issue is the design of technical
systems for fostering creativity. In the light of what we know about creativity in action in the real world, how can personalization in new technology contribute to enhancing creativity? In order to design for the
enhancement of creativity, we need to look beyond the surface issues of
the human–computer interface. This means that we need to go further
than designing customizable interfaces or configuring better programming
environments.

A technical issue that is not always directly identified by artists as
computer users is the flexibility that the computer system has in adapting
to the specific needs of a project. It may often seem that computers are

hard to use when, in fact, the software is simply difficult to configure in appropriate ways. Ways need to be found to provide this flexibility beyond programming from scratch using a basic computer language, such as C or Lisp.

Responsive Strategies

We need computing resources and software to enable the kind of guided or playful exploration of possibilities in which artists engage. At the very least, we must ask, if it is impossible to anticipate all the technology and support needs in advance, what basic provision will suffice?

More deeply, we need to understand just how the technology can allow the required degrees of flexibility. How can we ensure that the environment is responsive to the evolving artists' needs? One solution might be the creation of more artists' software tools that allow the artist access to deeper levels of the computer's programming system, as distinct from software applications that have been developed for specific tasks such as image manipulation. Such tools could provide a bridge between the use of an environment that requires programming knowledge and the 'closed' application, which does not provide sufficient flexibility. Perhaps it points us to the methods of the earliest digital artists, who learnt the computing trade and became programmers in order to advance their art.

A co-evolutionary process, in which practice-based action research is used to understand and develop the technology and that art practice in parallel, is the method that can help to answer these questions. In particular, this approach can aid the development of strategies for the provision of responsive environments for digital art practice.

Several issues have been identified about strategies for providing creative technology environments. These concern the network infrastructure, the hardware and software platforms and the tools and applications. In particular, the concept of flexibility is important in all of them: for example, the environment must be heterogeneous and support communication and data exchange between the different systems. Equally, it must be relatively easy to extend or add to the facilities. Often, we found that what existed did not match what was eventually needed. Producing art is a kind of exploration that needs flexible support. There is no exploration if everything has to be defined and fixed before you set off.

Our experience suggests that even today, with all the advances in software, the degree of programming and systems expertise is critical to having more artistic control over the developing process. Those artists who had such knowledge were in a position to make more interim decisions during the exploratory process that guided the next course of action. Those artists who depended on a technologist often felt uncertain as to how much control they might have to relinquish to achieve their goals.

There is no one solution to designing environments for creative use. Conflicting requirements, such as accessibility and ease of learning on the one hand, and a high degree of control by the artist on the other, may not be mutually achievable. Ways forward combine new technology, new ways of working and new collaborations. Each artist will choose a personal approach and the intersection of art and technology will lead along different paths in each case. Nevertheless, it is important to understand as much as possible about what is general in art and technology creative processes and how applicable different technologies are. The research studies discussed in the following chapters are an attempt to meet this need.

References

1. Harris, C.: Art and Innovation: The Xerox PARC Artist-in-Residence Program MIT Press: Cambridge, MA (1999)

2. Smith, D.C. and Johnson, J.: The Xerox Star: A Retrospective. IEEE Computer (1989) 15

3. Redhead, D.D.: The Lisa 2: Apple's Ablest Computer. Byte, December (1984) 106-114

4. Markoff, J. and Shapiro, E.: Macintosh's Other Designers. Byte, August (1984) 347-356

5. Windows: http://www.microsoft.com/windows

6. Photoshop. Adobe Systems Corporation. San Jose, CA, USA

7. Silicon Graphics Inc. Mountain View, CA, USA

8. Iris printer; CroScitex, Burnaby, British Columbia, Canada

9. Soft-board: Microfield Graphics: http://www.microfield.com

There is a need to establish empathy
with the individual being observed so
that they become comfortable with the
observer's presence. Tom Hewett

The legacy of the recent past is that
artists are individuals who work
exclusively on their own. While this
has probably never been true, the
art world remains fixated on the
individual. Compare this to scientific
research where claims for individual
ownership are less valid and there
is acknowledgement of group effort.
Ray Ward

Well you understand what I am doing,
where should I be starting from?
Michael Quantrill

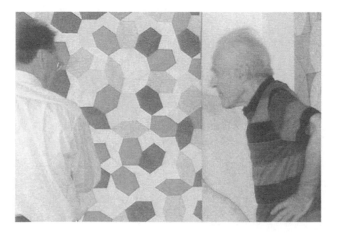

The characteristics of
any resources, materials,
tools or techniques that
form a part of the creative
work are in themselves
critical factors that
influence the process.
Linda Candy

3   Research

This chapter is concerned with research into art and technology. This is an activity that seeks understanding of the creative process and how it might be related to knowledge of other fields. Whilst artists and technologists collaborate in creating digital art, at the same time, researchers observe events for themselves and then collate and assess all the contributing sources of information. The goal of researchers is to arrive at a coherent view of events across a number of separate situations. A distinctive characteristic of this kind of approach is that actual digital art projects are developed in tandem with the research activity. The dual aim of the research is to acquire information that guides change in the existing situation and also to inform our broader understanding of art practice and future digital technologies.

Practice-based Action Research

Artists and technologists are exploring virtual and physical interactivity by pushing technology and art forward on several fronts, from programming tools to interactive installations combining sound, position and image. By putting such initiatives in place and, at the same time, providing a means of informing our general understanding, it is possible to learn from the experiences and apply the lessons immediately. In order to make that effective, it is necessary to bring to bear systematic approaches to acquiring knowledge using sensitive methods for gathering and analyzing necessary data. Additionally, if the knowledge acquired is to be immediately useful, it must be deeply rooted in the actual context and experiences of the participants.

Action research is a method that aims to identify existing assumptions in practice and then develop new strategies for change in the light of that knowledge. This process includes participant self-evaluation but does not rely on it alone. The practice-based action research approach that we have applied to the study of digital art and technology, embodies the integration of practice and research. Practitioner accounts of creative practice are combined with the observations of external researchers in order to arrive at a multi-view perspective on situated studies.

The research analysis draws upon two main sources of information: the collaborating parties' records of ongoing events and the records of non-participants, the observers. It is the task of the research to collate and analyze these multiple views and then to stand back from the events and try to evaluate them in ways that might be interesting to different audiences. Those audiences might be organizers of arts and media centres, research and development companies looking for improvements to the technology or, indeed, other artists and technologists wishing to learn from the experience of others. From an analysis of this rich set of information, answers can be proposed to research questions such as:

- What are the requirements for art-technology environments?
- What are the opportunities for technological innovations?
- What are the implications for creative practice?

Practice-based action research draws on the field of Human–Computer Interaction (HCI) from which a strong focus on *interaction* between people and technology comes. Because interaction between individuals, groups and many forms of digital technology is so important in digital art, there is much to draw upon from HCI. Moreover, HCI can gain from the creativity and innovation that drives the intersection between art and technology.

Human–Computer Interaction

HCI provides the basis for a practice-based action research approach to digital art studies. It is a discipline concerned with the design, evaluation and implementation of interactive computing systems for human use and the study of their use in practice. It is an interdisciplinary subject that exists within several mainstream disciplines: computer science, psychology, sociology and anthropology and industrial design. From a computer science perspective, the focus is on interaction and specifically, interaction between one or more humans and one or more computer systems. A range of interpretations of what is meant by interaction leads to a rich space of possible topics.

Take the notion of machine. Instead of workstations, computers may be in the form of embedded computational machines, such as parts of spacecraft cockpits or microwave ovens. Because the techniques for designing these interfaces bear so much relationship to the techniques for designing workstations interfaces, they can be profitably treated together. But if we weaken the computational and interaction aspects more and treat the design of machines that are mechanical and passive, such as the design of a hammer, we are clearly on the margins, and generally the relationships between humans and hammers would not be considered part of Human–Computer Interaction. Such relationships clearly would be part of general human factors, which studies the human aspects of all designed devices, but not the mechanisms of these devices. Human–Computer Interaction, by contrast, studies both the mechanism side and the human side, but of a narrower class of devices.

Or consider what is meant by the notion human. If we allow the human to be a group of humans or an organization, we may consider interfaces for distributed systems, computer-aided communications between humans, or the nature of the work being cooperatively performed by means of the system. These are all generally regarded as important topics central within the sphere of Human–Computer Interaction studies. If we go further down this path to consider job design from the point of view of the nature of the work and the nature of human satisfaction, then computers will only occasionally occur (when they are useful for these ends or when they interfere with these ends) and Human–Computer Interaction is only one supporting area among others. [1].

The HCI research agenda has been influenced by the drive to meet the needs of a changing population of users, and also by the very character of the disciplines that have come together in this field. HCI is multi-disciplinary and eclectic in its concerns and, for that reason, contending forces jostle for the central agenda. The philosophical and subject disciplines are diverse. For example, Lucy Suchman [2] and Terry Winograd [3] whose work has extended the range of HCI approaches, draw upon ethnography and conversation analysis for their theoretical frameworks.

HCI research methods are drawn from significantly different scientific principles: from predictive modelling [4] to prescriptive guidelines, tools and methods [5] and, more radically, the claim that "theories" are embedded in the products or artifacts themselves [6]. These approaches can be viewed as supporting both practice in design and engineering and the theoretical foundation vital to a strong scientific discipline [7].

A distinguishing feature of HCI research is the stress upon immediacy of results. The demand for new products and effective design principles places an intense pressure upon researchers to deliver immediately applicable knowledge that can be applied using the existing technology. As a result, the need for well-designed and engineered products often takes precedence over the quest for long term scientific knowledge. The drive to improve computer systems design by rapidly turning research results into products or artifacts has influenced the traditionalist approaches. This is exemplified by the work of Card, Moran and Newell [8] and Norman [9], where the methods are valued for their practical application.

There is an impetus in HCI to transfer research results quickly into sound applied principles which may be in conflict with developing longer scientific knowledge. There is a tension between achieving generalized principles and the context dependency of applied knowledge. Some have argued that a participatory action research approach [10,11] is the best way to acquire knowledge that can be applied in context [12]. A 'reflexive' approach, that is, one that recognizes a number of co-existing facets of scientific concern, can offer a positive way forward [13]. The need for making the stakeholders' viewpoints an integral part of the research activities is a key issue that has led to the notion of participatory research.

Participatory research has a long tradition, particularly in Scandinavia and now has a firm foundation in HCI. The term 'participatory' refers to the involvement of users in the design process and usually in the early stages when the initial requirements are defined [14]. There are well-recognized problems arising from the fact that users' views are not always articulated in a way that can be readily translated into system design characteristics. In addition, the initial requirements are unlikely to remain static. In participatory research, there is explicit recognition of the inter-related roles of the personnel involved. The matter of participation extends to system designers, prospective users, research investigators and any other person active in the project. All interested parties have participatory roles to play alongside the user. The research and design activities operate as an iterative cycle of investigation, analysis and feedback into design and development.

To improve the process of innovation, the methods include constant monitoring by participants on the basis of which modifications and adjustments are made. This involves the use of a number of data collection mechanisms: field diary notes, questionnaires, interviews, case studies. These provide multiple perspectives and feedback can be translated into modifications and directional changes. It enables improvements to be made in the current context rather than at a later time [15]. In this respect, it differs from traditional experimental research which seeks results that are relevant to the general case.

Research Methods for Studying Collaboration

We know that digital technology today is far from simple and its use in art even less so. It is also clear that much of the work being undertaken today involves collaboration and this in itself is an interesting issue to investigate. But, how can we study art and technology collaboration? How can we learn what is appropriate in terms of the environment of expertise and technology? How can we identify the requirements for new computer systems or environments? These questions require a research process that can address the complexities of an actual creative practitioner situation. A theoretical framework provides a route map for directing the overall aims and objectives of any research activity. An HCI-driven approach investigates how to acquire empirical data that can give rise to 'evidence-based' action. For gathering information about events and experiences of real practice, appropriate methods are needed.

The question that follows from this is what are the most effective methods for studying artists working with technologists in digital art? Artists are very individual and unpredictable in many ways. They are also inclined to be very strong-willed in the pursuit of their art and, therefore, not likely to welcome being treated as subjects in standard laboratory experimental situations. In truth, scientists and technologists are no different, it is just that they are often involved on the other side of the fence as the investigators. The methods to be used need to take account of the particular circumstances of the people involved. In research into human activities, controlled laboratory conditions are not achievable without sacrificing the context that gives them meaning. There are rich layers of meaning which are relevant to the description and interpretation of what is happening. When studies of creativity are carried out, the real-world context is an important consideration.

The starting point is to ascertain the artists' needs and expectations, not only in terms of technology required, but also access to the skills and knowledge of other experts. The requirements gathering exercise is an ongoing process that informs the acquisition of new technology and access to the technical expertise.

The scientific paradigm, based upon the rationalist tradition, has dominated computer system research and development, resulting in a preoccupation with the technology itself, its performance and formal characteristics. When the human user of the system is introduced, the tendency has been to use the same approach and contrive situations where the user and system can be observed and a limited set of variables manipulated. Unfortunately, human behaviour, especially creative behaviour, is too complex to be understood in much detail with this approach. One way forward is to conduct case studies of creative projects in actual development situations.

Case Study Method

A case study is an investigation of a specific set of events within a real-life context in which a number of factors are considered as evidence [16]. The units that are studied and analyzed may range from individual studies of outstanding people to histories of innovative corporate culture. The method is most applicable when events are not amenable to control by the investigator and when the questions posed are open-ended and multifactored. Questions are asked about why and how something took place in order to understand the meaning of specific instances. Explanations are based upon observations of existing events or recoveries of past events. The findings from such studies do not necessarily apply generally although it is common to compare results with other similar ones. A common use of the case study is to generate hypotheses about a wide range of events which may then be studied in single variable controlled conditions using traditional experimental methods. It is used widely in many research areas from medicine and public health to social science.

The case study method can be used to study exploratory projects developing new art forms in a collaborative environment where artists and scientists can work together as equal partners in the exploration of the use of digital technology in art practice. The following sections give an account of how this was achieved at C&CRS via the COSTART (COmputer SupporT for ARTists) project [17].

Artist Residency Studies

Artists-in-residence are opportunities for developing new approaches and works within specific art projects that are defined to meet the specification of the commissioning body. Normally, research is carried out by the artist to progress the work rather than for the benefit of general knowledge and a wider audience. Nevertheless, keeping a record of ideas and actions that documents the personal creative process is common practice amongst many artists. An extension of this practice is where the artist accumulates material towards an academic qualification. This kind of primary information is one view of events that practice-based action research uses.

The research process begins with the collection of many types of information about the activities, exchanges and outcomes of the art-technology residency projects. This is recorded, compiled and structured in transcription records and case study reports. This provides primary evidence for the extraction of features and the allocation of feature values. The results of this exercise may be applied to individual case studies which are then compared. An example of how this was done in relation to evidence about the nature of collaboration can be found in the next chapter.

In 1996, a series of case studies of artist-in-residencies took place at Loughborough University in the East Midlands of England. The events were monitored overall and before and after interviews conducted with the artist participants. In one case, the artist did not wish to use a virtual reality (VR) system to simulate what he called "real" reality [18]. He wanted a black space without the constraints of gravity in which to create sculptural objects, move them about in relation to one another and determine combinations of outcomes. To help him achieve this, a personal tool kit for creating virtual sculptural environments was created.

> In my work I have to emulate the struggle with gravity ...I never will be able to create real motion which I simulate in my normal art work which I can create and explore in VR...'By hand' I defined a relative complex rotation-movement of every shape around the sphere....The movement of these few forms make an extremely strong impression of depth and enough sense of orientation. The result was intoxicating. I finally could see the movement I imagined for years!
>
> *Ilgen on the use of a VR system*

The experience of using this digital medium had a significant effect on the artist leading to a change in his experience of creating art forms. The experience with VR inspired him to develop a kind of painting that visualizes the simulation of the colour space. He calls these "Virtual Paintings".

That experience, and those of other artists, demonstrated that more understanding of artistic practice and the role of technology in the creative process was needed. So, whilst the outcomes of the first residencies were interesting, it was apparent that there was a need to carry out more extensive studies. We also became more aware of the importance of collaboration in art and technology and, therefore, the role of technologists themselves figured more highly in the planning for the studies.

The COSTART Project

The COSTART project is concerned with the nature of creative collaboration in digital art practice. Two types of investigation were carried out: a survey of digital artists worldwide and a set of artists-in-residence studies. The areas surveyed fell broadly within the categories of visual art, animation, performance art, interactive installations and work in sound and image correspondence. Over 90 per cent of respondents indicated they were involved in collaborative activities with other people. A summary of the statistical results may be found on the project website [17].

The information acquired from the survey assisted with the development of resources and facilities at C&CRS in preparation for the artist-in- residency studies. Candidates for the residencies were identified from the survey respondents. The main criteria for selecting candidate artists were:

- evidence of the artist's involvement in collaborative work
- evidence of prior public exhibition of work
- close match between needs and resources
- ability and willingness of the artist to discuss their work.

The selected candidates were invited to a workshop when the opportunities and requirements were discussed with prospective technology support staff and researchers. It was particularly important that artists were prepared to participate actively in the research as it involved recording events as they happened and being willing to discuss openly their emerging ideas and problems encountered throughout the time in residence.

The resources available to the artists were to consist of more than a physical environment in which to work. They included daily support coordinated by a designated contact person and specialist consultations with technical experts throughout the residency period of five days and for follow up work after that time for one year.

The technical environment provided facilities for all residency projects, and a range of software and hardware in use or of value to many digital artists. The initial technical requirements had been identified from the earlier residencies and from our prior knowledge of the digital art world and digital technology. Specific needs of the projects for new software or hardware were met in response to the particular requirements of the artists as described earlier Chapter 2.

The Artists-in-Residence

Of the twenty artists who attended the orientation workshop, seven projects were found to be viable and the project planning began in earnest. Timing was a crucial factor. Each artist was allocated five days of full-time access and support during which time a technologist and an observer had to be available. As it turned out, it was possible to schedule the residencies on site for three weeks overall making a maximum of three artists working in any given week. This was fortunate as the load on facilities and, more important, people, proved to be a critical issue. Whilst the artists changed by week, the technologists and observers did not, making it essential that the degree of commitment and effort was high.

The response by everyone to the demands of the situation was extremely positive and the level of commitment was demonstrated by the universal demand for twenty four hour access to the buildings. Living on site was an opportunity for the artists to give full concentration and effort to the work and to take advantage of the separation from the demands of normal life. For most of the technologists, life outside the project carried on as usual which meant they were rarely free to give the totality of their time to the residency. However, in one case at least, it was not unknown for overnight stays to take place, often matching the artist's long hours. This is not to say that time resource had not been allocated for the technologists to support the work, but that the time available was not enough. The idea that for some, a part-time involvement, whilst continuing to do normal duties, would be possible within normal hours was a fond hope. But in truth, few of the people involved worked conventional office hours.

As for the observers, because their role was to observe, interview and discuss with the collaborating parties by arrangement, there was more control over the time commitment. Nevertheless, it was a full-time activity and the follow-up work compiling the information that had been collected when everyone else had gone home, was considerable.

Information Gathering

Each residency began with an initial planning meeting between artist, technologist and observer. The discussions were recorded on audio-cassette and field diary notes were kept by all. In addition, video snap-shots of activities were taken by the observers. Problems arose with sound quality in the recorded conversations due to some noisy equipment in the main studio. Also, for the video recording of the interactive sensor system, which required large projected images, the lowered light reduced the visual quality of the recordings. Where there were gaps in the chronology of events, we relied on the diaries to piece events together.

For each residency, in addition to the individual diaries kept by artists, technologists and observers, other records of events consisted of photographs and archives of work in progress, much of it in digital form. These data were documented as daily summaries and highlighted events into which transcription of discussions were inserted. The outcomes of the data collection were, for each residency, a set of transcription records and a case report based upon the transcription and the interview data. The transcription records form the basis of an ongoing record of artists' activities after the residencies and can be updated as new information is received.

Case reports on each residency project drew on the primary source data, i.e. the complete transcription records of the residency as well as follow up interviews and email communications about ongoing work. Artists provided feedback on the accuracy of their own case reports to complete the record. The case reports were then compiled according to the principal research topics. The information consists of primary sources from the first hand records of the participants in the studies including artists, technologists and observers. In addition, a secondary level is included which consists of comments by researchers on the chronological records structured according to a set of pre-defined research topics.

Case Study Records

To give a closer sense of the kind of records that were accumulated, extracts from one of the case studies now follow. Of course, to really gain a full sense of the history, the reader would need access to the whole narrative and all the associated images, videos and sound and, indeed, the opportunity to partake in the interactive experiences too. For such primary evidence to make sense, it also helps to have the motivation and fortitude of the historian, who might be happy to bury deep within the material of the past or, indeed, the recent present. So assuming the reader would prefer a snapshot instead, we begin with examples of the two main types of record, i.e. transcription and case study report, followed by an extract from each. They all refer to the same artist-in-residence project.

1. Transcription Record

The Transcription is a set of chronological records of the artist-in-residency for each project comprising all participants' field diary notes. Three distinct viewpoints on the events were compiled as a transcription by a researcher. This acts as a guide to the residency events as well as any associated material such as computer files, images, drawings, audio-video tape recordings which provide additional views of the events that a text record cannot supply.

In the first extract below, the initial planning meeting is recorded in terms of items such as the outdoor location, the subject of discussion, the terminology used, the drawing actions and the main topic: how the technologist is working to elicit constraints from the artist in order that the programming can begin. A verbatim extract from the observer's diary is also included. We know they went to Herbies (a university eating house) for the meeting, the start and end time of the session, whether diaries were used, and the fact that audio tape recording number one was taken but that no video recording was captured on this occasion.

Transcription Record Extract

A: Artist   T: Technologist   O: Observer   E: Other Artist
Date July 26 Location - 1 park table outside Herbies; 2 in C's Office; 4 in Studio

Session	Start	Finish	Activities	Diary	Video	Audio
1.	*14.33*	*15.35*	*Initial planning*	*Yes*	*No*	*Yes, Tape1*

First meeting takes place outdoors on picnic bench. T & A begin discussion of what A wants to accomplish during the residency time. A describes building an environment using ephemeral animation, with things growing inside forms... (Picture in A Notebook drawn to illustrate for T.) T begins to explore the constraints which A wishes to impose, e.g., "it must be light behind glass." A develops sketch to see if T has captured the concept. A expresses further constraints involving such things as "organic growth over time," with different objects having different growth periods and with various environmental inputs (e.g., temperature). Over most of the session T is working with A to elicit the constraints which must be identified before any programming can begin. They also spend time in discussion of a tentative plan for the day and rest of the week.

From Observer's field diary:
A and T discuss building an "environment using ephemeral animation". Using a sketchbook, A describes what she wants to achieve in the hope of learning about an alternative and how to bring in programming. T tries to get a grasp of what the constraints are within the piece. A wants to maintain some control to build shapes inside the sculptural form. A stresses the importance of growth occurring over time ("organic growth")as a central element of her piece. A was keen to understand how the piece could be achieved digitally and they both agree that the piece must work aesthetically. T explains how other artists have used digital media to set growth patterns of entities and describes the work that he and E have completed in order to illustrate his point. T suggests that A experiences the grid he and E worked on in order to get a true sense of what can be achieved. T considers

what is possible with software available and explains that it is relatively easy to program colour, transparency and objects. T and A discuss what their priorities are for the rest of the week. A wants to understand how the programming and technology works to produce the patterns that she wants to see within the piece itself. A is keen to make the programming unpredictable and for the environment itself to change the patterns in subtle ways. The environment will be directly affecting the piece...

End of Transcription Record Extract

2. Case Study Report

The Case Study Report consists of comments on the information from the transcription record. Additional information such as the prior survey response, the artists' curriculum vitae and subsequent activities are also included. This record is significantly different from the previous record because it includes commentary and interpretation by researchers associated with the source information from the transcription. The reports were structured according to the topics as follows:

- goals, outcomes and achievements
- support implications of artists using digital technology
- opportunities for digital technology
- impact of technology on art practice.

In the extract given, the researcher has not been able to find any indication of the artist's fundamental ideas from the transcription record and has turned to the survey results for evidence. This is followed by the artist's comments on the residency experience. She refers in detail to the nature of her creative process and the problem she has in communicating her ideas digitally when she does not know how to write programs. The technologist is satisfied with the outcome of the week too but expresses it in terms of progress in converting ideas into "a way of thinking that was modular". He is considering this from a systems analysis perspective because this is an essential precursor for the program design to begin.

In the section headed "Support Implications", the researcher speculates (possibly based on the artist's remark that is shown) that the success of this collaboration was because the technologist understood the artistic process well enough to help the artist define the technology requirements without compromising her preferred method.

In the extract headed, Opportunities for Computer Technology, the commentary weaves together the information about how the artist used traditional drawing media alongside new technology to distinguish between direct engagement with the media and indirect engagement through the support person. For the artist, there is also a distinction between tools for developing new ideas using hand drawings, and tools for delivery of the results of these ideas using computer technology. However, with exposure to new forms of technology, the potential for enhancing the creative process itself through better visualization techniques, becomes apparent. However, as the final extract on control of the creative process indicates, a critical problem was how to have access to the power of the technology for her thinking and making without sacrificing artistic control. An extract from the case study report now follows.

Case Study Report Extract

The artist does not refer to the ideas underlying her work in recorded interviews or conversations throughout the residency. Nor are these referred to within the diaries of the artist, support person or observer. In her original project proposal A described the main concerns underlying her work as "The relationship between architectural/light structures and programming".

In the survey, A described the concepts in her work as:
Aiming to make sensitive environments or architectural additions to environments. Continuing interest in how we experience spaces, travelling through them, resting and traces left in places...I always make work with the idea that it will be pleasurable or thought provoking to look at. A's response to Questions 109 and 113 of Survey

Although, as anticipated, no major "products" resulted from the week, A's ideas evolved during the residency, particularly the aesthetic qualities of her work in relation to the possibilities of the technology. This development work is perhaps indicative of the stage that the project had reached prior to the residency, as well as the method by which the artist usually works.

A on her achievements from the residency, in her diary:
The five days helped me to evolve a new approach to using digital technologies – something that I had previously considered but was uncertain how this would develop. I've been thinking about things like: how can I communicate the precise ideas I would like to achieve and be hands off (the computer). This has definitely included going through an instinctive creative process in drawing images in grids– which was effectively like an animation story board – then breaking this down and reforming it as programming idea.

T reflected on the overall achievements of the week in his diary:
We tried to look at A's ideas for image-movement. What I tried to do was help A to be able to convert her ideas into a way of thinking that was modular - as this was a stated goal at the beginning of the work. In balance, I think we went some good way to achieving this. T's diary

Support Implications

Art-led process: a key to the success of T and A's working relationship would appear to have been the level of knowledge that T had in relation to artistic process.

Working with someone who has a knowledge of the process of making an art work and programming seemed to allow many different ideas to emerge when at times the direction or desired outcome was not clear. A's comment

The technology support person's understanding of the artistic process enabled him to tease out the information that he needed in order to pursue her goals, working closely with her to help define how to achieve what she wanted using the technology. He took on board the artist's approach and worked with, rather than against, her method.

Opportunities for Computer Technology

Drawing using traditional media (such as pencil and paper) and the production of storyboards were devices used throughout by the artist, even though the end result will incorporate high-end technology. It appeared to be a very natural way for her to externalize her thought process. Pre-prepared illustrations were brought to meetings and drawings were created spontaneously when discussing work with support people. The development of the artist's work relied heavily on interplay between traditional drawing and mark-making techniques (which she was directly engaged in) and experimentation with new technology (which she engaged indirectly with through the support person). Paperwork was produced by the artist, from which the programming would be developed separately by the support person. The sensor position system was useful: being able to walk around and experience the effects on the body in the space immediately sparked off ideas. The artist made a distinction between tools used for the *development* of ideas (primarily drawing by hand) and tools utilized in the *delivery* of ideas (computer technology).

End of Case Report Extract

Examples of the two main types of case study record, i.e. transcription and case study report, followed by an extract from each have been shown. The transcription records and case study reports provide a store of primary information that can be accessed using different analysis techniques.

In the following chapter, some of the results of analyzing this information are discussed with particular reference to collaborative work in art and technology. Later, in Chapter 13, Tom Hewett discusses collecting observational data and the nature of expertise with reference to digital artists.

References

1. Hewett, T.T., Baecker, R., Card, S., Carey, T., Gasen, J., Mantei, M., Perlman, G., Strong, G., and Verplank, W.: ACM SIGCHI Curricula for Human–Computer Interaction (1992)

2. Suchman, L.: Plans and Situated Actions. Cambridge University Press, Cambridge (1987)

3. Winograd, T. and Flores, F. Understanding Computers and Cognition: A New Foundation for Design. Ablex Publishing Corporation, Norwood, NJ (1986)

4. Young, R.M., Green, T.R.G. and Simon, T. (eds): Programmable User Models for Predictive Evaluation of Interface Design. In Bice, K. and Lewis, C. Proceedings of CHI'89. ACM, New York (1989) 15-19

5. Long, J. and Dowell, J.: Conceptions of the Discipline of HCI: Craft Applied Science and Engineering. In Sutcliffe, A. and MaCaulay, L. People and Computers V. Cambridge University Press, Cambridge (1989)

6. Carroll, J.M., Kellogg, W.A. and Rosson, M.B.: The Task-Artifact Cycle. In Carroll, J.M. (ed.) Designing Interaction: Psychology at the Human-Computer Interface. Cambridge University Press, New York (1991)

7. Marchionini, G. and Sibert, J.: An Agenda for Human-Computer Interaction: Science amd Engineering serving Human Needs. SIGCHI Bulletin, 23 (4), October. ACM Press, New York (1991) 17-32

8. Card, S.K., Moran, T.P. and Newell, A.: The Psychology of Human-Computer Interaction. Lawrence Erlbaum Associates, Hillsdale, New Jersey, London (1983)

9. Norman, D.: The Psychology of Everyday Things. Basic Books, NY (1988)

10. Lewin, K.: Field Theory in Social Science. Basic Books, New York (1951)

11. Warmington, A.: Action Research: Its Methods and its Implications. Journal Applied Systems Analysis, 7 (1980)

12. Avison, D.E. and Wood-Harper, A.T.: Information Systems Development Research: An Exploration of Ideas in Practice. The Computer Journal, 34 (2) (1991)

13. Woolgar, S.: (ed) Knowledge and Reflexivity: New Frontiers in the Sociology of Knowledge, Sage Publications (1991)

14. Candy, L.: The Twin Paths of Research and Design: Reformulating the Computer System Development Process. Journal of Design Sciences and Technology, 4 (1) Europia Productions (1995) 57-72

15. Mumford, E.: Participative System Design: Structure and Method. Systems, Objectives, Solutions, 1 (1) (1981) 5-19

16. Bruce, M.: Case Study Method in Design. Design Studies, 14 (4) (1993)

17. COSTART Project Web Site: http://creative.llboro.ac.uk/costart

18. Edmonds, E.A. and Candy, L.: Computation, Interaction and Imagination: Into Virtual Space and Back to Reality. In Gero, J and Maher, M (eds), Proceedings Computational Models of Creative Design. (1999) 19-31

A creative process of experimenting with technology seems to provoke questions that may not usually be asked of technology. Esther Rolinson

Why is collaboration such an important part of the new century? With increased use of more and more specialized, complicated technology, it is far less productive to be an artist delivering a monologue alone in the studio. Jack Ox

Digital art challenges not just the nature of representation in art but the traditional methods of production and represents a new creative space. Sarah Tierney

4   Collaboration

Art and technology projects provide an opportunity to try to understand just what the ingredients of successful creative collaborations are. One of the research questions that was posed was how to identify the support requirements for art and technology collaborative projects. This chapter describes some of the characteristics of collaborative work that were identified from the COSTART residency studies [1]. The overall research approach and methods for gathering data were described earlier in Chapter 3. In this chapter, we examine the way the information was analyzed and the results of that exercise followed by a discussion of some implications for collaborative creativity. We conclude that the idea of providing supportive environments for art and technology needs to be broadened to encompass the establishment of ongoing collaborative relationships that are fostered by the organization.

Research Process

The research process began with the collection of many types of data about the activities, exchanges and outcomes of the art-technology collaborations. Figure 4.1 gives an overview of the process.

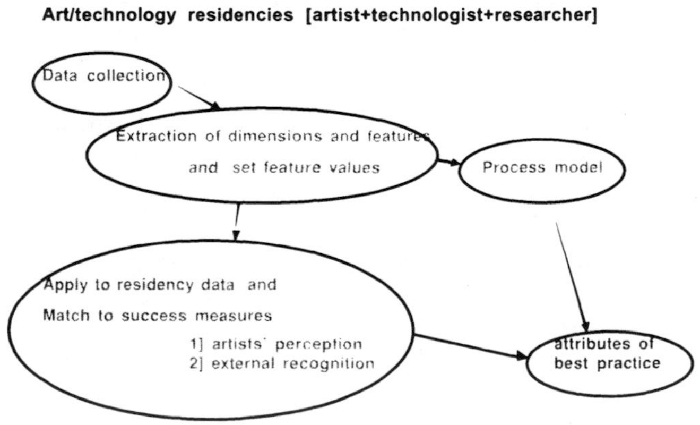

Figure 4.1 The research process

The research process includes the analysis framework and the mechanisms used to evaluate the art-technology collaborations. The information was compiled and structured in transcription records and case study reports which could then be analyzed by different researchers. This provided the primary evidence for the extraction of features and the allocation of feature values or descriptors of collaboration. This was carried out by two researchers who arrived separately at an independent assessment. Textual data can be subjected to various forms of analysis. The one used in this case was as follows:

- The first pass over the case study texts looked for features of collaborative behaviour that relate to an existing theoretical model of creativity including cognitive style, communication, knowledge [2].
- Values were then attached to the features: e.g. feature is, for example, approach: values are exploratory, open-ended, goal-driven, etc.
- The second pass over the texts assigned values to features for each case study (see Table 4.1)
- The results for all cases were tabulated and compared (see Table 4.2).

Cognitive Style Feature	Value Selected-Res. 1	Value Selected- Res. 2	Values Not Selected
Approach	Exploratory	Exploratory	Goal-driven
Role	Different	Different	Same/Interchangeable
Ethic	Art-Led	Neither/Both	Technology-led
Control	Important	Necessary	Optional
Methods	Digital	Mixture	Traditional

Table 4.1 Features with values for Case Study 7

Table 4.1 shows the values selected for a single collaboration by each researcher. The degree of agreement is exact for two features (approach and role) and close for three (ethic, control, methods). This pattern of agreement occurred also in the Communication and Knowledge features. Further discussion of the features of creative collaboration can be found later on in this chapter. To complete the explanation of how the data was analyzed, we now show how each case study was compared.

Comparisons across Case Studies

In order to characterize the different collaborations, the case study data was examined for each of the above features and associated values. The researchers then compared results and compiled the features and values as tables. The results were then compared (see Table 4.2 below).

The next stage in the process was to evaluate each case study in terms of two success measures: subjective and objective. "Subjective" was defined as the perceived views of the participants in the collaboration as to whether it worked well or not. "Objective" was defined in terms of outcomes (exhibitions, ongoing work, etc.) as public demonstrations of the value coming from the work done.

Case Studies---->	CS1	CS2	CS3	CS4	CS5	CS6	CS7	Result ALL	Result FULL
Cognitive Style									
APPROACH									
Exploratory	***			***		***		3/7	2/3
Goal Driven		***	***		***	***		4/7	1/3
ROLE									
Different	***	***	***			***	***	5/7	3/3
Interchangeable				***	***			2/7	
Same									
ETHIC									
Art-led	***	***		***		***	***	5/7	3/3
Tech-led									
Neither/Both		***		***				2/7	
CONTROL									
Important		***	***		***		***	4/7	2/3
Necessary	***			***				2/7	1/3
Optional						***		1/7	
METHODS									
Digital	***					***		2/7	1/3
Mixture		***	***	***	***		***	5/7	2/3
Evaluation									
Viewpoint (V)	V	V	++	V	++	++	V	4/7	
Outcomes (O)	O	O	++	++	O	++	O	4/7	
V+O	V/O	V/O	++	++	++	++	V/O	3/7	

Table 4.2 Comparison of features for all cases

Having identified which collaborations were successful or otherwise in terms of the two measures, it was then possible to look back at the features and descriptors for each case study and infer which was associated with success. By combining these with success measures, the quality of the collaboration was assessed. In three cases, the collaboration was assessed as successful both subjectively and objectively. These collaborations could be described as full partnerships and are shown in Table 4.2 above.

This exercise may be used in a number of ways. The results can provide a basis for generalizing the results in the form of models of collaboration [3]. Such outcomes provide a method for evaluating collaborations in terms of best practice. The method we have presented here is being refined for future use in the ongoing research.

Cognitive Style in Collaboration

The collaboration involved, amongst other things, three types of human activity: cognitive style, communication and the use of knowledge. For each of these types of activity, a set of features with associated descriptors was identified and values were ascribed to each collaboration. Here we focus upon the cognitive style area of creativity and discuss the features we identified in the case studies. The term "cognitive style" is used here to denote the characteristics of thinking and making in the creative process as revealed in external behaviour and self-evaluation. Five main features of cognitive style were identified as follows:

- the approach used to carry out the project
- the role adopted by the participants
- the ethic adopted that drove the process
- the value placed upon level of control over the process
- whether the methods used were wholly digital or traditional media combined with digital ones

As an example, an exploratory approach involves the generation of ideas, often from small details, in an iterative manner until a clear path is determined. The process may be tentative and opportunistic. By contrast a goal driven approach means setting a well-defined goal at the outset of a project and carrying it through with minor deviation only. The notion of an art-led or technology-led "ethic" arose from observation of the different priorities given to domain-oriented concerns. For example, in the art-led case, the importance of audience awareness or personal engagement and, in the technology-led case, finding the right solution first time or using best fit technical solutions.

The following quotations are direct quotations from the participants in the research: the artists, technologists and observers. They provide viewpoints on which the evidence of the feature values of cognitive style, knowledge and communication are based.

Approach: Exploratory versus Goal-Oriented

"A's approach to her work, is very developmental and hands-on, which essentially means that whilst she has a rough idea of what she wants to achieve, her ideas constantly develop as she produces the work." (Observer)

"Sometimes I believe I've resolved the problem with A but the next time we talk it seems he meant something else. It seems difficult to impress upon him the need to look at the problem logically and be very specific. This is not his fault but the problem must be expressed in sequential logical terms." (Technologist)

Role: Complementary versus Different

"The main focus of the collaboration was on a personal level rather than a goal in that we talked together about various things on a very personal level and it became apparent that our interests were very complementary...." (Artist)

"The work with A has been extremely enjoyable. It was a feeling as if we were both working together at times, gently changing roles, where I would suggest to her something from an art point of view and she would suggest to me things from a technical point of view." (Technologist)

"This was a collaboration in which the participants had separate background concerns driving their own art practice that, in turn, informed the individual contributions and direction of the collaboration." (Observer)

Ethic: Art-Led versus Technology-Led

"T does not think like an animator." (Artist)

"One of the main things I have found working with artists is their feeling that the resources are unlimited and bear no cost. I agree that they want high resolution for their work but with a little bit of technical understanding they could have the image they want and keep the cost down." (Technologist)

Control: Important versus Necessary

"Trying to adjust thinking to work more closely with programming...I want to make unexpected or unplanned patterns of animations but still control overall style. Discussed with T about the control that I could have over final work – Defining *all* the images would limit the sense of unpredictable growth and 'unseen' images evolving." (Artist)

"T raises question, 'how much control do they want over the sound?' A replies 'as much as necessary'. T says 'At the moment we've got absolute control over all the visual information... the reason that I wrote the code is that I wanted to have complete control over the sound which was why we had to go down to that low level'. (Technologist)

Methods: Traditional versus Digital

"Both were more comfortable with their preferred techniques and were not able to adopt the perspective of the other very easily. In this situation a traditional animator wished to explore the possibilities of augmenting conventional techniques with computer-based ones for which purposes an expert in computer-based modeling was essential. This meant that the blending or migration of techniques such as a frame-based approach to a digital one proved impossible. At the heart of the problem, was a lack of a shared vision of what the end result should look like." (Observer)

These quotations are examples of viewpoints by artists, technologists and observers that were used to identify features of cognitive style for each art and technology collaboration. The same procedure was applied to communication style and the use of knowledge as shown in the following examples.

Communication in Collaboration

Six features of collaborative communication were identified as follows:

- whether openness of communication was adopted by both parties or was restricted to one or none;
- whether the relationship existed only for the residency or was ongoing; whether the language as demonstrated by terminology used, was shared or restricted to one or other individual;
- whether the exchanges took place in a continuous manner or only intermittently;
- whether there was mutual flexibility in respect of the way communication was used;
- whether the process of arriving at an agreement involved affirmation of each party towards one another or was an agreement to differ.

Examples related to the problem of not having a shared language are shown below. In the first, the technologist thinks he is using too much technical language and in the second, the artist needs more understanding of the software application's procedures for development. These form part of a lengthy series of exchanges between the two collaborators during which they struggled to arrive at a common view of both requirements and software capability to achieve the artist's goals.

Shared Language

"We are now looking at lighting. I seem to understand what type of effect she wants with lights but I am not able to explain to her properly that lighting does not work in this software as she thinks it should. Maybe I am getting a bit too technical in my explanation." (Technologist)

"Having to re-do all drawing as once the objects have been manipulated, I cannot change the number of segments. This aspect of workflow is so important and it would be good to have had more of this pointed out as I am currently repeating tasks and I feel the process is getting messy. Maybe needed some more of the overall philosophy of the development process in relation to this particular software". (Artist)

Knowledge in Collaboration

The features of the use of knowledge in collaboration are concerned with:

- how each party to the collaboration acquired and used the knowledge required to carry out his or her tasks
- whether there was sufficient technical knowledge to achieve the tasks
- whether there was shared domain knowledge (art or technology)
- whether research proved necessary or not
- how critical the inter-dependence of the knowledge between the collaborators was to the success of the collaboration.

The quotations from the case reports that follow illustrate the features related to the artist's level of technical knowledge and the effect of this on the amount of support needed. A related feature was a need for further research despite an already high level of technical expertise on the part of the artist.

Technical Knowledge and Level of Support

"So far the initial idea that A would be a 'safe' artist to support is proving to be less simple than first thought. He has needed more constant presence to get started: O was drawn into it: he commented on lack of learning strategies." (Observer)

Need for Research and Learning

"In spite of the unusually high level of technological expertise in comparison with other artists taking part in the residency programme, particular gaps in the artists' knowledge about software and hardware meant that, on several occasions, they had to spend a great deal of time learning about the technology before they could make progress... some software required for the piece had to be learnt from scratch." (Observer)

Success Factors for Collaborative Creativity

The COSTART studies brought out several issues about the nature of art-technology co-creativity. In particular, we need to recognize that the artist may be seeking more than access to technology and expertise. Being able to develop a partnership, as distinct from having an "assistant" relationship was a significant plus point for the success of collaborative projects between artists and technologist.

Learning new skills and techniques is an important facilitator for creative practice. If the artist does not have the skills or the time to learn them, the role of a human collaborator is essential. Some artists may want to take full control of the reins of the technology because it is pivotal to the way they work whilst, for others a temporary need can be met by a technology assistant. However, technologists with little knowledge of art practice do not easily make good collaborators. Artists need collaborators who understand or are empathetic to their need to exercise control for themselves. Working through and with the eyes and hands of the person who provides technical expertise is not right for the core creative activities, although it might be acceptable for the more mundane ones.

Seeking a Partnership

One of the interesting things we observed was how much further the artists themselves wanted to extend the supportive relationship of their assistants. A significant number were looking for more than technical know how but rather were seeking a partner for an artistic exploration. For that to work, the assistants needed to engage more actively in the creative process and to resist imposing a standard technical solution. Likewise, the artists needed to be more open about their intentions and to be prepared to reveal tentative ideas that would normally remain hidden until they reached a more mature state.

Complementary Interests for Mutual Benefit

In a true partnership, complementary interests exist even where the outcomes by each individual may differ. Indeed, one of the most successful ongoing partnerships operates in such a way as to serve convergent interests but, at the same time, produces quite distinct artistic outcomes. In this way, the partners are able to achieve mutual benefit but, at the same time, retain ownership of their individual achievements. To be able to enjoy such mutual benefit, requires the relinquishing of individual control of the creative process: having differentiated but complementary roles appears to be best suited to achieving that end. Having a respect for differences in methods is also important to a successful partnership. The trick is for the people concerned to be able to identify in what way their differences in approach can benefit one another.

Art-led Versus Technology-led

Where the partnership is perceived as art-led by both parties, this seems to lead to better collaboration. The technology-led situation, on the other hand, may place the non-technologist at a disadvantage both in terms of control of the creative process and the eventual outcomes. If the implications of adopting a particular technology solution are not fully understood by the artist, then it may not be possible to steer the direction of the work to suit, resulting in a loss of artistic control.

For the technologist, the disadvantage of a technology-led assistant model lies in a lack of ownership of the project. This may occur even as they are providing critical input to the process through such contributions as software programming design. Where the relationship is of the assistant type, it is more productive if the artist explicitly acknowledges the value of the technologist's contribution and actively tries to learn from it. In some cases, the danger of one-sidedness for the technologist may be overcome if the artistic problem to be solved provides a sufficiently interesting technical challenge.

Sharing Knowledge

An effective working relationship exists where both parties exchange knowledge resources in order to progress the work and resolve difficulties of both a technical and artistic nature. The sharing of knowledge is an important facilitator of creative collaboration. It also depends upon the parties having complementary skills rather than at the same level. A partnership that aims to be self-sufficient must also know its limits and be willing to carry out the necessary research when the knowledge is insufficient. Indeed, self-sufficiency in technical know-how, or at least the quest for it through research, can be in itself a stimulus to creative thought. Being able to learn through knowledge sharing is beneficial and it particularly applies where having direct contact with a new way of thinking stimulates the generation of options. In one such case, as the process of programming became clearer, the artist was able to understand more fully the basic logic. This enabled her to consider more carefully her options and how the aesthetics of the piece could operate.

Communication Skills

Naturally the ability to communicate well with others is an important part of the collaboration process, but art-technology collaborations have particular requirements. For successful partnerships, being able to have a longer-term relationship during which trust and confidence can be built up, has real advantage. A communication barrier may manifest itself in a whole variety of different situations, bringing with it frustrations and problems. For example, a high degree of openness and flexibility and a willingness to engage in discussion with one another in a whole-hearted manner, facilitates the partnership whereas a lack of flexibility may indicate that there are unspoken differences about the way the project is developing. Difficulty with the language of communication sometimes reflected a different way of thinking about the problem in hand and how to go about solving it. Developing a common language (particularly when discussing technical issues) that both parties can understand and work with is essential if anything useful is to be achieved. Where an "assistant" style of collaboration operated, there was more difficulty in finding a shared vocabulary.

Requirements for Art and Technology Collaboration

A major lesson that came out of the first residencies was to do with the concept of "support" itself. In responding to the demand from artists for technological facilities and expertise, the preparation for the residencies concentrated on two things:

- the technology: the required software packages and hardware devices needed to carry out the artists' projects
- people with the technical skills to enable the use of that technology.

For the technology, we had an established base of 'high-end' computing equipment, network facilities and a repertoire of office and drawing software as well as specialized packages for 3D modelling and a position sensing system. Where a specific piece of technology was needed, it was acquired for the purpose of the residency. Whilst a number of the artists had well-developed skills in the use of some technology, because the projects were set up with a view to exploring *new* digital forms, we anticipated the need for help from experts in the more advanced technology.

For the experts, we turned to a sizeable network of willing experts at the university. We envisaged artists driving the projects and technical people supporting the process in response to their requirements. This did happen, of course, and the programmers, in particular, found their skills were in twenty four hour demand for the duration of the residencies. The support provided was, in fact, never really enough but there was no doubt that the artists appreciated the time and commitment that was given. That said, support for specific activities such as programming or digital video editing, was only part of the story. The idea of supportive environments for art and technology needs to be broadened to encompass the establishment of ongoing collaborative partnerships that are fostered by the organization.

A summary follows of a basic set of requirements for support for artists and desirable characteristics of technologists that can be viewed as essential for a successful partnership in this field. Further studies will explore these requirements and consider their relevance to other domains.

Artists need:

- heterogeneous resources for a broad range of needs
- access to high end facilities and tailored digital systems
- access to appropriate human expertise that is communicated well
- an ability to reflect and learn from technologists.

Technologists need:

- good communication skills as well as technical skills
- an ability to *listen* and learn from listening
- an ability to suppress the urge to promote a course of action that is technically feasible but not artistically valid.

Successful collaboration can be learned. Based upon the experience of this research, some basic requirements for sound and productive partnerships are:

- devise a shared language
- develop a common understanding of artistic intentions and vision
- engage in extensive discussions and "what if?" sessions
- give time to establish the relationship and recover from mistakes.

A number of artists have continued their association with the C&CRS and new people have joined. To be successful over time, creative partnerships needed appropriate organizational support. An environment for art and technology collaboration involves much more than the choice of which technologies and technical skills are needed, vital though that remains.

> The main support I observe artists needing is that of people support. It is not enough to have systems that artists can use, they need real contact with people who understand the technologies and that can effectively communicate with the artists. These people would be more than technicians. For the best results they would need to be sympathetic to the artists' concerns and not just interested in solving technical problems. (Artist)

Conclusions

The results of the COSTART studies are relevant to our understanding of the nature of collaboration. Art-technology collaborations benefit from a partnership model of collaboration. The assistant or support model of collaboration is also needed but for different purposes. The quality of the type of collaboration can be assessed in terms of its durability and stimulus to creative thinking. It follows from all this that learning *how* to collaborate successfully is very important and cannot be assumed to be a natural to everyone. Of course, we can facilitate it by making the environmental conditions more than sufficient but we need to be more aware of the critical human issues at play. For any organizations wishing to promote collaborative creativity, attention should be paid to ways of developing learning strategies for successful collaboration. Referring to the longer term nature of the personal creative process, Harold Cohen said:

> Creativity is not a random walk in a space of interesting possibilities, it is directed. The difficulty in tracking how the individual proceeds is that it is directed less by what the individual wants the single work to be than by what he wants his work as a whole to become. [4]

This implies supporting a sustained process. For sustainability to be possible in the context of digital creativity, that can only be achieved within an organizational context that is appropriate to a special kind of collaborative partnership. Therefore, understanding how good partnerships evolve and flourish is very important for developing creativity enhancing environments.

References

1. COSTART Project Web Site: http://creative.llboro.ac.uk/costart

2. Candy, L.: Computers and Creativity Support: Knowledge, Visualization and Collaboration. Knowledge-Based Systems, 10 (1) (1997) 3-13

3. Candy, L and Edmonds, E.A.: Modeling Creative Collaboration: Studies in Digital Art. In Gero, J. and Maher, M-L. (eds). Proceedings 5th International Roundtable Conference on Computational and Cognitive Models of Creative Design. December (2001)

4. Cohen, H.: A Self-Defining Game for One Player, Special Section on Creativity and Cognition, Leonardo, 35 (1) February (2002)

What fascinates me about a machine is the experience of a physical and intellectual extension of myself. Manfred Mohr

I want to refine my methods of working and find more ways of using the benefits with the pleasures of the tactile and physical. Joan Ashworth

The more than 150 years old history of the 'new medium' photography has already shown that a new technology definitely may add important creative possibilities, without ever really excluding painting or sculpture. Fré Ilgen

Using digital technology seems to give potential for creating a different type of relationship between object and viewer. Esther Rolinson

In digital art I want to go somewhere I have never imagined going in painting or performance. Ray Ward

5   Practice

Since the mid-1960s, artists have been actively and successfully using digital technology in their practice. Many of these artists can be classified as 'computer expert'. Bringing the expertise of art and technology together has usually been the achievement of one person working alone. As we consider more recent digital art, increasing collaboration can be seen between people of different disciplines and skills. The paradigm for digital art seems to be shifting towards collaborative practice as a norm. A survey revealed that 90 per cent of the artists who were experimenting with digital technology were also collaborating with people in other fields [1]. Whether this pattern of collaborative practice continues to grow or not will, perhaps, change as education develops and responds to the art and technology developments presented here. We may see a growth in the number of artists who are expert in computer technology to a similar level as those in print-making, carving or welding. On the other hand, the advantages of collaboration extend beyond merely the acquisition of technical skills. Collaboration provides opportunities for more ambitious creative projects. Furthermore, the many funding initiatives that explicitly encourage joint activities also contribute to this growing trend.

The artists' reflections in the second part of this book raise issues about the role of digital technology in relation to creative practice as it is seen today. A number of artists have noted how involvement with computers has stimulated them to move forward in their conceptual thinking. They have been encouraged to break with previously established conventions and explore new methods. One artist discusses the importance that digital technology has had in encouraging him to shift the very idea of what he considered to be art. Another found that using a virtual reality (VR) system was the trigger that caused him to reconsider the nature of his paintings. Others found that involvement with computers caused them to reformulate the boundaries of their artistic scope, for example, by adding time as a dimension of the work. In general, the challenges inherent in working with digital technology can have a positive influence in encouraging artists to break with their existing conventions, a development that is a core element of truly innovative practice.

For most digital artists, the importance of using and having access to expert technological knowledge cannot be over emphasized. As the study of collaboration described in Chapter 4 revealed, some find it vital for each member of the team to have a clear and well-defined role. On the other hand, by their own account, some artists have been struck by the way in which digital art collaborations lead to the blurring of the distinction between artist and technologist. In both situations, access to expert knowledge and opportunities for the collaboration needed in order to acquire that expertise, prove to be essential in enabling the realization of successful digital projects. An interesting aspect of collaboration is the way in which it provides participants with more than one viewpoint about the nature of the creative process. One artist notes how the process of collaboration with a technologist, and the kind of discussion that it requires, encouraged her to reflect on different views about how to proceed with the work and what method to use to produce it. Collaboration helps the participants to address tasks via a number of parallel channels of thinking, which draw upon different types of knowledge. From this process, entirely new understandings can emerge that transform the outcomes of the creative work.

Studies of Creative Process

Understanding the ways in which creative process has been influenced by the growth of computer use is a key concern of this book. Studies of the creative process, as distinct from studies of the outcomes or artifacts of this process, have been much more extensive in the field of design than in art. Although there are many differences between the fields of design and art, they have many similar characteristics in terms of the creative process involved. It is therefore useful to broaden the discussion to examine the issues surrounding creativity in general, but particularly in design practice.

There has been considerable research into how designers carry out design activities. In both product design and software design, common characteristics have been identified. In particular, the view of design as an hierarchically organized planned activity as opposed to design as an opportunistically driven mix of top-down and bottom-up strategies has been explored in a number of empirical studies, e.g. Guindon [2] and Ullman [3]. Maccoby [4] studied prominent designers and engineers whose contribution to their fields was unquestioned by their peers and the world at large. Although they represent a spectrum of different fields and cultures, they exhibit similar ways of thinking and working. Most are "holistic thinkers", in the sense that they look for an overall broad scope before moving into specific detail. Other studies indicate that design is often solution-led, in that the designer proposes candidate solutions early on in order to scope the problem better. Designers impose constraints that narrow down the number of solutions and help generate new concepts. They also change their goals and add constraints during the design process. Boden [5] makes a good case for the claim that changing a constraint might be at the core of creative thinking.

Taking account of these studies and our own investigations into innovative designers, various characteristics of the creative process have been identified with a view to identifying the kind of computer system that could be supportive to the designers' creative practice [6,7]. New ideas do not just come out of thin air. The conditions for creativity are very important and outstandingly creative people seem to be able to arrange for the right conditions to be available. The use of complex tools, such as computers, forms a significant part of the context in which these conditions for creativity exist. The studies referred to above identified aspects of the creative process that are relevant to art and technology practice. Most interestingly, they relate to artists' observations on working with computer technology that were discussed earlier. Examples of the aspects identified are:

- *Breaking with convention*
  Breaking away from conventional expectations, whether visual, structural or conceptual, is a key characteristic of creative thought. Events that hinder such breaking with convention are avoided, whereas positive influences are embraced.

- *Immersion*
  The complexity of the creative process is served well by total immersion in the activity. Distractions from this immersion are to be avoided.

- *Holistic view*
  The full scope of a design problem is only fully embraced by taking a holistic, or systems, view. The designer needs to be able to take an overview position at any point and, in particular, to find multiple viewpoints of the data or emerging design important.

- *Parallel channels*
  Keeping a number of different approaches, as well as viewpoints, active at the same time is a necessary part of generating new ideas. The creative person needs to work in *parallel channels*.

The creative process includes the following activities, each of which has its own characteristics. Some of the key elements are:

- ideas generation
- problem finding and formulation
- applying strategies for innovation
- acquiring new methods or skills
- using expert knowledge.

Digital artists are very involved in finding support for the last two of these. Much of the collaboration that we observe in the artist's discussions and from the studies of their residencies is addressing these activities. Digital artists are concerned with finding and creating the environments in which they can work productively. The early digital artists had little choice but to acquire the necessary computer expertise themselves if they were to be able to achieve anything at all. Their experiences were rarely collaborative in the sense we mean today where people of different skills and backgrounds combine their efforts to make the technology accessible for art practice.

As an example of the role of digital technology in the development of an artist's expert knowledge, it is interesting to consider two artists whose contribution to computers in art has been very significant over many years.

Digital Technology and Creative Knowledge

Harold Cohen's computer system, AARON, is the best known and most successful example of a computer program that creates drawings and paintings autonomously [8]. Cohen's artistic knowledge about creating drawings and painting was captured in the form of a computer program which could then create new works itself. In the process of developing the program, the artist's process involved evaluating AARON's drawings and re-examining the knowledge in the programs in the light of his judgement. He then modified the program many times to include the new insights in the program. The creative process was one of externalizing his existing drawing and painting knowledge and then, once it was "made visible" by the computer, evaluating the outcomes and making further changes for which he often needed to acquire new knowledge. When he began this work, the drawings were concerned with strictly organizational issues in the sense that they were basically abstract. Cohen has since moved into expressing knowledge about colour in the computer program which, for some time has been generating figurative art works. The figurative knowledge in the computer system required more knowledge about the world, e.g. plant pot relationships to the ground area and the physical composition of human faces, as distinct from the earlier drawing object relationships e.g. perceptual groupings.

For Cohen, creativity is something that is a process of continuous change, as distinct from single events. That change, as his work exemplifies, is in the mind and actions of the human and the process is essentially a directed one. There have been many cycles of his exploratory, pioneering work but during all that time, his goals have been consistent. His work is unique and the basic concept of developing an autonomous creative computer has rarely been taken as far as this. Cohen explores the implications of his work for art practice and the changes that it has brought about in concepts of art and who owns it later in Chapter 7.

Another artist who has made pioneering contributions to art and technology in quite different ways is Manfred Mohr, whose work has been transformed by the visualization possibilities of technology. Mohr's work involves the construction of two-dimensional views of six-dimensional cubes (hyper-cubes). His goal is to express geometric knowledge about the cube which is encoded in the computer system using a programming language. The computer program then generates graphical entities from which he makes artworks using conventional media such as canvas and laser cutting and often special computer output devices to implement his intentions. The goals of two parties to the process, i.e. the artist and the computer, are clearly differentiated: the computer program generates purely geometric objects whilst the artist makes aesthetic choices on the basis of which he goes on to make artworks. The artist cannot do the bi-dimensional geometry in his head and the computer requires the artist to specify the geometric knowledge in a computationally tractable form. For Mohr, the interactive process with the computer is one with which he extends his capability as an artist:

what fascinates me about a machine is the experience of a physical and intellectual extension of myself. [9, p. 5-7].

A productive relationship with the computer is dependent upon both the power of the programming language used by the artist and his own ability to develop its capability to achieve his goals. Mohr's approach is to retain ultimate aesthetic control over the final outcomes rather than leaving the final choice to the computer

This symbiotic interaction differs from that of Harold Cohen's. Cohen's primary goal is to have the computer system make the artworks. The role he chooses for himself is to specify to the computer the critical underpinning knowledge about art from which the computer generates the drawings and paintings. In using a computer language to make a computer create works, rather than a software application to create the drawings and paintings himself, he is expressing a fundamental premise on which his whole approach is based, exemplified in the statement:

I inevitably get nervous about the notion that somebody could make art without a profound grasp of the underlying disciplines involved. [8, p.14].

Cohen's artistic vision places high value on expert knowledge about art and its role in computer-generated art. Mohr's vision involves exploring generative processes that are not accessible to human perception but are, nevertheless, able to be specified using the method he has chosen. The final artworks remain the province of his artistic decisions. For each artist, the particular points in the creative process when he chooses to interact with the computer language and the outcomes it generates, are different.

Contributors

The second part of the book contains articles written by artists and technologists who have been associated with the Creativity and Cognition Research Studios from 1996 to 2000. The articles are personal statements about individual and collaborative explorations in art and technology.

Both Harold Cohen and Manfred Mohr took part in the Creativity and Cognition conference and exhibition series along with Bettina Brendel, Joan Truckenbrod, Stelarc and Roman Verostko, all distinguished international artists. They represent a broad spectrum of digital art practice both in terms of artistic intentions and the purposes for which they employ computer technology.

Roman Verostko has dedicated himself to algorithmic art in which, as he puts it, the computer program acts as a *score* for visualizing the forms. He has a drawing machine, a multi-pen plotter, which is driven by his computer programs and produces his final work. These do not necessarily look as if they have anything to do with a computer, yet they could not exist without it. Verotsko has developed algorithmic systems that, despite their apparent formality, generate soft and quite organic results. He takes his inspiration primarily from artists in the constructivist tradition whilst, from the complex behaviour of his computer programs, he generates work that is far removed from the formal geometric forms with which one associates that tradition. He provides insights into his formative experiences and development as a digital artist in Chapter 12.

Bettina Brendel and Joan Truckenbrod both relate strongly to organic life, whilst finding inspiration in science. Brendel has drawn on analogies from physics for more than 40 years and she has a deep scientific interest. From that perspective, it was not difficult or surprising for her to adopt the computer as part of the armory of her studio. In her case, it did not bring special new conceptual issues into her work, rather it was a natural addition in the context of her interest in physics, as she makes clear in her statement in Chapter 6. In the case of Truckenbrod, on the other hand, the virtual worlds of computing and the Internet add a new dimension to her concerns. The differences and correspondences of virtual worlds and physical ones and transformations between them forms the driving concern for her digital work. See Chapter 11 for her account.

Stelarc has pushed the boundaries forward in a different sense. He is a performance artist who came to the realization that he could explore his human self by exploring the intersection of the technological and the organic. His work challenges our understandings and expectations of that intersection by treating technological devices and communications capabilities as extensions of himself. For Stelarc, the technology that he uses is at the centre of his conceptual interest. In order to make his work he has to become deeply involved both in the workings of the technology and in the science of biology in respect of the implications for each of the interchanges that he studies. Chapter 10 gives a flavour of the kind of dramatic work he performs using some remarkable and complex technologies.

The artist-in-residencies at Loughborough University in 1996, were held under the auspices of Creativity and Cognition [10]. Three of the four artists concerned went away without complete technological solutions to the problems they had brought to the table. The specific questions they were asking did not have ready-made software or hardware answers. Moreover, the artists themselves found they had to work through the generality of some of the problems they were posing with an expert in another discipline, in order to define more precisely the implications. Until you work through potential solutions, it is sometimes difficult to know what exactly is the right question to ask in order to solve the problem. Sometimes, until it has been worked through, it is not even clear what the problem is.

Of the 1996 residents, Fré Ilgen, Michael Kidner and Jean-Pierre Husquinet have contributed chapters to this book. The artist residencies that followed during 1999 and 2000 were both research and art led. The COSTART (Computer Support for Art) Project, funded by the Engineering and Physical Science Research Council of the UK, which provided support for residency accommodation and subsistence, undertook in-depth studies of collaborative art and technology projects [11]. Of the COSTART artists, chapters by Joan Ashworth, Dave Everitt, Beverley Hood, Anthony Padgett, Michael Quantrill and Esther Rolinson are included. For these artists, collaboration with technologists was vital. Technologists, Colin Machin, André Schappo and Manumaya Uniyal provide their own version of events. The YOTA (Year of the Artist) and AA2A (Artists' Access to Art Colleges)[1] schemes provided financial support for materials only and were aimed at educational and public exhibition outcomes. Of the artists funded by these schemes, Marlena Novak, Jack Ox, Juliet Robson and Ray Ward have contributed chapters.

The Artists

For Jean-Pierre Husquinet and Michael Kidner, artists-in-residence in 1996, the expectation that their work could benefit from computational support was a reasonable one. They were both seeking answers to complex problems that required a significant amount of prior analysis before a work could be executed: the first was in the area of knot theory and the second in Boolean nets. It did not seem far-fetched to assume that a computational solution would be possible, but before that could be achieved, the first and most important task was to specify the nature of their problem and then discuss with an expert how this could be realized. Working with mathematical and software engineering experts, revealed just how much knowledge was needed and how much effort would have to go into the solutions. They describe their experiences in Chapters 20 and 22 respectively.

In his residency, Fré Ilgen explored his perception and understanding of reality in its various aspects using a simulation of complex movements in three-dimensional objects. Interaction with a VR system proved to be a critical event in the artist's creative process that gave rise to new developments in his art. The technology did not perform a task on the artist's behalf nor did it produce artistic outcomes, but rather it stimulated him to generate new ideas and techniques. In Chapter 21, he gives his own account of the events and outcomes.

The 1996 residency artists were almost entirely new to digital technology. Initially, there were high, and perhaps unrealistic, expectations of what the technology could do to help solve their problems. For the organizers, one important lesson that was taken on board for future residencies, was just how vital it was to provide targeted support from technical experts. These residencies highlighted the fact that using new technology does not necessarily lead to a dependence or focus upon the technology itself, but rather to a change in the artist's understanding of his or her own creative process. It also demonstrated a need for greater understanding of the artist's process on the part of the technologists. We came to understand most particularly, that the availability of a support environment for art and technology explorations required the right combination of human expertise and the technological tools.

All of those experiences in turn led to the formation of the Creativity and Cognition Research Studios (C&CRS), a joint operation between the Computer Science Department and the School of Art and Design at Loughborough University, UK, as described earlier in Chapter 1.

The C&CRS artists who came in 1999 for the COSTART Project were all familiar with digital technology of one form or another. Some had already made extensive use of the technology in their work. These residencies were established as collaborative projects and had a dedicated technical environment allocated to them. Lessons from 1996 were applied to the development of resources and facilities as discussed earlier in Chapter 2.

Joan Ashworth, Professor of Animation at the Royal College of Art, London, is a professional filmmaker, animator and teacher who has first-hand experience of the rapid changes taking place in the film industry as digital technologies take hold. Her desire to bring such technology into her personal creative practice, without abandoning the tactile qualities of traditional animation methods, shapes her approach. This had an influence on her collaboration with the computer animator, Manumaya Uniyal. It was an intersection, not only between people of different knowledge and skill but also of goals and communication styles. Just as her "Stone Mermaid" project had a long gestation, so the partnership between artist and technologist required time to develop successfully. For this artist, her initial scepticism at the outset developed into an understanding of what was technically feasible and, moreover, where learning would have to take place on her part to make it an enduring process. The collaboration opened up new avenues and encouraged her to learn new skills in order to exercise more control over the process. She discusses her views in Chapter 17.

Beverley Hood's residency had some parallels with that of Joan Ashworth. However, her work is primarily directed towards developing static visual models rather than time-based work. She characterizes her creativity as a form of "hybrid invention" in which she explores the relationships between disciplines (e.g. sculpture) and diverse media (see Chapter 19). She has embraced digital technology as an artist but feels strongly that, without access to good digital facilities combined with the skills of technologists, there will be serious limitations to the take-up in the art world more generally. Ashworth points out that it is already the case that prejudice against computers operates within art circles, where the results are perceived as either computer generated (and, therefore not the artist's own) and/or "computer-styled" (i.e. bearing the hallmarks of the software rather than the artist). Either way, both the art world and the technology world have an uneasy relationship at this point in time.

Joan Ashworth and Beverley Hood both explored the possibility of using VR technology to realize their aims for the computer modelling of two-dimensional objects. For different reasons, they decided to use standard three-dimensional animation software believing that a VR environment was detached from important points of contact with the physical environment. By contrast, for Fré Ilgen, it was the unique ability of the technology to provide a non-physical environment that appealed to him. For example, he was able to work with sculptural objects without gravitational pull. For someone whose models were heavy and difficult to manipulate in the world, the out-of-world experience of VR was a liberating experience.

Both Ashworth and Hood are concerned with the interrelationship between the physical and digital worlds and what this means for their personal creative process. Hood is exploring the connections and differences between traditional and digital forms at the conceptual level, whilst Ashworth is keeping both traditional and digital techniques in play because neither satisfy all her creative needs. She is trying to utilize the benefits of the digital and yet retain the pleasures of a tactile experience. This

arises, in part, from her frustration with the limitations of digital technology in its familiar forms. She writes of the stifling effects of the
mouse, keyboard interaction methods on gesture and movement and effort required to develop creative ideas. Typical interaction with a computer is not only a sedentary activity but also a tightly restricted one,
where all the effort goes into finger-tip movement or small slight traces
of a pointing device across a tiny mat. Haptic environments that incorporate force-field interaction, offer a way towards addressing the need for
physical interaction through gesture and movement. An example is the
Reachin Technologies system [12].

One factor that influenced Ashworth's decision not to pursue the VR
route was the requirement to specify the conditions and parameters of
the environment to be modelled in advance. This, she felt, limited the
opportunity for a more spontaneous process of developing ideas. For a
software engineer, the artist's preference for an opportunistic, iterative
approach is not only an unfamiliar way of working, but is usually considered to be undesirable. These differences between the intersecting disciplines of software engineering and art practice in formulating ideas and
making artifacts can lead to mismatches.

When both computer science and art disciplines co-exist in the same
person, there can be conflicts that create blocks in thinking, as Mike
Quantrill discovered. This situation illustrates that working with the
complexities of real or simulated physical worlds can be problematic.
Quantrill is that rare person who is formally trained in computer science
but whose central concerns are with art. He assumed the role of technical
expert providing advice and programming support for the projects of
Anthony Padgett and Esther Rolinson. At a different time, with Dave
Everitt, he formed a joint residency project in which he was able to pursue his personal artistic goals. This collaboration developed into a partnership that proved to be successful and sustainable. His contribution in
the book focuses upon his own work. In Chapter 26, he describes how the
close coupling between mind, hand and body and the technology itself is a
transformational experience. He characterizes his work as an intertwining
of human and machine processes leading to unexpected outcomes such as
the time-based dimension of the work.

Quantrill reflects on his interest in how the use of the technology could
lead him to new understandings. Finished artworks are of a lesser concern.
A problem that is often referred to in relation to the use of computers is
their relative lack of support for sketching and tentative processes. The
pencil seems much better for this purpose. Quantrill, however, describes
much of his computer-based work in terms of producing "sketches". His
drawing on the electronic Soft-board [13] consisted of physical mark
making with felt-tip pens and could be termed sketching where an infor-
mal or tentative approach is being taken. On the other hand, his work
with the sensor grid in the interactive environment did not involve

making marks at all. In this case he refers to his computer programs as 'sketches'. He approaches programming in a way that takes deliberate account of the tentative and uncertain process that he is involved in. Each version of a program is seen as a tentative experiment leading to ideas for the next 'sketch'.

There is also a much more important sense in which Quantrill's work with the sensor grid extends the notion of sketching. He is experimenting with interaction spaces in which the position and movement of people, the participants, constitute the primary or only input to a computer system. Whilst the participants are not making marks on paper, their physical activity is recorded and leaves a trace within the computer system. In effect, Quantrill sees them as sketching with their body. One way that he looks at his work is as an investigation into languages of interaction: this is a form of correspondence between human movement and formal representations within the computer. Understanding such processes forms the core of his explorations. In doing this, his relationship to the technology is very close and he explicitly refers to its role as actively informing the work. For this artist, the computer is much more than just a tool.

Dave Everitt, in his collaboration with Mike Quantrill, experimented with interactive pieces using the sensor grid. He describes his way of working as maintaining a number of simultaneous lines of enquiry from which ideas emerge and bear fruit at times in the form of art projects. He draws on mathematics through contact with the Magic Cube interest groups on the World Wide Web and works increasingly in collaboration with programmers to develop his ideas. During his residency, he worked with computer scientist, Greg Turner, who helped him to realize his magic square concepts in computer programs that drove interactive artworks. His approach is eclectic, concerned with issues that have cultural, social and artistic implications. The creative driver for much of the work of Everitt seems to come from the intersection of disciplines and is brought about largely through collaborations of various kinds, from direct partnerships to Internet discussion groups. He discusses these issues and poses a number of questions about art and technology in Chapter 18.

Another artist for whom collaboration is central is Jack Ox. The primary goal of Ox's work is to create an intimate correspondence between visual and musical languages. In Chapter 24, she describes what she does as a form of 'translation' of music into sets of visual languages. To achieve this, she has to determine structural parameters of the piece of music to be visualized, which take the form of operating principles and data sets that are encoded in MIDI files in the Color Organ. A critical part of the process over many years has been her collaboration with composers and experts in digital technology. She has moved on from the formula of having a technological assistant to one of having a technological equal partner and co-author of her art. She also finds that such collaborations provide the triggers for significant creative advance. The importance of finding the right people to interact with creatively has driven her to seek out particular individuals over a wide geographical area. She acknowledges the fact that the kinds of works she is interested in are expensive to develop and difficult to market. However, she has no patience with the idea that an artist should rely on financial subsidies and has been exploring ways of using the Internet to make available high quality prints from electronic works for sale. Her participation in conferences, giving talks, writing papers and demonstrating her works is part of an entrepreneurial spirit that seeks to disseminate innovative ideas to international cultural communities and the public at large. In doing this, Jack Ox is not just promoting art. It is her experience and firm belief that, in the technology and art collaborations that she finds so necessary, the technologist has much to gain and that the artist should positively engage in achieving such benefits as well as progressing their own art practice.

Marlena Novak is also very positive about the importance of collaboration, both with technologists and with artists in other fields, particularly in music. The most significant conceptual step that the computer has enabled her to make is to add a time-base to her previously static work. It is from this step that the concern with correspondences between time-based visual art and music arose. As well as adding a new dimension to her work, it seems that there was feedback from the music. Her direct concern was with composed, rather than improvised, music. That is to say, the time-base from the music was fixed and the sequence of sounds determined. From a visual point of view, this directly relates to film. Naturally, therefore, Novak was able to make great use of software tools that had been constructed to support film making. Her time-based work could not be called film, but its fundamental structures correspond to those used in film, hence the tools work for her. Whereas most film represents real or imagined worlds, Novak's work is generally abstract. Nevertheless, a correspondence at the level of the underlying structure of the work is sufficient to enable the same tools to be employed. She provides interesting insights into her formative ideas and the development of her recent work in Chapter 23.

Esther Rolinson works with natural elements and architectural structures and creates installations in the physical world. She is developing an interest in using digital technology to control her light structures and to explore the way it affects the relationship between the object and the viewer. The project she carried out during her artist-in-residency involved collaboration with two technologists, Colin Machin and, with his technology hat on, Mike Quantrill. The work involved the development of both hardware and software for the piece itself, but it also became apparent that the ability of the computer to provide visual simulations of the intended work was also valuable to her development process. A third technologist, Dave Garton, eventually joined the team to develop this simulation, as described in Chapter 14 by Machin.

Iteration and flexibility in the creative process proved to be important as Rolinson's ideas evolved in response to new developments as they emerged. In her case, the enabling of the flexibility was very much a technologist's problem. She chose not to develop specific expertise herself but to rely on her partners, putting her efforts into defining and communicating her intentions. This is always particularly hard in relation to software development, on which she worked with Mike Quantrill. She stresses how important it was that he was also an artist, and therefore, that the communication between them about complex issues was eased. Nevertheless, from time to time, she indicated concern about how much control over the process she might have to relinquish to the technologists because of her lack of programming knowledge. In Chapter 28, she describes some of her experiences in collaboration and the influence of this on her artistic development.

Anthony Padgett began as a sculptor exploring different forms of bringing art and nature together. The spiritual dimension of his experiences has taken him into the potential of digital technology for extending the range of interaction between artist, viewer and the physical and spiritual world. He has found the interactive sensor grid system an experience that frees the participant and blurs the distinctive boundaries between technology and human being. He is not the only artist to have found this system a liberating experience from the usual forms of interaction with computer systems. Although Mike Quantrill also had a similar view, Padgett saw the opportunity in explicitly spiritual terms. Spiritual as his viewpoint might be, he was very clear about the importance of well-organized teamwork. He draws an analogy between digital art collaborations and film crews, in which each person has a clear well-defined and distinct expert role. It is also interesting, as he describes in Chapter 25, that he ran an experiment involving art students using the Soft-board as part of his exploration of the creative space that the device offered.

Ray Ward is another artist who sees himself working as part of a collaborative team. He accepts that he may not have all of the skills needed to make a work and points out that there is a long tradition of artists working with others in this way. Being adept at communicating with other members of the team is, however, a vital skill. The research studies reported earlier also noticed that there is much more than the need for help from others required for making a collaboration work. Particular kinds of communication and collaboration skills are important if teamwork is needed. Ray Ward noticed how important it was to learn to understand just how slow the development of computer systems can be. The speed of the computer does not equate with the speed of the development process. As he points out in Chapter 29, digital artists have to understand

and to come to terms with this if they are to be successful in their collaborations with technologists.

Juliet Robson, on the other hand, found how important the attitudes and availability of the technologists were to the creative potential of her work with technologies. When successful, her collaborations were characterized by the existence of clear and distinct roles. As with Padgett's film crew analogy, Robson was more concerned with the best way to facilitate communication than with finding the best way to learn everything herself. The communication aspect of collaboration was more important to her than simply getting things done. It was also a significant stimulus to creative thinking. The intersection of disciplines through the meeting of experts in those disciplines seems to have been a significant trigger for her work. The most important trigger, of-course, was the very particular constraint that disability brought with it. The viewpoint of a wheelchair user led to some very innovative use of the technology. Perhaps the most important aspect of her relationship as an artist with the technology was to insist that the "normalizing" of her use of it was not the main point of her work. In Chapter 27, she describes how she sought ways of reconceptualizing the technology from the point of view of her physical situation by, for example, abandoning the wheelchair and exploring the opportunities for relating to and through the technical systems from that perspective. For example, she used a movement tracking system that is often applied to the identification of physical problems in order to explore and, indeed, celebrate her own "language of movement". [14].

All these artists are concerned with issues of art practice and reflect upon the changes that digital technology is bringing to their practice. In their writing, it is not the "nuts and bolts" of practice that concerns them most, but conceptual shifts and opportunities for extending collaboration. Where the artist cannot find a way to exploit the technology, the reasons are rarely a failure of the usability of the software alone. As these artists demonstrate in their own words, the mapping of artistic goals and intentions to digital methods often requires transformations not only in the technical solutions but also in the artist's thinking.

Notes

[1]   YOTA and AA2A are two examples of support for residencies from publicly available sources that were acquired for C&CRS artists: YOTA (Year of the Artist) 2000 was a UK Lottery Funded Scheme and AA2A (Access to Art Colleges) 1999–2000 was supported by the National Association for Fine Art Education in collaboration with the National Arts Association of the UK.

References

1. COSTART Survey 1999 Report: follow links: http://creative/lboro/co/uk/costart

2. Guindon, R., Krasner, H. and Curtis, B.: Cognitive Processes in Software Design, Proceedings of the 2nd IFIP Conference on Human Computer Interaction-INTERACT'87, North-Holland (1987) 383-388

3. Ullman, D.G., Dietterich, T.G. and Stauffer, L.: A Model of the Mechanical Design Process Based on Empirical Data. AI EDAM, 2 (1) (1988) 33-52.

4. Maccoby, M.: The Innovative Mind at Work. IEEE Spectrum (1991) 23-35

5. Boden, M.A.: The Creative Mind: Myths and Mechanisms. Weidenfeld and Nicolson, London (1990)

6. Candy, L. and Edmonds, E. A.: Artefacts and the Designer's Process: Implications for Computer Support to Design. Journal of Design Sciences and Technology. 3 (1) (1994) 11-31

7. Candy, L. and Edmonds, E.A.: Creative Design of the Lotus bicycle: Implications for Knowledge Support Systems Research, Design Studies. 17 (1) (1996) 71-90

8. Cohen H.: The Robotic Artist: Aaron in Living Color. The Computer Museum, Boston (1995)

9. Gomringer, E.: Manfred Mohr-Cubist in the Computer Age. In Algorithmic Works (Manfred Mohr), Josef Albers Museum, Bottrop (1998) 5-7

10. Creativity & Cognition Conference: creativityandcognition.com/

11. COSTART Project Web Site: http://creative.llboro.ac.uk/costart

12. Reachin Technologies AB: http://www.reachin.se

13. Soft-board: Microfield Graphics: http://www.microfield.com

14. CODA System: Charnwood Dynamics: http:// www.charndyn.com

Part 2

6   Windows to a New Dimension

Bettina Brendel

In my work, I visualize the sub-atomic world of elementary particles, photons and electrons, and how their interactions create patterns and symmetries. These are magnifications of processes that occur in nature, but are inaccessible to the human eye except through the use of powerful instruments. I see the artist as a participant in the creative discoveries and inventions of our century.

Over the years I have worked towards developing a symbolic language to express ideas that deal with the physics of light and energy. Imagine that we had a seventh sense that could penetrate matter, magnify it and reveal its secrets to us. Imagine that this penetrating power could defy time and place, preserve what is perishable, predict what is still distant in the future, and then realize that we have this instrument with us every day. It is our mind which explores the unknown, which can enlarge and focus on hidden details in nature and enter into vibrations of energies from the past to the future. The abstract world of particles and fields, symmetries and balances is available to us through thought. This world is a world in motion and we, within our individual limitations create an ever-changing path of discovery to it. Being witness to a contemporary vision we nevertheless find our own interpretations, a visual metaphor that might also become meaningful to others.

First Steps with a Computer

I started to work with computers in 1988, rather late in my career. We were a small group of artists-in-residence at the California Museum of Science and Industry in Los Angeles. Our job was to give demonstrations to the public and explain how the computer works. In return we had free time on the latest computer technology and programs. I loved to tell science fiction stories on the screen for the schoolchildren who came to the museum with their teachers. There was a simple program for colour-cycling available on the computer that added animation to the screen. There was always 'hands-on' time at the end of the session when it was obvious that the children picked up the sequence of required steps faster than the adults. When the museum discontinued the program, I acquired my own computer.

Inspirations

Science, especially Physics has been the inspiration for my work for the last 40 years. Looking at the current work of internationally known, exhibiting artists, I continue to come across specific ideas in their art that originated in my mind many years ago. In 1969, I studied the technology of holography and wrote a poem about the holographic structure of thought and suggested that light is involved in both processes. I proposed using a sphere for the reconstruction of the image [1].

The known photographic technique called holography, records a subject, not by ordinary photography, but by recording the wave-fronts of light coming from the subject. The basic principles were originally described in 1947 by Dennis Gabor, but only after the introduction of the laser did the method become practical for commercial purposes.

Holograms can produce very realistic three-dimensional images of objects in black and white and in multi-colours. There are two stages in the holographic process: the recording stage and the reconstructing stage which requires a laser beam, mirrors and lenses [2]. The theoretical physicist, Michio Kaku, suggests in his book, Visions, that the total information shared by all the computers of the world may one day be stored in a single holographic cube [3].

On the Invention of a Spherical Hologram

A Ball of Light...

A ball of light rolls on the metered track,
And where its coating of emulsion
Receives the gentle touch of beam,
The pattern of an image, coherent message,
Inscribes itself onto the surface
Until the angled light inside the sphere
Illuminates for one brief second
The memory of now and then.
Thus while the trundling eye
Rotates from dawn to dusk,
From birth to death,
Through years of space and living:
The secret code of every thought
Is glowing presence in the mind.

We live in changing moments of perception,
While the diffused image of the hologram
Continues to appear as past, as future,
Behind, beyond the four dimensions of reality.

Bettina Brendel, 1969 [1]

Presently, in the year of the 75th anniversary of the discovery of Quantum Mechanics, one of the fundamental laws of Physics, I am working on a series of images that visualize the particle and wave nature of light and energy on which the theory is based. This visualization is, of course, done within the means of two-dimensional imagery and is a subjective proposal which has to satisfy the requirements of imagination and artistic integrity. Needless to say, the many thought and images connected with Quantum Theory, particles within waves, and waves created by particles, would require the introduction of motion, motion in space, or in "virtual space" as on the computer. But suppose the motion has been arrested for a second – what would the process look like?

The assumption of a Universal Atomic Length, a third universal constant as proposed by Werner Heisenberg, would suggest a particle portrayal of short, straight, thin lines vibrating within waves of energy.

Visual Parable

Heisenberg, one of the founders of Quantum Mechanics, deals with the question of observation, description and imagery in his book, *Ordnung der Wirklichkeit (Order of Reality)*. He speaks about those aspects of the world that can only be talked about in "parables", and says that the great philosophers were aware of the "floating character of all discoveries". [4]

Figure 6.1 Quantum waves No. 5: digital giclé print, 2001 © Bettina Brendel

I consider my picture, Quantum Waves No. 5 (see figure 6.1) to be such a visual parable as spoken of by Heisenberg. It was printed on a giclé printing press, and is number five of a series of seven. It was created on an IBM computer, using a magnetic drawing pen as part of an advanced art program. This program is especially designed for artists. It has a choice of 16 million colours. It offers various sizes of pens and brushes, transparent overlays, reduction and enlargement of parts of the picture, repetition and shading. First of all, the screen can be cleared of all icons and menus and the image is created by the artist in the same way as a drawing or painting on the paper or canvas. Only the light on the screen illuminates the image and adds magic and depth to the vision.

The painting, "Windows to the Micro-World", from the year 2000, shows three rectangular areas, windows, that display the magnification of a random motion of particles. The circle in the centre, like a magnifying lens, enlarges the pattern to a much higher degree, and we discover that each particle line is creating its vectors of energy that multiply indefinitely into the distance [5] (see Plate 8 in colour section).

Every New Discovery is a Window to a New Dimension

What now are the new dimensions of the twenty-first century? From Physics and Biology, nuclear powered microscopes would enable us to investigate cells and atoms to a higher degree. There will also be advances in medicine and healing. And what is important to me personally, is that there will be new forms of communication, such as computers interacting with brainwaves. Those advances in technology have to be regulated and limited by law and informed consent to experimentation by humans is required. In my estimation, these and many others, are the new dimensions of the twenty-first century. The immediate future holds unknown possibilities for the individual creative mind. Modern technology has given us new forms of communication; it has facilitated the exploration of outer space and advances in medicine. However, it has also afforded new ways of isolation and opened up the possibility of exploitation such as a loss of control experienced by the creative individuals over the singular invention of their minds.

References

1. Brendel, B.: On the Invention of a Spherical Hologram, 1969. In Whenever in the World, Poems, Jon Press, Los Angeles (1977)
2. Pennington, K.: Advances in Holography: Lasers and Light. Freeman, San Francisco (1968)
3. Kaku, M.: Visions, Anchor Books, New York (1997)
4. Heisenberg, W.: Ordnung der Wirklichkeit, R. Piper, Munich (1989)
5. Brendel, B.: Symmetry and Sequences. Exhibition Brochure, Beverley Hills, CA (2000)

7   A Million Millennial Medicis

Harold Cohen

A client visited my studio recently to see what new work I had. But instead of buying a painting, she invested about a quarter of what a painting would have cost on a new computer, a data projector and a license to run my computer program, AARON, from the output of which the paintings had been made. If you were to visit her apartment in New York now, you would find one wall of her living room serving as a screen on which you would catch AARON busily generating original images, a new one every two minutes or so.

AARON has been under continuous development since the early 1970s. It is still modest in size by today's standards, about 12 Mb including the code I've written myself and the LISP environment in which it runs. That is equivalent in size to ten rather fat novels. Given a cable modem on your computer, you could download it all from the World Wide Web in about four minutes.

The program also needs around 32 Mb of internal memory to run in, which is also modest by today's standards; the machine I work on today has four times that much and could hold a good deal more.

Around the time AARON began, nearly thirty years ago, the first computer I owned had only 8000 bytes of internal memory. So in nearly 30 years the internal memory I have had to work with has increased from 8000 bytes to 128 million; that is, 16,000 times as much. My current machine's hard disk holds 20 Gb – enough to store about sixteen hundred copies of the program – but there is really no way to calculate the increase in mass storage over the same period, because my first machine had only paper tape for storage. Punching the tape at ten characters per second, it would have taken almost two weeks to store the program, assuming you could get enough tape. That was not an issue at the time, though, since the first versions of the program ran to a couple of thousand bytes, not 12 million. My current machine, running at 866 MHz, is almost 20 times as fast as that cutting edge "minicomputer" of 30 years ago. The vice-president of the company that made it told me he did not think the price of minicomputers would ever fall below the $10,000 I paid him for mine, because it would never be worth anyone's while to make them for less.

Have you ever tried counting up to 12,000 million, or catching an eight-hundred-millionth of a second as it went by? How did our numbers get to be so far outside ordinary human experience?

Moore's Law says that computer power per unit cost doubles every eighteen months. My five-year old daughter can count to eighteen and doubling is easy enough to understand; but think about what doubling every eighteen months actually means. This is the contemporary version of the old tale about the crafty advisor who bankrupted the king by requesting payment for services rendered with one grain of rice on the first square of a chess board, two grains on the second and so on – 2^{64} grains of rice turned out to be a lot of rice. In AARON's thirty years I've seen twenty eighteen jumps, which means that the computing power per unit cost available to me today is greater than it was when AARON started by a factor of 2^{20} power, which is over a million.

A million-fold increase in anything is pretty impressive, but since Moores' Law deals only with raw computing power, it only scratches the surface of what these immense numbers imply for people. Just as computing power increases exponentially, the number and the range of applications computing makes possible proliferates exponentially also. Just as AARON in its present state would never have been possible thirty years ago, we did not then – *could* not then – have had global weather prediction, CAT scans, the mapping of the human genome, digital imaging, ... the list goes on and on. Most important of all, we could never have had the revolution in communications that is going on right now. No email, no World Wide Web, no instant access to libraries full of information, no e-commerce, no way of receiving the equivalent of ten fat novels in four minutes.

Every day, we see more and more indications of how different things are from what they were yesterday. Yet most of us still find it extremely difficult to grasp the fact that the process of technological change that brought us from yesterday to today is now sweeping us into tomorrow at ever increasing speed. Doubling every eighteen months means that the next eighteen months will see as much change as all the previous changes put together. And when our current silicon-based computing technology finally runs out of steam, its successor technology, molecular computing, quantum computing, whatever it turns out to be, will make Moore's Law seem like a masterpiece of understatement. A recent article in *Scientific American* described the next generation as follows: if you imagine the entire page of the magazine to represent one logical unit in a silicon-based computer, the same unit in a molecular computer would be as big as one period on the page.

Not Speed, Acceleration

And this is not merely a technological revolution. We are being swept forward in an accelerating cultural revolution of unprecedented scale.

As an artist, I have always believed that art is a cultural undertaking much more than it is a personal one: that, inevitably, the health of art reflects its relationship to the culture it serves. It is not clear any longer what that relationship is to be in the decades ahead, because it is not clear any longer how the culture will evolve in the decades ahead. Traditionally – in Western cultures, at least – the arts have been supported for the services they provide, not directly to the culture at large, but in return for the luxury objects they provide to those relatively few patrons wealthy enough to afford them and willing to do so. Today, at the same time that the Internet is effecting truly global communications for the first time in history, it has also been manufacturing wealth at a rate unprecedented in history; at the height of the internet boom, reportedly sixty new millionaires a day!

That should mean that the arts can look to a rosy future with patronage for all, should it not? Lots of luck! Rumour has it that in his multimillion dollar home Bill Gates, Mr Microsoft, has some very large, custom-made computer screens upon which he displays reproductions of Rembrandt paintings; paintings he could afford to buy if they were on the market. If art-as-luxury-object is the name of the game one can understand that a Rembrandt painting is more of a luxury than a painting by Harold Cohen, but a *reproduction* of a Rembrandt? We owe the existence of the great luxury objects of Western art to the fact that the Medicis of the Renaissance supported *living* art. Clearly Bill Gates is no Medici and I think we should not assume too much about how many of those new millionaires will be. Yet the big question is not how many Internet millionaires will become art patrons, but whether it really matters.

Why is this so? Because even as this new wealth is being created, its cultural influence is being sidelined by the very communications revolution that is creating it. Let me explain. When I was exhibiting paintings fifty, forty, thirty years ago, an exhibition in one of London's leading galleries meant that perhaps two or three hundred people would see my work. A museum show might mean a thousand or two. Fifteen years ago, when I represented the USA in the World Fair in Japan, it was reported that a million people went through the US pavilion and saw one of my drawing machines at work over a six-month period. Five years ago, an exhibition at the Computer Museum in Boston was attended, physically, by the old-style numbers, a mere couple of thousand; yet my total audience, reached by television coverage, syndicated newspaper reports, magazine articles, the full range of media coverage made possible by an increasingly powerful and pervasive communication system, was estimated to be more than thirteen million. Since then, and while I may be the only artist remaining in the Western world who does not have a web site of his own, I am shocked to find my work referenced on almost a hundred other sites. I cannot even begin to guess how frequently those sites are accessed. To get some sense of the kinds of numbers we will have to consider in the years ahead, I heard recently from a curator at the Tate Gallery in London asking for permission to reproduce works of mine in their collection on their web site. Launched just last year, he told me, the site is now recording 170,000 hits a day!

One can hardly suppose that the arts will somehow avoid being impacted by rapidly changing patterns of patronage. It is hardly surprising that more and more artists today are looking to the World Wide Web, rather than to the hundred-year old gallery system, to provide a way of getting their work out to a potentially planet-sized audience. It is not clear, however, that the Web will actually pay off for them. According to Yahoo's Web reference book published last year, "there are more than fifty million websites residing on servers all over the world and the number is growing by thousands every day." The success of the gallery system rested upon a sophisticated marketing apparatus, and without an equivalent apparatus to support it, any work on the Web is likely to be lost in the sprawl, unlikely to be seen by anyone other than by accident.

In any case, I do not believe that the point for the artist is to reach the largest possible audience at any cost, but to reach an audience capable of hearing what he has to say, without compromising what that is in the process. And it is prone to compromise. No matter how original and valuable his internal thoughts may be, there is simply nothing to disseminate if they stay inside his head. At the same time, there is nothing automatic and nothing neutral, about the business of getting them out of his head and into the external world. The external image has to be produced and what the individual is able to say is heavily mediated by whatever technology of production he can muster, just as it will then be mediated by the technologies of dissemination.

That has always been the case, of course, although for most of Western history, both the means of production and the means of dissemination stayed stable enough for long enough – I am oversimplifying a bit – that they could be largely ignored as active elements of art-making. The Industrial Revolution changed both, from painting in the studio with traditional earth colours to painting outdoors with factory-produced metal-oxide colours of unprecedented vividness; from traditional patronage to the beginnings of the dealer system.

But those changes were marginal compared to what we are facing now. For the means of production and the means of dissemination – computing and communications – are not merely changing as rapidly and as radically as everything else, they are the central issues, the engines that are driving the technological revolution. I believe that from now on they will figure as active components of art-making, to a far greater degree than history and training have ever suggested.

It is thirty two years since I met my first computer and by simple virtue of having been around for long enough in this revolution I am able now to discern with reasonable clarity the influence of these two components upon what has played out in my own work. Just a couple of weeks after arriving in San Diego on a one-year visiting professorship I met a graduate music student who seemed intent on teaching programming to anyone in the arts he could grab, and I simply allowed myself to be grabbed. To explain why I allowed myself to be grabbed I will need to say something about what I had been doing before it happened.

For most of the 1960s I had been preoccupied with what I still regard as the core mystery of image-making: the curious fact that we are able to use marks on flat surfaces as representations, surrogates, for events and objects in the real world. My paintings were driven by that preoccupation: they were *about* representation, without being representational in any obvious sense. But by the end of decade I was feeling that all I had succeeded in doing was cataloguing some of the ways in which marks serve as representations, without ever developing anything I could consider to be a broad theory of representation. I was feeling not only that I understood as little about the mystery as I had at the beginning, but that I evidently lacked the means to elucidate it further.

The Meeting with my First Computer was Unintentional

In a state of frustration, it seemed to me that there were more interesting things happening outside my studio than inside it and, once the opportunity was presented to me, I thought that computing might conceivably be one of those things. The meeting was thus unintentional and, in the event, bewildering. If I pushed beyond the first encounter, it was not because I immediately saw the future in a great flash of light, it was simply that I found programming to be an exciting and invigorating intellectual exercise. No doubt Pascal was right and fortune does indeed favour the prepared mind, but the mind is not always well enough prepared to accept the favour as soon as it is offered. It took me about six months before I began to develop a suspicion that this new technology, this new means of production, would allow me to get back on course, and to examine what was in my head in a clearer way than I had ever been able to do by painting alone.

All this was several years before my own first minicomputer and computing was even more unlike the way we know it today. The interactive, Windows-like environments we take for granted did not exist. Programs were punched in IBM cards, a line to a card, and the entire deck of cards was submitted to an operator who fed them to the university's central computer, a room-sized machine with considerably less power than the cheapest PC has today, and which the user never saw. You went back the next day for the output and if you had misspelled something or left a semicolon off a line, as I always did, you re-punched that card and re-submitted your job, to come back the following day for another error and another re-submission. It could take days to do what it now takes minutes to do.

Perhaps most trying of all for someone new to this new technology, there were no precedents that you could look to for justification, no one to say what computing might do for someone in the arts.

This may all sound very negative and certainly I would never want to go back to that primitive state. But it was not actually a negative experience. From my own perspective, the most significant difference between then and now is that today the user's biggest problem is to know which of the many programs being thrust at him by marketing moguls on the Web to buy.

In 1969, there were no programs to buy and no Web, nor even computer stores, to sell them. If you wanted a program you wrote it. I have never thought there was anything negative about that. On the contrary, I cannot begin to express how fortunate I feel myself to be that I came to computing at that time, prepared to do it the hard way, and with a growing suspicion that it might provide me with a way of refocusing upon my core preoccupations, my concern with the nature of representation.

I reasoned that if an artist's images could mean anything at all to people he had never met, it had to reflect some commonality much deeper than individual experience and probably had something to do with the fact that all human beings, regardless of their culture, use essentially the same cognitive system. I figured, then, that I might learn something about how human beings make images and how they read them if I could simulate, in a computer program, a few of the low-level cognitive functions we all share – the ability to differentiate between figure and ground, the ability to differentiate between closed forms and open forms, and so on. And since I didn't want to subvert any chance of acceptance by producing obviously mechanistic drawings I paid a good deal of attention to structuring the simulation in terms of the feedback mechanisms that pervade all human behaviour, whether in driving a car, steering a forkful of food to the mouth, or doing freehand drawing.

I thought that the test of the program's success as a simulation and an indication that I had learned anything in designing it, would be whether its output would be accepted on the same terms as, interchangeable with, human output. Obviously it could not be interchangeable in the sense of including those agreed upon, specific meanings in paintings that belong to a single state of a single culture. I regard artworks as meaning generators that evoke meaning in the viewer rather than inform the viewer what someone else, some artist remote in time and culture, intended to communicate. So, when a woman at one of my exhibitions told me she knew I must live in San Francisco since the program had just drawn one of the city's landmarks, Twin Peaks, I felt I could claim that my program was functioning as an evocation machine, doing just what it was supposed to be doing; and not one jot less so because I was living in San Diego, not San Francisco, and AARON had no concept of Twin Peaks.

That phase of AARON's development took the better part of six years and I could probably write most of the code today in a couple of afternoons. The difference reflects the fact that I was working both at the limits of available computing resources for that period and also at the limits imposed upon my means of production by my own programming skills. And during that same period I was also trying to resolve questions about the third element – the means of dissemination – that had arisen because of the other changes. Thinking conventionally in terms of exhibitions, it was clear that the little ten-inch monochrome screen upon which I was doing my programming would not suffice for an exhibition; only one or two people could actually see it at any one time.

By 1975, I had built my first device intended explicitly for exhibiting – a small computer-controlled turtle that rolled around on huge sheets of paper, leaving a trail of black ink behind it. Lots of people could see that at the same time. But the little turtle had so much 'personality', attracted so much attention to itself, that I became convinced that people could not actually see the drawings because they were focusing so completely on the turtle. I used it only twice – once at the international Documenta exhibition in Germany; and once at the San Francisco Museum of Modern Art. I abandoned it then in favour of more anonymous, conventional drawing machines, still big enough that at least a dozen or so people could stand around it and see what was being drawn.

I went on using machines of that same conventional sort for the next ten years. Yet it was clear even from my very first clumsy attempt at engineering that the nature of exhibitions – the means of dissemination – had changed for me as much as it had changed for the audience. As a painter I recognized that my paintings had a public role, but I never thought I had one myself. However, I was not just showing paintings in the mid 1970s and information about the sort of thing I was doing was not widely available as it is today. The public seemed to be divided pretty evenly between un-sceptical believers and unbelieving sceptics. The believers were happy to believe that computers could do anything and consequently accepted the idea, with neither difficulty nor understanding, that mine was making art. The sceptics thought computers were just complicated adding machines and, consequently, experienced insurmountable difficulty and equally little understanding, in believing that mine was doing what I said it was doing. One gentleman in Germany even announced that, of course, I was only doing this turtle stuff to make money, which gave my two unpaid assistants and me the biggest laugh we had had in weeks.

I was presenting this two-sided public with something it had never seen happen before, forcing both sides to ask questions, and I felt I had some responsibility in trying to provide answers.

From that point on, my exhibitions became extended conversation events in which I had the central role to play. I was repaid for my loss of privacy with some remarkable conversations. During my exhibition at the Tate Gallery in London, for example, one visitor remarked that he thought it a bit sad that the program had to be limited to doing what *I* wanted instead of being able to do what *it* wanted; particularly so because it had not been taught to do its own colouring and needed me to do it. I experienced no sudden flash of enlightenment; but looking back from much later I was able to see that even though the early stages of AARON's development were intended as a simulation of human behaviour, the idea of the program's *autonomous* behaviour had been implicit from the very beginning. In pointing to the possibility of an autonomous, self-determining program the man's remark rang a sort of advance warning bell for a change that did not complete itself until several years later.

Figure 7.1 AARON drawing in black and white 1985 © Harold Cohen

Before moving on to that change, and collapsing a long and complicated story into a couple of paragraphs, I should fill in briefly what had been happening to what I had in my head, what I wanted to say, along the way. When I started on the program – AARON as evocation machine –

it had seemed to me that I could continue to develop it indefinitely by adding more and more cognitive 'primitives' to its repertoire. After a while, as it turned out, I could not identify any more primitives to add. I started to suspect that the human cognitive system is the way it is, not because of a huge array of primitives, but because a relatively small set of primitives develop complex interactions in coming to terms with the external world. At that point, sometime around 1980, I started to look beyond what the textbooks told me about cognition to see how children's drawing behaviour actually develops. Having watched my own children when they were very young, I knew that drawing starts with scribbling, and that at some point a round-and-round scribble migrates outwards from the rest of the scribble to become a sort of container, an outline. It had also seemed to me that this was the point at which my children started to think of their drawings as representations for the familiar things of their world.[1]

I never had any great success in trying to simulate this key phase of children's drawing. However, the principle of generating a core figure and then drawing an outline around it turned out to be amazingly powerful. In applying it I found AARON's drawings becoming much more 'thing-like', so much more like representations of things in the world than anything it had done previously, that I concluded finally that I should really tell the program something about the real world. It took one final prod from a curator who wanted AARON to draw the Statue of Liberty for a bicentennial exhibition for me to add some rudimentary knowledge of how the human figure is constructed and how it moves and AARON crossed over into figuration, dragging me along with it. And the rest, as they say, is history.[2]

Figure 7.2 Drawing by Zana aged four years

The things one has in one's head do not come in isolated packages, and they do not all operate on the same level of control. Important as the change from abstraction to figuration was for me, it was paralleled by an increasing preoccupation with the notion that AARON should be able to do its own colouring. The way both issues worked themselves out was being determined to a very large degree by the fact – on a higher level of control – that AARON had been built as a simulation of human behaviour. Providing enough knowledge to deal with the human figure was giving the program independent control over a larger range of performance and, to that degree, eroding its identity as a simulation; but without causing a total revision of that identity.

In fact, it was the problem of giving AARON independent control over its own colouring that finally caused that fundamental re-evaluation; the realization that what I wanted to say, what I *needed* to say, had to do with autonomous program behaviour, not with the simulation of human behaviour.

But why colour? Why could colour force a change of direction in a way that the move to figuration had not done?

The problem of independent colour control was proving to be the most difficult I had ever faced. For about two years I experienced the same kind of frustration I had experienced at the end of the 1960s; the feeling that I lacked the intellectual means even to think about the problem, much less to do something about it. The first sign of a breakthrough came when I asked myself what elements of colour human artists had control over and realized that I had known the answer for as long as I had been painting and teaching. I still do not know why it took me so long to bring it into focus. The most important element of colour is, in fact, not colour at all, but brightness. If the artist has control over the brightness structure of his image he is half-way home with respect to colour. And when I showed the program how to control the brightness structure of its images, it was able very quickly to generate satisfactory colour schemes, some of which I could transpose directly onto the paintings I was making from AARON's output.

But that was, after all, only half-way: it was satisfactory but not masterful. And still linked too tightly to the simulation model to go the rest of the way. I had not yet fully grasped the fact that the simulation model could not solve the problem, for the simple reason that the program's strategies as a colourist could not possibly simulate the human colourist's strategies. But what *are* those strategies? How *does* the painter choose what colour to make some area of a painting? Colour is a sort of ultimate abstraction for human beings. We can use it, sometimes at a high level of expertise, but we cannot say how we do it. If I could not explain my own educated intuitions to myself, then how could I possibly write a program to simulate them?

Figure 7.3: AARON painting 1999 © Harold Cohen

As inexplicable as the human colourist's strategies are, what is clear is that they depend on the physical apparatus he has at his disposal. Human artists have eyes, and they know what colours they are mixing because they can see them. They mix colours in feedback mode as they do everything else in feedback mode, continuously adjusting the individual colours in a painting by eye until their educated intuitions tell them they have it right, without ever needing to say – without being able to say – what they think is right about it. My program did not have eyes to provide a feedback path, so continuous adjustment was out of the question. What it did have was the ability to construct a complete colour scheme "in its head", so to speak, and that is an ability human beings lack completely: so completely, in fact, that we can hardly imagine any mode other than our own existing, much less construct one. So it required a major change in mental set to understand that, while programs can be designed to do many of the things only expert human beings can do, and to do them at an expert level, all performance is apparatus-dependent and they cannot go about doing them in the same way when they do not use the same apparatus. That, of course, is just another way of saying that externalizing what one has in one's head is mediated by the means of production, that is, the technology one uses to externalize it. AARON's strategies would have to be built on its own ability to construct a colour scheme in its entirety and it would have to have rules that would guarantee getting it right first time. If that sounded like a daunting proposition – and it certainly did – it looked less so to me than the alternative, because I knew that if AARON did have eyes, I would then be forced into trying to simulate precisely the behaviour I already knew I could not describe.[3]

Once I had set myself on the path to making AARON an autonomous colourist, I had also to figure out what I would do about the means of dissemination, given that I wanted to continue to show, not merely the results, but the process. Colour displays of quite high quality were available by this time, but they were still too small to be considered as exhibition devices. I suppose it was just a bit too obvious, having built several generations of drawing machines, to think I had to build a painting machine.

Notice that I referred to the human colourist as possessing, not simply intuition, but educated intuition. He may get by without a detailed knowledge of any of the standard theories of colour, but he does not paint with theories of abstractions, he paints with paint. Paint gets its colour from a wide range of physical materials, each of them having distinct physical and optical properties, and what we mean by expertise in this domain is, among other things, a detailed knowledge of how these materials interact with one another. The physical properties of paint are not an issue when you are working on a computer display, but they certainly are for computer programs designed to work in the real world. I needed to be able to develop the program on the display, but the program had to make decisions in terms of what would happen on the machine. That is precisely the opposite of what industry wants of its colour output devices, which is to reproduce, as faithfully as possible, what the user does on the screen. It took the better part of a year to provide adequate knowledge: deciding on a suitable range of water-based dyes and suitable papers, making over a thousand samples from carefully measured mixtures and measuring the colour composition and brightness of the results.

I built three machines in all. The first served to show me how little I knew about engineering and never made it out of my studio. The second served me for a single exhibition at the Computer Museum in Boston. The third has been filmed in my studio for several TV programs, including, most recently, *Scientific American Frontiers*, but it has never been used in a 'live' exhibition and it won't be. It will shortly join the historical collection of the Computer Resource Center in Silicon Valley. The truth is that my experience of exhibiting with this machine was uncomfortably like my earlier experience with the turtle: a complicated technology, extremely difficult to keep stable, garnering much more attention than the program it was supposed to be serving. I could not help noticing, for example, that what really turned on the audience was not so much what the machine was painting, but the fact that it washed out its own cups and cleaned its own brushes. The principal reason for abandoning the machine was different, however. I reached the conclusion that there's something fundamentally regressive about trying to drag nineteenth century moving-parts technology into the twenty-first century. I should be looking forward, not backward.

But Where is Forward, Exactly?

I want to refer back to one of those museum conversations I mentioned earlier. This particular conversation took place during my exhibition at the Brooklyn Museum in New York. The show used four drawing machines, and a man had been standing watching one of them at work for some while, at first asking me questions, then engaging other people in conversation and trying to answer their questions, watching other people buying drawings for $25 each but never buying one for himself. Then, about fifteen minutes before closing time, as I was getting ready to do a last drawing, the man said suddenly "I want to buy the one it's starting now!" I pointed out that he had been watching the machine for hours and had already seen at least a couple of dozen finished drawings. Didn't he want to choose one of those, to see what he was buying? He frowned for a moment, then he said "The Medicis didn't know what they would get when they commissioned Michelangelo to do something, did they?" And I thought, Marvellous! For $25 this man has bought himself a place in history and won a new understanding of his relationship to art.

I suggested earlier that the enormous wealth being created by the Internet, rather than providing a new generation of Medicis in the old patronage model, was actually being sidelined as a cultural force by the very communication system that generated the wealth. I was not thinking about the millions of individuals who access the Web every day, but more particularly about this self-appointed new-style Medici in the Brooklyn Museum and all the hundreds of others like him – not millions yet – who bought original drawings in this and in other museums for $25 each.

If one thinks of dissemination in terms of art museums and art galleries, then almost inevitably one thinks in terms of art objects. Even so, I started to see about a year ago that data projectors, widely available today, would make much better exhibition devices, providing a far better fit to what it is I want to disseminate, than low-level robotics technology that grabbed the viewer's attention away from what the program was doing. And if physical art-objects are still required – and I am sure they will be – I could use one of the large-format printing machines that can produce museum-quality originals directly from the program's digital output; in minutes, instead of the six hours my painting machine required.

It occurred to me also to question the underlying assumption that dissemination has to involve galleries and museums. I have no doubt that they will evolve to serve changing public needs, as, indeed, they have been evolving, and continue to exist. At the same time, I started to see that the new communication media, the Internet and the World Wide Web, could enable me to make the entire art-making process, not just the art objects, available to this new breed of Medicis, without needing the gallery context at all. I could make the program itself available, so that anyone could download it off the Web and watch it generate original images all day long if they wanted to. They could run it on their personal computers in exactly the way I see it running on mine, even making prints for themselves if they want physical art objects. The logic of my situation seemed obvious, but that did not make its implications one bit easier to accept for someone who has spent half a century in the "official" art world. What if these new Medicis were in reality no more than a figment of my imagination? And if they did actually exist, what if they would not want what I have to offer? There are always a million reasons for not doing something. Finally I was able to stop myself asking "what if?" and arranged with a distributor, who can provide a Web-based equivalent to the marketing machinery of the orthodox dealer to market licences to the AARON program.

Today, anyone with enough interest, a computer with a modem and not much more than my Medici paid for his drawing fifteen years ago, can download a copy of AARON, doing just what I see it doing in my own studio. And, like the client with whom I opened this story, they can do what Bill Gates never understood that he could do. Why exhibit static reproductions of Rembrandts on your living room wall when you can not only display an infinite number of new, original images, you can have the privilege of being present while the artist is making them?

Will it work? Technologically, of course, it will work: it is working now. But, I believe that the health of art rests upon its relationship with the culture it serves. We may view the future that is rushing towards us as exciting or terrifying, infinitely desirable or infinitely depressing. We cannot have any very clear idea what it is going to be like and there is no way back. Whether AARON will help to establish a viable relationship with the culture as the future reconfigures it, I cannot possibly know. But, while I wait for the results to come in at least I have the feeling that, without being able to see more than a very little way down the road, I do have my head pointing in the right direction. That is a feeling every artist needs.

Notes

1   See A Self Defining Game for One player for a discussion of creativity, drawing and AARON available on the website and in a short version in *Leonardo*, 35 (1) (2002)

2   This part of the history is covered in several papers available on my web page. Follow links from Centre for Research in Computing and the Arts (CRCA): http:www crca.ucsd.edu/

3   I am skipping over detail when I say that today I regard AARON as an expert colourist. The story is covered in three papers which are available off the website.

8   Structure in Art Practice

Ernest Edmonds

My personal development in the use of digital technology in my art practice began more than thirty years ago. I used a computer for the first time to perform an art task for the construction of a work [1]. I was making a wall hanging relief consisting of twenty separate pieces, but I was struggling with what seemed an intractable problem. I had many bits and pieces and I wanted to arrange them according to certain rules. I found it very hard. Whenever I made an arrangement, it broke one of the rules I wanted to satisfy. It was as if I was setting out a chess game but at least one of the pieces was always in an illegal place. Luckily, I was able to gain access to three hours of computer time, which was almost enough to solve the problem for me. I had to switch the computer program off after three hours because someone else needed it but I still had not quite solved the problem. However, my program had reduced it into something I could solve myself. I finished solving the problem by noticing that I could make a small change to the computer's partial solution and complete the task. Thus, with a little help from me, the program then solved the problem.

That was a good beginning but I did not find this way of using computers very exciting. Later it became clear that many of the structural issues that had concerned me, such as the co-existence of two colours in the same space, could be tackled by moving from static to time-based work. By this time, such work was made possible by the fact that computing technology had moved on and could support it in a unique way.

The use of computers in abstract, constructivist,[1] art has mostly been in the production of static objects or series of objects and yet an important property of the computer is that it can handle complex activity developing in time. Indeed, computer technology has had an important impact in music from the specialized research at IRCAM[2] to extensive exploitation in Rock music. It is true that computer-generated images and videos are widespread, and, in so far as they aspire to art, they are often classified as "computer art", which is often understood to refer to work that has a strong technological feel about it. Recent developments in computer art have often placed a strong emphasis on constructing abstract models of three-dimensional worlds from which views are selected to make the final work. That may be too simple a description, but it certainly is the case that most of that work is not constructivist. More often, it might be more related to surrealist art. The use of the computer to represent imagined realities has been dominant.

The use of computers for constructing and manipulating images has received considerable attention and there is no doubt that most of us are quite amazed at what can be achieved technically. The exploitation of these possibilities in art practice, so far, has been largely influenced by one type of computer graphics, known as geometric graphics. In this approach, the basic elements, manipulated in order to produce images, are either geometric abstractions such as lines, circles and polygons, or three-dimensional entities such as spheres, cuboids and surface patches of one sort or another. We are so used to these notions that often, we forget that they are abstract. The abstract concept of a line, for example, is of something of no thickness and yet when we actually draw a line, it unavoidably has one. Of course, the physical line has many other qualities not attributable to the abstract one. Why else would we care about the difference between a 3B and a 2H pencil? Therefore, in using geometric computer graphics, careful attention has to be given to how the abstract descriptions of images constructed in this way are realized as perceivable images.

The technology itself encourages a view that the realization of the image is only an approximation to the perfectly formed abstraction. In the early days of the use of computer in the visual arts, this approach was used in order to generate drawings produced by automatic drawing machines called graph plotters. Inevitably, when it came to producing the drawing, one of the key concerns was the particular pen to be used and the speed that it was moved over the paper. Computer-generated video images, or sequences, showing views of imagined worlds constructed within the computer, are typical of modern work of this type. The concrete reality of the work is somewhat subsidiary to the abstract notion of it.

Video Constructs

The work that I am concerned with now is what I have come to call "video constructs" [3, 4]. A video construct is a work that is specified in a program. The structure of the work consists of visual elements comprising shapes and colours each with a set of physical or geometric relationships and time-based ordering relationships. The pieces are time-based, in that they exist in time just as music and film do. The concrete and final destination of the images is a video monitor. In no sense are the images seen on the screen a view of some other reality. They do not represent paintings or drawings any more than they relate to images seen in television news programmes. The work is concerned with precisely what exists on the monitor.

Figure 8.1 Six stills from Jasper video construct, 1988 ©Ernest Edmonds

The fact that an artwork is generated through a computer system allows considerable attention to be paid to the generating structures that underlie both the images, and their movement in time. However, the image is not a view of an abstract world hidden behind the screen. The image on the screen is the concrete and only reality of the work.

To take a specific example, the video construct, Jasper (Figure 8.1) is based upon a number of overlapping squares of reducing dimensions, each of a different gray tone. The work starts with the gray levels stepping evenly from black to white, starting with the largest square and ending with the smallest. This order is disrupted at the beginning and the work proceeds in a search for a new resolution. The search itself is the basis of the work. The image pulsates as the tones shift between the static squares in a way that is, perhaps, closer to the so-called minimalist music than normal video material. It changes with a regular persistent rhythm and has a sense of continual repetition, even though in reality it never quite repeats itself.

In a later example, Fragments ver5,[3] a matrix of squares is explored in a similar way, except in colour. Here, the piece moves through a portion of the colour space. Whilst the local rate of change can be fast, with some specific images only lasting for a fraction of a second, the general shift of colour is slow enough for the work to be quite different in the mid-afternoon from its mid-morning state. This work cannot be understood satisfactorily in the context of, for example, film. Rather, it is a changing exhibit having, perhaps, more in common with light dappling on water as the sun slowly rises and eventually sets than with the simple geometry that is, at first sight, its basis.

Control and Structure

It has become clear that a detailed technical control of the computer system for producing video constructs is as important to me as having control over oil paint were I currently painting in oils. Having control is largely a matter of the availability of specification methods that are clear and brief enough to be understood. For me, the most exciting element of the video construct is the careful and very terse way in which a specification of what occurs in time is possible. The brevity of the specification is extremely important in the development of my ideas. The inevitable exploration is so strongly supported by this aspect of computer use that new thinking about works emerges during my creative process [5].

The exploration of time-based constructive work made possible by modern computer technology is more than a new way of doing something. The conceptual development that goes along with the art practice is something new that has implications beyond video constructs. The new thinking and evolving concepts that come from the digital work will inevitably influence drawing, painting and construction as much as they are influencing the video.

The computer enabled me to express, at a much higher level than I was used to, what I wanted to achieve. I was able to write computer programs that specified the structures and the internal relationships and correspondences of the time-based work. The structures that I provided to the system specified the time-based development of the images as well as the colour and physical relationships that can be used in any single still, the transformations that can be used between stills and the strategy for progressing through time. The system has built-in knowledge that can be used to move from these structures to the actual realization of a work.

The system enabled the structure I had specified in my program to be generated in visual form. I could then look at that visual form, reflect on it and evaluate it. This meant that I could start to think about the implications of the structures in ways that were not possible before. Generating time-based work of this kind was transformed by the computer. It was not just a matter of a speeded up process but one that was changed in kind, in the sense that the way that thinking about the work was enhanced was entirely new. This work developed into a specific approach to the use of computing to augment creativity in which the expression of knowledge in the system and the interactive development of that knowledge was very important to my creative process.

Interactive Video Constructs

Recently, I have returned to my interest in the development of interaction techniques within artworks. Today, it is possible to use image-processing technology in order to build interactive works [6]. In my case, the time-based video constructs have become *interactive* video constructs [7]. Structures in time can be constructed so as to react to events detected by sensor systems. In the example of Kyoto (2001),[4] a real-time image analysis facility is incorporated into the generation of the work. The system includes a digital video camera that points towards the space in front of the work: it looks at the audience. The system uses motion analysis designed to detect human activity and so reports to the video construct computer about the presence of people and about the degree of motion (e.g. fast waving of a left arm). The behaviour of the piece then reacts to participant behaviour. The generative system at the heart of the work has a real-time correspondence with the participant's movement and, in turn, a visualized correspondence with the images displayed.

Kyoto, and similar work, incorporate a human motion recognition system designed to operate with a single person in front of a camera. A video stream from the camera is taken as input and processed in real time. Continuous interpretation of motion is provided from the images in the video stream. The system builds a model of human movement in front of the work and analyzes it, in real time, to the computer controlling the images. The model can represent the following:

- presence/absence of a person
- distance from the camera
- quantity of motion
- general direction of motion
- number of separate motions
- which body part caused each motion
- position of each motion
- recognition of specific motions (e.g. waving).

Conclusion

I have described some of the thinking behind my time-based and interactive art up to the current work employing image recognition. The work allows me to reflect on the implications of the organizing principles and the compositional elements that comprise the structure underlying my artworks. Generating time-based and interactive work was transformed by using the computer because it enables the effective construction of inter-relationships that provide computational models for building correspondences between forms and systems. The point is that the computer enabled me to express my ideas for the artworks in a way that gave me access to general strategies for constructing and evaluating the outcomes. I can specify rules and relationships between objects in a computer program, which then generates visual sequences. From this I can see the how this realization reveals the effects of the underlying structure. This means that I can explore and evaluate different structures for their effects and make changes in the rules that govern the structure according to personal criteria. It makes it possible to concentrate on the essential features of the work, such as how an interactive piece behaves rather than just how to build it. The comparative ease with which interactive artworks can now be created is helping me make a much fuller use of the conceptual advances that the computer has offered in terms of understanding structures in time and for interaction.

Notes

[1]   Constructivism is a movement characterized by geometric abstract forms with its origin in early twentieth century Russian art

[2]   The Institut de Reserche et de Coordination Acoustque/Musique, Paris, founded in 1977 under the leadership of Pierre Boulez. It is devoted to advancing the techniques of music, particularly in electronics and computing.

[3]   Fragments, Kyoto: more information on my work is available on my website: http://www.ernestedmonds.com

[4]   As note 2.

References

1. Edmonds, E.A.: Structure in Art Practice: Technology as an Agent for Concept Development. Leonardo (2002)

2. Cornock, S. and Edmonds, E.A.: The Creative Process where the Artist is Amplified or Superseded by the Computer. Leonardo 6 (1973) 11-15

3. Edmonds, E.A.: Logic and Time-Based Art Practice. Leonardo Electronic Art Supplemental Issue (1988) 19-20

4. Edmonds, E.A.: Vers Vidéo Constructs. Mesures Art International 3, Mesures, Liège (1989)

5. Edmonds, E.A.: Knowledge-Based Systems for Creativity. In Gero, J. S. & Maher, M-L. (eds): Modeling Creativity and Knowledge-Based Creative Design, Erlbaum, New Jersey, USA (1993) 259-271

6. Fels, S. and Mase, K: Iamascope: A Musical Application for Image Processing. Proceedings of the Third International Conference for Automatic Face and Gesture Recognition (FG'98), (1998)

7. Edmonds, E.A. and Dixon, J.: Constructing Inter-relationships: Computations for Interaction in Art. In: Gero, J.S. and Maher, M-L. (eds): Modeling Creativity and Knowledge-Based Creative Design, Sydney University (2001)

9   Generative Art

Manfred Mohr

In my artistic development I did not have the typical constructivist background [1]. I was an action painter and jazz musician. Through a development of consciousness, I detached myself from spontaneous expressions and turned myself to a more constructivist and, therefore, geometric expression [2]. Beyond this, my art developed into an algorithmic art in which inventing rules (algorithms) is the starting point and basis of my research. These compositional rules are not necessarily based on already imaginable forms, but on abstract and systematic processes. My rules are parametric rules, which means that at certain points in the process, conditions have to be set for which, in some cases, random choices can be employed.

In my work, similar to a journey, only the starting point and a theoretical destination is known. What happens during the journey is often unexpected and surprising. Even though my work process is rational and systematic, as well as controlled by visual criteria at all times, it is always open to surprises. With such parametric rules, the actual image is created as the result of a process. Since 1973, in my research, I have been concentrating on fracturing the symmetry of a cube, without questioning the structure of the cube as a "system,,. This disturbance or disintegration of symmetry is the basic generator of new constructions and relationships. What I am interested in are the two-dimensional signs, "etres graphiques,, resulting from the projection of the lines of a cube. I describe them as unstable signs because they evoke visual unrest.

My artwork is always the result of a calculation. At the same time, however, it is not a mathematical art, but rather an expression of my artistic experience. The rules I invent reflect my thinking and feelings. It is not necessarily the system or logic of my work I want to present, but the visual invention which results from it. My artistic goal is reached when a finished work can dissociate itself from its logical content and stand convincingly as an independent abstract entity. These algorithms can become very complex, that is to say, complicated and difficult to survey. In order to master this problem, the use of a computer is necessary in my work. Only in this way is it possible to overlay as many rules as necessary without losing control. It is inevitable that the results – that is, my images – are not readable at first glance. The information is deeply buried and a certain participation is demanded from the spectator, a readiness to interrogate this material.

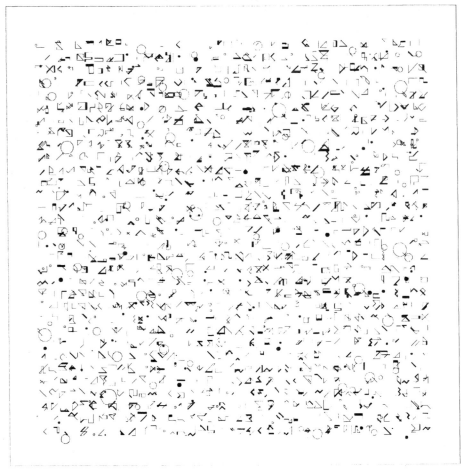

Figure 9.1 P-049/S: Plotterdrawing ink/paper 1970 © Manfred Mohr

In principle, all my work can be verified and rationally understood. This does not mean that there is no room for associations and imagination. On the contrary, the rational part of my work is limited basically to its production. What one experiences, understands, learns, dreams ... or interprets because of the presence of the artwork rests solely in the mind of the spectator. An artwork is only a starting point, a principle of order, an artist's statement, intended to provoke the spectator to continue his investigations. The steady increase of complexity in my work forced me to reconsider the use of the binary system black and white in order to find a more adequate visual expression. Adding colours to my work describe spatial relationships which are not based on color theory. The colours should be seen as random elements, showing through their differentiation the complexity and spatial ambiguity essential to my work [3].

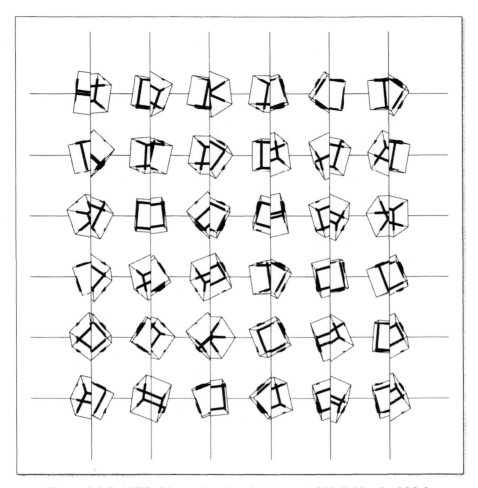

Figure 9.2 P-197/S: Plotterdrawing ink/paper 1977 © Manfred Mohr

My colour work is shown as inkjet images, and also on a flat screen presenting a slow motion animation, so that time after time a different image appears. This work phase (as well as all my work since 1990) is based on the six-dimensional hyper-cube. This geometrically defined structure has 32 diagonals. The endpoints of each diagonal lie diametrically opposite in the structure. A "diagonal-path„ is the connection of two such diametric points through the network of edges of this complex structure. In a six-dimensional hyper-cube, each of these 32 diagonals have 720 different "diagonal-paths„. For each work a random selection of four "diagonal-paths" from this repertoire of 23,040 (32*720) possible paths is made (thick lines) and are ordered from 1 to 4. The corresponding vectors are connected with thin lines. Thus, vector pairs are created and together with the thin lines, form planar quadrilaterals or colour fields.

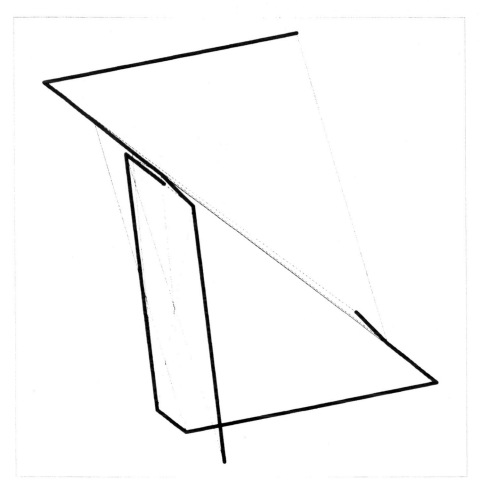

Figure 9.3:P-503/U   Plotterdrawing ink/paper 1997 © Manfred Mohr

In each work, two colour fields must stay white. The two outer "diagonal-paths,, (one and four) are connected in the same way but without thin lines, wrapping the image around the outside of the bounding rectangle. The hypercube is rotated in six-dimensional space and then projected into two-dimensional space. The resulting image overlays the colour fields from front to back. Together with the "diagonal-paths,,, the resulting image creates unimaginable constellations.

References

1. Rickey. G.: Constructivism: Origins and Evolution. G. Braziller, New York (1967)
2. Keiner, M., Kurtz, T. and Nadin, M.: Manfred Mohr. Waser Verlag, Zürich (1994)
3. Mohr, M.: Space.Color. Museum für Konkrete Kunst, Ingolstadt (2001)

10   From Zombies to Cyborg Bodies: Extra Ear, Exoskeleton and Avatars

Stelarc

This chapter is about what is seen to be meaningful in performances and the ideas that are generated by the actions in them. Sometimes, existing available instruments and technology are used. For example, in the body amplification performances with the Third Hand, medical instruments to monitor and pre-amplify body signals were used. The Third Hand was based on prosthetic devices and research at the time, but as a constructed object, it is unique. However, it is not always possible to simply access technology. The Stomach Sculpture that was inserted inside the body for the Fifth Australian Sculpture Triennale was an object constructed from scratch. To achieve it, the assistance of a jeweller and a micro-surgery instrument maker were needed. The team used an endoscope to track the insertion and to document it on video. Also with the Exoskeleton, there has been research and construction of small walking robots. A new contribution was the design of the six-legged spider-like robots large enough to support a human body. The control system is unique too. The leg motions are controlled by arm gestures; magnetic sensors on the segments of the jointed exoskeleton, which wraps around the upper body, indicate to the computer which mode of locomotion and the robot's direction is selected.

Zombies and Cyborgs

The body is an evolutionary architecture that operates and becomes aware in the world. To alter its architecture is to adjust its awareness. The body has always been a prosthetic body, one augmented by its instruments and machines. There has always been a danger of the body behaving involuntarily and of being conditioned automatically. A zombie is a body that performs involuntarily, that does not have a mind of its own. A cyborg is a human-machine system. There has always been a fear of the involuntary and the automated. Of the zombie and the cyborg: we fear what we have always been and what we have already become.

Issues of identity and alternate, intimate and involuntary experiences of the body, as well as the telematic scaling of experience, are explored in accounts of recent performances. Technology is inserted and attached. The body is invaded, augmented and extended. Virtual–actual interfaces enable the body to perform in electronic spaces. What becomes important is not merely the body's identity, but its connectivity, not its mobility or location, but its interface. The Stomach Sculpture is an object inserted into the stomach cavity. It is actuated by a servo-motor and a logic circuit tethered to a flexi-drive cable. It opens and closes, extends and retracts and has a flashing light and a beeping sound. The Stimbod software makes possible the remote choreography of the body using a touch-screen interfaced muscle stimulation system. In the Fractal Flesh performance, people at the Pompidou Centre in Paris, the Media Lab in Helsinki and the Doors of Perception Conference in Amsterdam, were able to access and actuate the artist in Luxembourg. Exoskeleton is a pneumatically powered six-legged walking machine actuated by arm gestures. Hexapod is a more compliant and flexible six-legged walking robot and although it looks like an insect, it will walk like a dog. Movatar is an inverse motion-capture system – an intelligent avatar that will be able to perform in the real world by accessing and actuating a body, whereas in previous performances the artist has attached prosthetic devices to augment the body. Now the body itself becomes a prosthesis, possessed by an avatar to perform in the physical world. The Extra Ear is a proposed project to surgically construct an ear that, connected to a modem and wearable computer, becomes an Internet antenna able to hear real audio sounds to augment the local sounds it hears with its actual ears.

Surface and Self: The Shedding of Skin

As surface, skin was once the beginning of the world and simultaneously the boundary of the self. But now stretched, pierced and penetrated by technology, the skin is no longer the smooth and sensuous surface of a site or a screen. Skin no longer signifies closure. The rupture of surface and skin means the erasure of inner and outer. An artwork has been inserted inside the body. The Stomach Sculpture, constructed for the Fifth Australian Sculpture Triennale in Melbourne, whose theme was site-specific work, was inserted 40 centimetres into the stomach cavity, not as a prosthetic implant, but as an aesthetic addition. The body becomes hollow, not the Body Without Organs, but rather a Body with Art. The body is experienced as hollow with no meaningful distinctions between public, private and physiological spaces. The hollow body becomes a host, not for a self but simply for a sculpture. As an interface, the skin is obsolete. The significance of the cyber may well reside in the act of the body shedding its skin. The clothing of the body with membranes embedded with alternate sensory and input/output devices creates the possibility of more intimate and enhanced interactivity. Subjectively, the body experiences itself as a more extruded system, rather than an enclosed structure. The self becomes situated beyond the skin. It is partly through this extrusion that the body becomes empty. But this emptiness is not through a lack but from the extrusion and extension of its capabilities, its new sensory antennae and its increasingly remote functioning.

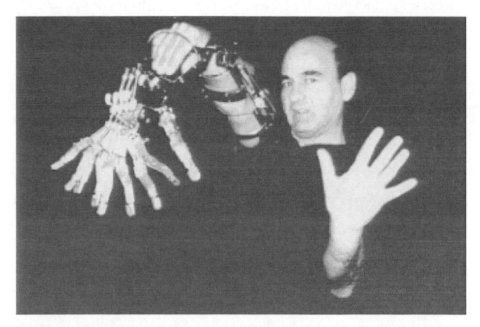

Figure 10.1 Extended arm; Melbourne/Hamburg. Photo T. Figallo © Stelarc

Fractal Flesh

Consider a body that can extrude is awareness and action into other bodies or bits of bodies in other places. An alternate operational entity that is spatially distributed but electronically connected. A movement that you initiate in Melbourne would be displaced and manifested in another body in Rotterdam. A shifting, sliding awareness that is neither "all-here" in this body nor "all-there" in those bodies. This is not about a fragmented body but a multiplicity of bodies and parts of bodies prompting and remotely guiding each other. This is not about master-slave control mechanisms but feedback-loops of alternate awareness, agency and of split physiology. Imagine one side of your body being remotely guided whilst the other side could collaborate with local agency. You watch a part of your body move but you have neither initiated it, nor are you contracting your muscles to produce it. Imagine the consequences and advantages of being a split body with voltage-in, inducing the behaviour of a remote agent and voltage-out of your body to control peripheral devices. This would be a more complex and interesting body, not simply a single entity with one agency but one that would be a host for a multiplicity of remote and alien agents.

Of Different Physiology and in Varying Locations

There may be justification, in some situations and, for particular actions, to tele-operate a human arm rather than a robot manipulator. If the task is to be performed in a non-hazardous location, then it might be an advantage to use a remote human arm, as it would be attached to another arm and a mobile, intelligent body. Consider a task begun by a body in one place, completed by another body in another place, or the transmission and conditioning of a skill. Consider the body not as a site of inscription, but as a medium for the manifestation of remote agents. This physically split body may have one arm gesturing involuntarily which is remotely actuated by an unknown agent, whilst the other arm is enhanced by an exoskeleton prosthesis to perform with exquisite skill and with extreme speed. A body capable of incorporating movement that from moment to moment would be a pure machine motion performed with neither memory nor desire.

Stimbod

The Stimbod is made possible by a touch-screen muscle stimulation system. A method has been developed that enables the body's movements to be programmed by touching the muscle sites on the computer model. Orange flesh maps the possible stimulation sites whilst red flesh indicates the actuated muscle(s). The sequence of motions can be replayed continuously with its loop function. As well as choreography by pressing, it is possible to paste sequences together from a library of gesture icons. The system allows stimulation of the programmed movement for analysis and evaluation before transmission to actuate the body. At a lower stimulation level it is a body prompting system. At a higher stimulation level it is a body actuation system. This is not about remote control of the body, but rather of constructing bodies with split physiology, operating with multiple agency. Was it Wittgenstein who asked if in raising your arm you could remove the intention of raising it what would remain? Ordinarily, you would associate intention with action (except, perhaps in an instinctual motion, or if you have a pathological condition like Parkinson's disease). With Stimbod, though, that intention would be transmitted from another body elsewhere. There would be actions without expectations. A two-way tele-Stimbod system would create a possessed and possessing body – a split physiology to collaborate and perform tasks remotely initiated and locally completed – at the same time in the one physiology.

Extreme Absence and the Experience of the Alien

Such a Stimbod would be a hollow body, a host body for the projection and performance of remote agents. Glove Anaethesia and Alien Hand are pathological conditions in which the patient experiences parts of their body as not there, as not their own, as not under their own control – an absence of physiology on the one hand and an absence of agency on the other. In a Stimbod not only would it possess a split physiology but it would experience parts of itself as automated, absent and alien. The problem would no longer be possessing a split personality, but rather a split physicality. In our Platonic, Cartesian and Freudian pasts these might have been considered pathological and in our Foucauldian present we focus on inscription and control of the body. But in the terrain of cyber complexity that we now inhabit the inadequacy and the obsolescence of the ego-agent driven biological body cannot be more apparent. A transition from psycho-body to cyber-system becomes necessary to function effectively and intuitively in remote spaces, speeded-up situations and complex technological terrains. There are also cyber-sexual implications with Stimbod. If I was in Melbourne and my remote lover was in Rotterdam, touching my chest would prompt her to caress her breast. Someone observing her there would see it as an act of self-gratification, as a masturbatory act. She would know though that her hand was remotely guided. Given tactile and force-feedback, I would feel my touch via another person from another place as a secondary and additional sensation. Or, by feeling my chest I can also feel her breast. An intimacy through interface, an intimacy without proximity. Remember that Stimbod is not merely a sensation of touch but an actuation system. Can a body cope with experiences of extreme absence and alien action without becoming overcome by outmoded metaphysical fears and obsessions of individuality and free agency? A Stimbod would thus need to experience its actuality neither all-present-in-this-body, nor all-present-in-that-body, but partly-here and projected-partly-there. An operational system of spatially distributed but electronically interfaced clusters of bodies ebbing and flowing in awareness, augmented by alternate and alien agency.

Parasite: Event for Invaded and Involuntary Body

A customized search engine has been constructed that scans, selects and displays images to the body, which functions in an interactive video field. Analyses of the files provide data that is mapped to the body via the muscle stimulation system. There is optical and electrical input into the body. The images that you see are the images that move you.

Figure 10.2 The Third Hand: Japan. Photo S. Hunter © Stelarc

Consider the body's vision, augmented and adjusted to a parallel virtuality which increases in intensity to compensate for the twilight of the real world. Imagine the search engine selecting images of the body off the World Wide Web, constructing a metabody that in turn moves the physical body. Representations of the body actuate the body's physiology. The resulting motion is mirrored in a VRML (Virtual Reality Markup Language) space at the performance site and also uploaded to a Website as potential and recursive source images for body reactivation. Real-Audio sound is inserted into sampled body signals and sounds generated by pressure, proximity, flexion and accelerometer sensors. The body's physicality provides feedback loops of interactive neurons, nerve endings, muscles, transducers and Third Hand mechanism. The system electronically extends the body's optical and operational parameters beyond its cyborg augmentation of its Third Hand and other peripheral devices. The prosthesis of the Third Hand is counter-pointed by the prosthesis of the search engine software code. Plugged-in, the body becomes a parasite sustained by an extended, external and virtual nervous system.

Exoskeleton

A six-legged, pneumatically powered walking machine has been constructed for the body. The loco-motor, with either ripple or tripod gait moves forwards, backwards, sideways and turns on the spot. It can also squat and lift by splaying or contracting its legs. The body is positioned on a turn-table, enabling it to rotate about its axis. It has an exoskeleton on its upper body and arms. The left arm is an extended arm with pneumatic manipulator having eleven degrees of freedom. It is human-like in form but with additional functions. The fingers open and close, becoming multiple grippers. There is individual flexion of the fingers, with thumb and wrist rotation. The body actuates the walking machine by moving its arms. Different gestures make different motions – a translation of limb to leg motions. The body's arms guide the choreography of the locomotor's movements and thus compose the cacophony of pneumatic and mechanical and sensor modulated sounds.

Hexapod

What is explored is a walking architecture that exploits gravity and the intrinsic dynamics of the machine to generate dynamic locomotion. By shifting body weight and twisting and turning the torso, it is possible to initiate walking, change the mode of locomotion, modulate the speed and rhythm and change its direction. The body becomes the body of the machine. The machine legs become the extended legs of the body. It is a more intuitive and interactive system that does not function through intelligence but rather because of its architecture. It is a more compliant and flexible mechanism. It looks like an insect but walks like a dog. Hopefully, this hybrid human-machine operation will initiate alternate kinds of choreography. It is 5 metres in diameter and weighs about 250 kilograms. It was first presented at the NOW Festival in Nottingham, England.

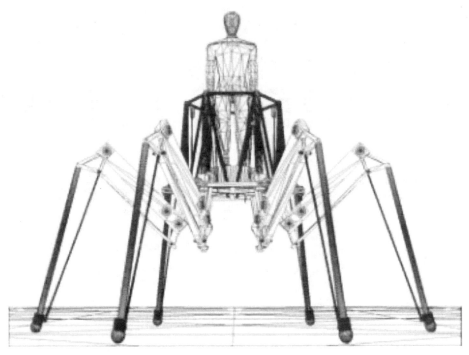

Figure 10.3 3D modelling of the HEXAPOD robot. © Stelarc

Movatar: An Inverse Motion Capture System

Motion capture allows a body to animate a three-dimensional computer-generated model. This is usually done by either markers on the body tracked by cameras, analyzed by a computer and the motion mapped onto the virtual actor. Alternatively, it can be done using electromagnetic sensors, like Polhemus or Flock-of-Birds, that indicate position and orientation of limbs and head. Consider though, a computer entity, a virtual body or an avatar that can access a physical body, actuating it to perform in the real world. If the avatar is imbued with an artificial intelligence, becoming increasingly autonomous and unpredictable, then it would be an AL (Artificial Life) form performing with a human body in physical space. With an appropriate visual software interface and muscle stimulation system this would be possible. The avatar would become a Movatar. And with appropriate feedback loops from the real world it would be able to respond and perform in more complex and compelling ways. The Movatar would be able not only to act, but also to express its emotions by appropriating the facial muscles of its physical body. As a VRML entity it could be logged into from anywhere, to allow your body to be accessed and acted upon. Or, from its perspective, the Movatar could perform anywhere in the real world, at any time with a multiplicity of physical bodies in diverse situations and remote locations.

Extra Ear

Having developed a Third Hand, consider the possibility of constructing an extra ear, positioned next to the real ear. A laser scan was done to create a 3D simulation of the Extra Ear in place. Although the chosen position is in front of and beside the right ear, this may not be the surest and safest place anatomically to position it. An inflating prosthesis would be inserted under the skin and then gradually inflated over a period of months until a bubble of stretched skin is formed. It is then removed and the cartilage ear structure is inserted and pinned beneath the stretched skin. A cosmetic surgeon would then need to cut and sew the skin over the cartilage structure. Alternatively, the ear could be constructed on the forearm and reposition later. But this would also require microsurgery to guarantee blood flow. Rather than the hardware prosthesis of a mechanical hand, the Extra Ear would be a soft augmentation, mimicking the actual ear in shape and structure, but having different functions. Imagine an ear that cannot hear but rather can emit noises. Implanted with a sound chip and a proximity sensor, the ear would speak to anyone who would get close to it. Perhaps, the ultimate aim would be for the Extra Ear to whisper sweet nothings to the other ear. Or imagine the Extra Ear as an Internet antennae able to amplify Real-Audio sounds to augment the local sounds heard by the actual ears. The ear is not only an organ of hearing but also an organ of balance. To have an extra ear points to more than visual and anatomical excess. It also points to a re-orientation of the body.

Where next?

The future is what you're constructing now – the Extra Ear project is being pursued at the moment but it is unrealized as yet. The ethical and surgical problems about constructing it are particularly important. It might have to be constructed on an arm and then relocated beside an actual ear. But that would require some orthopaedic surgery (to pin the ear to the cranium) and micro-surgery (to guarantee blood-flow). This creates the necessity to have even more specialist practitioners involved. It is hard enough to get cosmetic and reconstructive surgeons involved. If the project is not physically realized, it is not important. The idea does

not suffice in itself as interesting or meaningful art. The computer modelling and animated gif on the website was not meant to be an image for
itself, but rather an indication and exploration of the positioning and
appearance.

Residencies

Residencies have been undertaken at the Advanced Computer Graphics
Centre, RMIT, Melbourne University, Kansas City Art School, Carnegie
Mellon University, Ohio State University and Flinders University. They
have provided specific facilities not found elsewhere. For example, the
Virtual Arm project would not have been possible without the expertise
and computer facilities at RMIT. The Studio for Creative Inquiry at Carnegie Mellon provided free access to the Biology, Robotics and Computer
Science areas. At Ohio State University it was possible to access and experiment with a state-of-the-art Motion Capture System. Exoskeleton
was funded by a performance space in Hamburg, Kampnagel, with all the
pneumatic actuators supplied by SMC. It was constructed with the assistance of F18, a group of artists/engineers. This was a project completed
as part of a residency for Hamburg City.

The current position held is Principal Research Fellow in the Digital
Research Unit, Department of Visual and Performing Arts at the Nottingham Trent University. The new walking robot, a project jointly done
by The Nottingham Trent University and Sussex University is even more
unique. Designed by Inman Harvey from the Evolutionary and Adaptive
Systems Group, this robot will not be tethered and its locomotion, speed
and direction will be controlled by shifting the body's weight, twisting its
torso and turning the body. It is a more compliant and flexible structure
that is a more dynamic loco-motor. It is a large robot approximately five
metres in leg-spread. None of the collaborations have been artistic, rather
they have been technical. The artist has to be opportunistic as the projects are not easy to realize. As these projects have involved specialist
medical, computer and engineering skills, technical assistance is always
needed.

Acknowledgements

The Muscle Stimulation System circuitry was designed by Bio-Electronics, Logitronics
and Rainer Linz in Melbourne with the box fabricated with the assistance of Jason Patterson. The Stomach Sculpture was constructed by Jason Patterson in Melbourne. The Fractal Flesh and Parasite software were developed by Gary Zebington and Dmitri Aronov in
Sydney. Exoskeleton was completed by F18 as part of a residency in Hamburg, coordinated by Eva Diegritz from Kampnagel. Hexapod is a collaboration between the Digital
Reseach Unit, Nottingham Trent University and the Evolutionary and Adaptive Systems
Group at Sussex University with funding from the Wellcome Trust. The project team
includes Barry Smith (Project Coordinator), Inman Harvey (Robot Designer), John Lux-
ton (Engineer) and Sophia Lycouris (Choreographer).

11   Tears in the Connective Tissue

Joan Truckenbrod

As cyberspace races towards the future, there is a cry for the hand in this virtual ecology. Linking to cyberspace, where is the touch, the tactility, the physicality of experience? The reach out and touch of telephone mythology has become the banner of the World Wide Web. Email and the Internet provide a long distance touch with an immediacy, simultaneity and multiplicity of connection. But the behaviour and feel of linking to and through computers is flat, a projected world connected through a flat light screen. In this mono-dimensionality, the visual dominates other perceptual senses. Computing is superimposed upon our physical world with little or no attempt to integrate the sensory perceptions into the digital experience. Computing should be constructed with sensory experiences like touch, rather than the language of the machine. The connective tissue linking the natural world with the virtual world through the body and mind is disjoint.

Experiences are kinaesthetic in which there is a synthesis of hearing, seeing, tasting, smelling and touching. The fragmentation of sensory experiences occurring in the cyber-world began with the invention of the printing press. According to McLuhan the invention of print and the printing press is responsible for segmenting sensory experiences. Our ability to think and feel kin-aesthetically, in such a way as to bring hearing, seeing, tasting and touching together, has diminished with the development of print. Words became divorced from related modes of expression, such as voice, gesture, dance, song and animated behaviours such as ritual and storytelling. When an individual perceptual sense like vision, becomes locked in a technology, it becomes separated from the other senses. This portion of one's self closes, as if it were locked in steel, whereas prior to such separation, there is complete interplay among the senses [1].

Computing is obsessed with creating virtual experiences that simulate forms, materials and behaviours from nature. Virtual experience "overthrows the sensorial and organic architecture of the human body by disembodying and reformatting its sensorium in powerful, computer generated, digitized spaces,, [2]. Cyberspace disengages from physical reality. Sensory experience is reduced to a mono-medium of digital coding.

Digital imaging mediates between these different realms of experience. The screen, the digital print, digital fibre creates portals to electronic worlds, spiritual dimensions and personal realms. The computer imaging cosmos is multi-planar, not in the three-dimensional nature of Cartesian space, but with multiple planes of imagery from different realms of experience existing simultaneously. The physicality of real space is imaged photographically, and carries the social and emotional baggage of reality. Imaginary spaces are created by hand using digital drawing and painting tools. Subterranean, invisible, interstitial happenings are sculpted with the light of the digital media. I create multiple planes of simultaneous existence in the social world, the emotional realm, the spiritual world, the natural world, and the virtual world. Some of these planes of experience have a clarity, like looking into a deep clear lake, while others are oblique, circuitous, nebulous, and intimate.

This intermingling is similar to looking through a car window on a rainy night. The world outside is transformed through the streaks of rain. As a shadowy reflection on that distorted image, I see my own face, and I feel that I am looking at the inside of the mask. The facial image is torn by shreds of the outside world flowing down the windshield with the pouring rain. This is not a crisp, bright image in a mirror, but hints of an image that pulsates with the sheets of rain. It appears to be the animating force peering out from behind the shadows of the streetlights, even more variegated with the strikes of lightning. The image as spirit has been summoned up by the ritual pounding of the rain under the cover of the darkness.

Was the image on the inside of the car window a real reflection or a virtual image? And how did the image connect to the distorted image of the real world viewed through the rain? The simultaneity of these disjunctive images connects them and creates overlapping experiences. I use the indigenous nature of computing to evoke symbolic multiple connections between layers of images, mediating between these real and virtual worlds and between spirit and matter.

This synthesis embraces the idea of convergence mythologies in African art in which the differences between worlds are linked. Each African culture has a specific explanation for the convergence of spirit and matter. For example, people of Yoruba conceived the cosmos in terms of two distinct yet inseparable components. Aye is the visible, tangible world of the living while Orun is the invisible, spiritual realm of the ancestors, gods, and spirits. In some societies, a dream and the dreaming person are the point of intersection between the human and the spirit realms [3]. The dreaming person is the intermediary of communication. Headrests are important agents in this process and are usually carved with mirror images of animal heads because these two realms are viewed as mirror images.

To bridge the experiential world and the imaginary world, I use different modes of digital representation simultaneously. Pictures that are photographic in origin refer to the experiential world while painted or sketched images refer to the world of imagination. Each mode of representation carries with it an intent which is injected into and becomes part of the image. A photo is a framed image that accurately represents the people, place or event on the other side of the lens. Photos, until the era of digital manipulation, have usually implied reality, a realistic view with a true narrative of an event or situation. There is, however, the photographer's perspective superimposed on the image as a result of the framing of the scene through the lens of the camera. Scanners and digital cameras are the photographic agents for computer imaging. The real world component of my artwork is created using digital photographic techniques. Here, the manipulation is extended to every grain (pixel).

Digital painting, on the other hand, projects a view from the imagination. There is a dream, a perspective, an opinion, or a personal experience of the subject. Paintings are infused with moods and emotive gestures. The process of painting by hand brings to the surface a probe of experiences not normally visible. Painting becomes a performative and ritualistic activity. Body painting in the Aboriginal culture exaggerates this because of the physicality of painting in conjunction with spirituality. Body painting is a sensuous, tactile form of social interchange in which stories are shared as the body is painted. The combination of touch and hearing increases the empathetic power and intensity of this form of communication. In the Aboriginal view, the meaning of symbolic experience is fully understood when it is absorbed through languages that affect both body and mind.

Computer imagery bridges the physical and the virtual worlds by using languages of both body and mind. The gesture of the hand with the stroke of a digital brush is an agent of the inside world, a portal between worlds. The hand is a vehicle for uncovering the layers of one's consciousness. In African mythology, the hand is a source of action and an instrument of creativity. It is the vehicle that transforms the ineffable, invisible abstractions of thought into objects of tangible, material reality. The hand is a way in which the unseen image can be conveyed visually through a dialogue of presence and absence that stretch meaning across the boundaries of experience and envisioning. According to African mythology, the hand dreams to visualize the invisible and bring extraordinary aspects of existence into human reach [3].

Body world experiences in 1998 jarred my way of being in the world. The social world, the natural world and more so the intimate world warped like the chaotic molecules in the stretch of a rubber band. Words were silenced simultaneously with an explosion of connections to the intimate dimensions of nature. Intensified in my everyday experience, wind brings tears as it patterns the sunshine with shadows of trees and undulating leaves. Colours embody light molecules themselves. Charging molecules, reshaped with light as my patterns, patterns of my body, of my soul are reshaped with blasts of light. Winds move the water, continuously reforming the pattern of one's life, translucent layers move spontaneously to reveal and conceal simultaneously.

These images are a fluid synthesis of photographic and scanned images. They confront the viewer with their scale, ranging in size from 50 inches high by 38 inches wide to 58 inches high by 40 inches wide. The viewer is engulfed: it is analogous to the tide moving in, swirling around and capturing the vision as if caught in a tide pool, a microcosm. With the tension of the undulating tide on the threshold of revealing secrets that again become concealed.

The ritual transformation in these prints creates a threshold into unsettling worlds. A radical transfiguration embodies the conflict of optimism with trauma. Chemicals applied to farmlands and foods, hormones and antibiotics in animal feed create an artificial mantle of wellbeing while playing havoc with our bodies. These substances mimic hormones and disrupt endocrine systems, causing cancerous tumors. The dichotomy of the view of beauty on the surface subverts the reality of invisible poisons underneath.

In my current artwork, the images embody transformation and rebirth. Water is the conduit as narratives ride on the surface of undulating waves. Directed by the moon, the tides in their circadian rhythm reveal the mythology of the underwater world, and then reverse direction conceal its secrets. Waves move in opposite directions creating strong undercurrents that are masked by the light patterns on the surface. The magic of light captures my imagination as it fills the surface of water with image, a synthesis of the place of the tides and the story beneath.

I work digitally to create a recombinant montage of these realms: the world of light and the underwater world. I create digital prints and digital fibre artworks using the dye sublimation process.

Silk as water, embodies the mythical spirit of its creation. This vitality resonates through the silk fibre, engaging with the imagery. The printed tapestry resonates a powerful synthesis. My intrigue with silk fibre was peaked during a visit to the famous fabric shop in Como, Italy. In this shop, unlike American fabric shops, the walls were lined with tall, stately, dark wood shelves stacked high with bolts of elegant fabrics.

In the middle of the shop were very long dark wood tables, a bit wider than the width of fabric. Upon inquiring about a particular silk fabric I was treated to an incredible experience that I still see in my mind's eye. The fabric was taken off the shelf, unrolled off the bolt and propelled down the long table in elegant rushing waves. There in my mind were my images riding on the surface of that wave. Silk fibre and the sea share the same language. My images are digitally printed on fibre which is, for me, analogous to the tide. The silk fibre originating from nature has a resonance with one's life spirit. It maps onto the undulations of air currents, echoing waves in the ocean.

Figure 11.1 Thresholding,[1] 1999 © Joan Truckenbrod

Images are continually juxtaposed in a virtual sketchbook, floating in my consciousness and periodically erupting through the surface. Tension emerges as unlike or conflicting images are woven together in a non-linear digital montage. Images I create are layered to expose different sections of each original image.

Analogous to the ocean with strong currents pushing and pulling on the sea life, images swell to the crest of the wave, leaving traces on the surface of the image. I am influenced by the turbulence of the sea and its connection to our own personal jarring transformation and renewal.

My working palette includes the underwater world and the reverberations of the spirits that dwell there. This is represented by the light patterns on the water that project themselves onto objects that I place in the water. These worlds that I create become womb-like, evoking transformation and renewal. I place bodice tissue patterns from women's clothing in the water because they capture the twisting and transformation of the ocean's current. Sunlight carried on the surface of the waves is projected onto these patterns. These undulating patterns of light make me think of ceremonial symbols that are painted by the Aborigines on their bodies in the secrecy of night only to be revealed by firelight as they perform ceremonial dances around the fire.

Notes

---

[1] Firelight in a ceremonial dance protecting the secrecy of symbolic forms painted on the body. Limited Edition Roland Print on Capri Paper, 56 h × 40 w (1999)

References

1. McLuhan, M.: The Gutenberg Galaxy: The Making of Typographic Man, University of Toronto Press, Toronto (1988) 265

2. Tomas, D.: quoted by Jim Elkins in There are No Philosophic Problems Raised by Virtual Reality, Computer Graphics, 28 (4) November (1994) 251

3. Nooter Roberts, M. and Roberts, A.F.: The Shape of Belief, Fine Arts Museums of San Francisco, San Francisco, CA, (1996) 13

12   Algorithmic Fine Art: Composing a Visual Arts Score

Roman Verostko

I was born in the year of the great depression, 1929, in the coal fields of eastern United States. Sixty years ago, at the age of 12, I made my first painting using a paint set I bought from a Montgomery Ward catalogue. Later I worked my way through art school, then attended college and spent some years in monastic life. By 1960 I found myself in the milieu of the abstract expressionists in New York.

Beginning in the late 1950s my interest turned to several faces of pure visual form: geometry, spontaneous brush strokes and automatic writing. I became an avid purist seeking an art of pure form that transcended the material world.

For over 40 years I have worked with pure visual forms ranging from controlled constructions with highly studied colour behaviour to spontaneous brush strokes and automatic drawing. Various terms for this art include 'abstract', 'concrete', and 'non-objective'.[1] In its purest form such art does not *re-present* other reality. Rather it *is* the reality. One contemplates a pure form similar to the way one might contemplate a fine vase or a seashell. For me, at its best, this art evokes a transcending cosmic experience. My study of Mondrian provided my first awareness of this experience.

A New Frontier

Radically new procedures for creating such art emerged in the last quarter of the twentieth century. With the advent of computers I began composing original detailed instructions for generating forms that are accessible only through extensive computing.[2] These instructions, called algorithms, opened a vast array of pure form, an uncharted frontier of unseen worlds waiting to be discovered and concretized. Those drawn to view culture with neo-Darwinian spectacles will relish the evolution of this art. Writing on the new biology of machines Kevin Kelly identified The Library of Form, a frontier hyperspace of form pioneered by Karl Simms [1]. My on-going work concentrates on developing my program of procedures, the 'score', for visualizing these forms. By joining these procedures with fine arts practice I create aesthetic objects to be contemplated much as we contemplate the wondrous forms of nature.

Algorithmic Form Generators

When I was a child a 'computer' was a human person hired to do computation. Algorithms for computation in accounting and engineering were carried out by humans, as were those for the tessellations in Islamic art. In recent times, we have come to apply the term "algorithm" more broadly to the detailed instructions for carrying out any task whatsoever. The algorithm driving the bread making machine embodies a recipe (the detailed instruction) for making bread.

From prehistoric times human craft has been algorithmic. The procedures for weaving baskets, fashioning hunting tools gradually evolved and passed from one generation to the next. A better algorithm meant a better product! From a broad perspective, algorithms in the arts would include the composer's score, the architect's plan and the choreographer's dance notation. Given sufficient detail and an adequate computer language, any procedure for executing a task can be translated into an instruction (algorithm) for executing the task. A computer, connected to appropriate machinery, can execute instructions for playing music, drawing a form, or displaying a figure moving in space.

The greater part of my creative work in the past fifteen years has been developing art form generators (software) that I integrate into my exploration of "unseen form". These are original detailed procedures, for initiating and improvising form ideas. The detailed procedures are designed to be executed specifically as pen drawn lines, and sometimes as brush strokes, using pen plotters driven by a PC.

Such form generators may be likened to biological genotypes since they contain the code for generating forms. The procedure for executing the code, somewhat analogous to biological epigenesis, grows the form.[3] The creation and control of these instructions provides an awesome means for an artist to employ form-growing concepts as an integral part of the creative process. Such routines provide access to a new frontier for the artist.

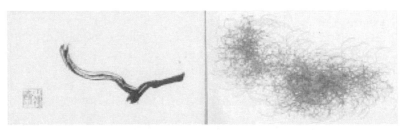

Figure 12.1 Frontispiece with plotted brushstroke[4] 1990 © Roman Verostko

The Work

Works are executed with a multi-pen plotter (drawing machine) coupled to a PC driven by my software. The plotter, choosing from an array of pens loaded with pigmented inks, draws each individual line. Most works require thousands of lines with software controlled pen changes[5]. An optional brush routine allows the occasional substitution of a brush for a pen. Brush strokes are plotted with brushes adapted to the machine's drawing arm. One series of illuminated digital scripts is reminiscent of medieval manuscripts. Many of these works are enhanced with a touch of gold or silver leaf applied by hand. However, the design elements illuminated with gold are always code generated and machine plotted.

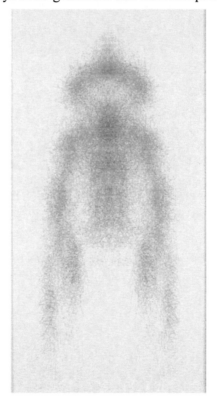

Figure 12.2 Epigenesis: the growth of form,[6] 1997 6ft× 3 ft © Roman Verostko

Content and Meaning

Over the years the software has evolved by stages yielding a series of works for each stage – *Pathway, Gaia, Glyph, Scarab, Apocalypse, Ezekiel and Cyberflower*. Each of these series has distinctive formal qualities associated with its form generators. None of the works are made with intentional representations in mind. Rather, each work presents one more adventure into an uncharted world of forms. This art does not represent some sort of subject or object. Just as a botanist might label a newly discovered flower so also I label this or that newly made visual form or series of forms. Titles are arbitrary and often derived from evocative qualities associated with the work.

The art works are visual manifestations of the dynamic procedures by which they grew. The finished works invite us to savour the mystery of their coded procedures whose stark logic yields a surprising grace and beauty. These procedures provide a window on those unseen processes from which they are grown. By doing so they serve as icons illuminating the mysterious nature of our evolving selves.

Creativity and Cognition, Loughborough

In 1996, Creativity and Cognition[7] at Loughborough provided an opportunity for me to reflect on my work and measure some of my ideas in a foreign context. The experience allowed interaction within a milieu of artists specifically interested in coded procedure. This allowed me to assess my algorithmic procedures alongside those of colleagues whose work was new to me. This led to questions as well as affirmations relative to my work. I learned that pen plotted work on paper could hold its own in varying contexts and the direction I had taken continued to be worthwhile even in the face of seductive newer technologies.

As an active artist for over 40 years, I always placed a great deal of value on mastering a tradition and a technology. As a painter I did not change paintbrushes every two or three years! One of the problems with the digital revolution is that the technology undergoes continuous change rapidly. Must we artists keep changing our technology or can we settle on a specific technology for a long term in order to become a master of that technology?

When I exhibited my first algorithmic work in 1985 I realized the technology could occupy me for a lifetime. My practice today employs the same DOS environment, the same ink pens and plotters, and the same command language. My refinements concentrate on algorithmic invention and the quality of the pen plot. My concerns become more and more tuned to the nuances of various rag papers, ink viscosities, the limits and character of pen plotted lines, and the unique form properties derived from intense algorithmic procedure.

My Loughborough experience helped confirm my direction. Since then I have acquired even more of the old equipment and have continued my commitment to work with this technology into the future.

Reflections: From the 20th into the 21st Century

Reflecting on the past forty years, I find myself on the same search that I began in the late 1950s, namely, the search for pure visual form that evokes transcendent experience. Close to twenty years ago I had my first glimpse of a new frontier of form made accessible with computing power. Since then I have gained a glimpse of this awesome array – too vast to hold – infinities of form. As the twenty-first century unfolds I envision a return to pure form. With algorithmic procedure forms will grow beyond the dreams of first generation twentieth century abstractionists[9] who will emerge as pioneers of twenty-first century formal art.

I recall visiting Michel Seuphor in Paris back in 1963. He glowed with his vision of a visual world that could lead us beyond mundane social conflict. Clearly the artists who pioneered the new reality saw it as a springboard to a greater cosmic consciousness. They envisioned a visual art somewhat like a symphony of sound. Note how the symphony transcends political conflict and invites us to be in our bodies with a total sense of hearing and simultaneously leads us beyond the material world. Diverse audiences can share the same symphony without respect to their social and political differences.

This phenomenon was very clear to Kandinsky who wanted his art to embody pure form free of political and social conflict [2]. His art stood on its own visual form without describing some "other" object or ideology. Following this path I have sought a similar goal. The project, Epigenesis: The Growth of Form, exemplifies a procedure that I believe will emerge very strongly in the visual arts of the twenty-first century. In this instance the procedure grows a series of improvisations based on the visual relationship of an arbitrary set of coordinates. The procedure, somewhat like a composer's musical score, generates a series of improvisations based on the initiating visual form. In effect there are eleven variations on a visual theme achieved through thousands of lines. Each pen line, distributed and shaped by the score, builds an intricate network of variations within a self-similar visual structure. By analogy to a 'sym-phony', the harmony of sounds, these visual improvisations become a 'syngraphy', a harmony of visual forms. Today, one can create a score for harmonic graphic generation in many ways similar to the way composers score for sound [3].

The vision I have held for the past twenty years has been gradually emerging as the new reality. With the emergence of the genetic algorithm and the growth of the software industry, artists, without laborious programming, will eventually grow algorithmic generators for their form preferences. The algorist programs of my time will then fade into an archaic past and our code will look quaint. I hope I live long enough to savour the rebirth of this neo-formalist art as it springs forth with vibrant life in the twenty-first century. All will marvel in a wondrous world of form as in a newly found Garden of Eden – an arcadia of great delight.

There are moments when one wishes that someone, the likes of a Mondrian, could appear for a brief moment in our historic time... and be able to experience his own "Broadway Boogie Woogie" in today's New York – ecstasy revisited!

Notes

1. First generation pioneers whose work opened this new reality for me included Mondrian, Kandinsky, Malevich, Hepworth, Kupka, Gabo and Pevsner. The "non-objective" and "new reality" artists included Mondrian, Barbara Hepworth, Max Bill, Ozenfant, Malevich, Gabo, and Pevsner. The "New Reality" for them was the art object they created; their forms did not represent other objects.

2. Other *algorists* following a similar path were unknown to each other at the beginning. Pen plotter artists who had achieved a mature body of work by 1990 included Harold Cohen, Mark Wilson, Vera Molnar, Jean Pierre Hebert, Manfred Mohr and Hans Dehlinger: see www.solo.com/studio/algorists.html

3. The term "epigenesis" borrowed from biology, refers to the process whereby a mature plant (phenotype) is grown from a seed or genotype (DNA). By analogy, the artwork (phenotype) is grown from the algorithm (genotype). The procedures for growing the work may be viewed as epigenetic. The algorithm (genotype) for each series of works is capable of generating a family of forms with each being one of a kind.

4. Figure 12.1 shows one of 125 different brush strokes plotted for a Limited edition of Chapter 3 of "An Investigation of the Laws of Thought..." by George Boole, L.L.D. Macmillan 1854. Chapter III. "Derivation of the laws of the symbols of logic from the laws of the operation of the human mind. Limited edition of Chapter 3 with illustrations by Roman Verostko, St. Sebastian Press, Minneapolis, MN, USA, 1990.

5. See Art and Algorithm (www.verostko.com/alg-isea94.html), which addresses procedures and issues related to an artist's use of algorithms.

6. Figure 12.2 shows one of 11 pen plotted units spanning 40 feet at Frey Science and Engineering Centre, University of St Thomas, St Paul Minnesota, USA see verostko.com/st/mural.html

7. Creativity and Cognition http://creativityandcognition.com

References

1. Kelly, K.: The Library of Form, a Frontier Hyperspace of Form pioneered by Karl Simms Chapter 14, Out of Control: The New Biology of Machines, Social Systems and the Economic World, Perseus, New York (1994)

2. Kandinsky, W.: Concerning the Spiritual in Art and Painting in Particular. R. Motherwell (ed), Documents of Modern Art, Wittenborn, Schultz, Inc. New York (1947)

3. Verostko, R.: Epigenetic Painting: Software as Genotype. Leonardo: Journal of the International Society for the Arts, Sciences and Technology, 23 (1) 17-23 Pergamon Press, New York (1990)

13   An Observer's Reflections: The Artist Considered as Expert

Thomas T. Hewett

This chapter offers a particular perspective on some of the rich set of results of the COSTART project residencies [1]. In the first section comments are made on certain important aspects of the process of collecting observational data and how some of the classical problems of observational studies were dealt with. This is followed by a short review of the nature of expertise, some observations on human knowledge, the uses of external representations of that knowledge, and how the research into those topics relates to the artists being studied. In the third section of the chapter an extensive set of quotations that were collected from digital artists during the residency periods is presented. These quotations will enable the interested reader to participate in the process of evaluating some of the observations and conclusions drawn in this chapter and in the book as a whole. Finally, some of the findings of the project relevant to digital artists considered as experts as summarized.

On Being an Observer

In any type of case study observations the observer, especially when conducting observations live and in real time, has to continually attempt to maintain a balance between two conflicting goals. First there is a need to establish a certain degree of familiarity or empathy with the individual(s) being observed so that they become comfortable with the observer's presence and possible questions. The other need is to maintain a certain distance and objectivity which allows the observer to record information relatively uncontaminated by personal biases.

In the case studies reported here the individuals who played the role of observer for the various residencies spent time before each residency period began discussing and refreshing their perspective upon the goals of the project, the role of the observer, and nature of the observations to be recorded. Each of these sessions had three fundamental purposes. The first purpose was to establish and re-establish basic ground rules for the role of the observer and how it was to be fulfilled, in other words the concern was to establish consistency between observers and across different weeks of the residencies. The second goal of these sessions was to review and discuss ways to deal with any unexpected or infelicitous events that might arise during the residency period of an artist (e.g. the loss of technical support time, etc.). The third goal of these sessions was to establish consistency between the observers as to the fundamental questions being addressed by the study.

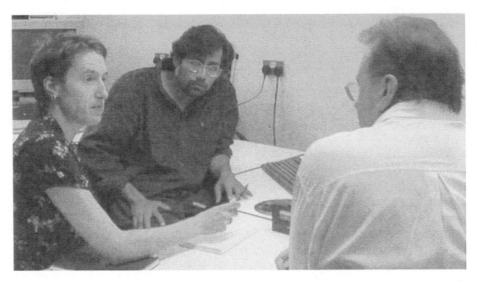

Figure 13.1 COSTART project discussions

Expertise and the General Characteristics of Experts

Each of the artists selected for the COSTART residencies was an expert in their area of artistic endeavour. Some were more expert than others by virtue of more years of experience, but part of the selection criteria for inviting artists to participate in the COSTART project was that the individual had to be above a certain threshold level of expertise in their endeavours. For example, every artist taking part in a residency had a degree of public and collegial recognition as being a successful artist. Each of them had made a personal commitment to the practice of digital art. Each of them had had one or more juried shows. Each of them had sold examples of their art.

To frame the context for the observations and conclusions reported below it is helpful to have a short discussion of some general characteristics of expertise. In an important review of the literature on the nature of expertise and the differences between novices and experts, Glaser and Chi [2] point out some important characteristics of experts which distinguish them from novices and which characterize the ways in which those experts deal with their professional activities. First, experts tend to excel mainly in their own domain of expertise, i.e. expertise in one domain does not generalize to other domains. Experts tend to perceive large meaningful patterns in their knowledge domain and tend to be fast at what they do when working on routine activities within that domain. When confronted with novel domain-related problems, experts tend to spend much of their time analyzing problems qualitatively. Typically they see and represent the problems they work on at a deeper or more abstract level. Finally, experts also tend to have good self-monitoring skill, i.e. they are more aware of their errors and make corrections. In addition, Ericsson [3] has pointed out that one key factor in the development of expertise is that experts, and experts-to-be, engage in "deliberated practice". Deliberated practice involves consciously working with the domain and with the elements and relationships in the domain to improve domain-related knowledge and skills.

The relevance of this brief review of expertise to the material that follows can be seen by considering the types of activities in which one might expect to find in an artist engaged during their preparation for and execution of a new piece of work. First, we would expect the digital artist to have some knowledge of digital resources and their capabilities but that their view of those resources is that they are a means to an end rather than an end in themselves. Secondly, we would expect the artists to have an overall vision, or partial vision, for what they want to accomplish but to have not necessarily worked out all the details or the implementation of that vision. Thirdly we would expect them to be willing to spend large amounts of time trying to articulate or realize that vision in a way that is satisfactory to themselves. Finally, we would expect the artist to be willing to engage in extensive, guided experimentation, working with the raw elements out of which they intend to create an instantiation of their vision. Even a cursory review of the quotations below reveals a consistency between these expectations and what the artists say about their working processes.

External Representations, Knowledge, and Knowledge Development

In a highly readable book, Norman [4] explores a number of issues related to well-designed and badly designed artifacts. In the process he discusses the importance of the distinction between knowledge in the head and knowledge in the world. Knowledge in the head consists of our memories, which may not always be present in our consciousness when needed. Knowledge in the world consists of information that exists in our environment that enables us to remember or activate information in memory when needed. For example, we typically do not remember all of the details represented on a standard piece of coinage, but we are able to remember the meaning of those details when the coin is visible. In other words, information in the world represents an external storage location. The world, just by being there, helps us remember and keep track of things.

In a related book, Norman [5] discusses the importance to the human mind of being able to create external representations with which to think as well as remember. He points out that the power of certain artifacts in our environment derives the knowledge embedded in the artifact. For example, imagine trying to drive in the United States from Gainsville, Florida to Muskegon, Michigan without looking at a map. Not surprisingly, when one is attempting to give someone directions on how to get from known point A to known point B it is often useful to draw a map. Furthermore, this construction of an external representation can reveal that there are many details of the route between points A and B which are not known until the map is constructed. In other words, development of an external representation can lead to the development of new insights or new knowledge. For example, the author once had an extended and almost heated discussion with a colleague who had lived in Vienna for several years. The topic of the debate was the number of exits from underground to the surface at a particular subway stop. The debate was only resolved when a sufficiently detailed map had been consulted.

Figure 13.2 COSTART project discussions

The relevance of this discussion of knowledge, external representations and knowledge development lies in the series of quotations presented below. From these quotations from the case studies, it becomes quite clear that a number of the artists made comments indicative of the need to create an external representation with which to experience and think about their developing vision or to enable them to clarify what that artistic vision actually was.

Extracts from the COSTART Case Studies

The pursuit of meaning through art is an act of embodiment. It is an unspoken dialogue between the self and the state that is to emerge.

The context for the technology is that of a medium for the creative work. Fundamentally, an attempt is made to allow the nature of the technology to be embraced rather than forcing metaphors from traditional creative tools upon it.

Much of this I could do by memory but some aspects I had forgotten... If I had to do this without the Whiteboard [and playback of the sequence of drawings] I would be using memory that might interfere with the creativity...

I felt my creativity was lessened if different systems were used and this was a problem... I knew that it [the preferred system] would achieve the effect I required whereas other systems might not achieve that effect.

Certain things you work on but to make it interesting to shoot, to keep it alive, you leave certain things undecided and also a bit loose. You know the parameters but how you actually perform it can change... So it's not just a mechanical process...you are actually performing through the model.

I've been working on the idea for about two years.

But as the week has gone on and as I started formalizing more in my head, now I can see the end piece I have visualized.

Technology is a two-way compromise. It encourages one to expand their working ideas and practices and yet also prevents one from creating as so much new information has to be learnt.

I always used to deliberately exploit the grain. I blow up images and they are very grainy and I still do that but with pixels.

I mean a lot of the time I do refer to the technology itself. It can be embedded within the actual work during the process itself. But I try to get it so that it's not using technology for technology's sake.

The entire thing has been on the boil... for about a year, but it's only been sort of, there's been different aspects of it... that I've been able to do to a timetable and this is one that I've just very much done tests for...

The process is vital because it informs the work itself.

The more I think about it the more I'm thinking I need to go back to the processes and the relationship between... the fundamental part of the work and how it would be disrupted by VR [Virtual Reality] by the very nature of it.

So to me it's quite strange coming in and sitting and watching and not being hands on.... ...when you're trying to make an object a particular shape... it's easier for me if I can do that myself....

...when working with the display environment I want to do some mock ups for the actual installation [of the work of art] in 3D. I like the idea of taking the spaces they create on the screen or mocking up a real space and then re-drawing the real space according to what the screen space is.

These things too...from a mathematical point of view they're very tricky...but from another point of view. Let's assume something else here...There has to be a tight nature with the material...the whole thing's integrated in this system as far as possible but there's no plan. But it implies something.

It's very exciting you know, thinking it would be good to have a sound trap. You see what he's done don't you? So one could play with those models more....

If we do a collaboration, you don't want my trademark.

Well you understand what I'm doing, where should I be starting from?

Discussion on what may be possible in programming terms influenced the shape of visual ideas, which were then in turn relayed back to the requirements of the programming. Crossing between the two forms was very useful as it has allowed the ideas to emerge out of a process rather than by designing a predefined object or environment.

A creative process of experimenting with technology seems to provoke questions that may not usually be asked of the technology. Examples of this are using simple techniques but within an unusual context and working with technology that is most appropriate to the concept of the work....

Using digital technology seems to give potential for creating a different type of relationship between the object and viewer... the potential to surround the body with a responsive and evolving environment...

Reflections on Providing Support for Digital Artists

For those experts in digital technology who would provide technical support for digital artists there are several lessons to be learned from thinking of artists as experts. One of the key features of creative work is the importance the artists give to the locus of control. For most, being able to determine exactly how and in what way the creative process takes place is a matter of paramount importance. This does not mean that they necessarily need to personally handle every single aspect of that process once it is understood and mastered. They are often willing to allocate the priorities and delegate tasks when they have a sense of what the results can be expected to be. This is crucial to how successful the generation of ideas and artifacts is perceived to be. It also means that being driven or diverted by unsolicited factors, such as a tool that keeps breaking, or a technology support person who keeps trying to do things that are not understood by the artist can be damaging to the process in hand.

Another factor to be remembered is that creative people are not afraid to choose pathways that are fraught with risk and full of pitfalls. In fact, one can argue that such exploratory activities are essential to the development of a creative work of art. Experimentation with concepts, materials and tools may, in the first instance lead to failure but those failures are often fertile ground for learning quickly how to move out of the conventional space of possibilities. This experimental approach to the creation of a new work of art means that the artist will not be easily deflected from a chosen route and, if it involves a hard struggle, i.e. learning a difficult technique, then they will do so in service of their goals. Creative people are not inclined to look for easy ways, or for rigid formulaic ways, to do things at the expense of achieving a creative result. This avoidance of rigid methodologies, however, can sometimes lead the artist to introduce rigid, inefficient formulaic approaches of their own for the well understood portions of what they do in order not to disrupt the flow of their work on the development of the novel and, perhaps creative, product.

While learning new skills or techniques is an important facilitator for creative practice, the role of collaboration for digital artists is integral to that process. In many respects the technology is new and only incompletely understood by the artist. Some artists may want to take full control of the reins of the technology because it is pivotal to the way they work. For others, it meets a temporary means to an end that can be met by a supportive collaborator. Typically technologists with little knowledge of art practice do not easily make good collaborators. The training and expertise of the technologist are oriented around providing the most economical and efficient solution to a problem. When an artist is in the process of experimentation with the development of external representations to be tested and evaluated, the last thing that they want to be concerned with is the constraint of machine efficiency or with a premature solution to problems perceived by the technologist but not understood by the artist. Artists need collaborators who understand or are empathetic to their goals and their need to exercise control for themselves. Being on a voyage of exploration and discovery they want to find their own way. They are typically not interested in being shown a solution unless convinced that the person they are working with understands what they want to accomplish. Working through and with the eyes and hands of the person who provides technical expertise does not work well for the core creative activities although it might be acceptable for the more well-understood ones.

A Final Note

As might be expected from the brief look at the literature on expertise here, it is often the case that the initial creative process does not concentrate upon the surface qualities of the work, such as the texture of the paint or the quality of sound from a particular instrument. A focus by artists on the underlying structure of art works shows clearly in the residency reports of the interactions between the artist and technology support person. It appears from the evidence so far that computer use in art has an impact on the concern for underlying structure of the creative product as distinct from its outward physical and virtual object realization. The most likely case is that the artist as expert is concerned with making an underlying structure explicit and the nature of the computer becomes a way of facilitating that activity in ways that cannot be achieved without the computer. Rather than start with surface considerations, the artist as expert will start with fundamental structuring considerations. This may represent a case where a significant opportunity for computer augmentation using a variety of programs or even intelligent agents. By being able to use software to generate the concrete and visible realizations of various possibilities inherent in the structure decisions, the artist would be able to see within very short intervals of time the implications of choices. In other words, a significant role for the computer in the user interaction with individuals engaged in creative work would be to enable the artist to think and act in terms of underlying structures. After setting the computer to do the work of developing alternative surface representations so that the artist can quickly see the instantiations and make choices at various deep structure points.

References

1. COSTART Project: http://www.creative.lboro.ac.uk/costart
2. Glaser, R., and Chi, M.T.H.: Overview. In M.T.H. Chi, R. Glaser, and M. J. Farr (Eds.), The Nature of Expertise. Erlbaum, Hillsdale, NJ (1988)
3. Ericsson, K.A. (Ed.): The Road to Excellence: The Acquisition of Expert Performance in the Arts and Sciences, Sports and Games. Erlbaum, Mahwah, NJ (1996)
4. Norman, D.A.: The Design of Everyday Things. New York: Doubleday (1988)
5. Norman, D.A.: Things That Make Us Smart. Addison-Wesley, Reading, MA (1993)

14 Realizing Digital Artworks

Colin Machin

Artists who aspire to using digital techniques in their artworks often require assistance from electronics and software engineers. The artist's desire to produce an artwork that, in some way, portrays motion or even reacts to its environment requires controlling electronics [1]. The simplest solution is to provide the artwork with intelligence through the use of a computer system. It is the job of the electronics and software engineers to collaborate in order to provide two elements that will provide this intelligence. First, and rather obviously, the electronics engineer must provide the computer-based hardware that will control the artwork and, if the artwork is to respond to its environment, the sensing electronics also. It is a relatively straightforward task to design and build a controller based upon microprocessor technology. The techniques are well established and are indeed merely simple manifestations of the type of solutions applied to industrial control applications. Typically a microcontroller would be used as the computing element. Once the hardware is available, the software engineer can provide the embedded software required in order to control the artwork.

Controlling the Artwork

The software that is embedded into the controller for the piece simply manipulates outputs on the hardware, which are connected to real-world elements. A simple item of this kind could be a Light-Emitting Diode (LED). These components produce small individual points of light, which may be combined to produce patterns. In a typical piece, the LEDs could be illuminated in some kind of sequence in response to the passage of time and/or external stimuli. In the first and simpler of the two cases, the piece follows a fixed sequence whose timing is predefined, much like a set of traffic lights at a busy junction. Even where sensors are involved, the response to the stimulus from a given sensor may be predefined. This behaviour is also seen in traffic lights. When a vehicle on a minor road arrives at an intersection it triggers the traffic light controller to enter the sequence that allows it egress on to the main road. We could borrow terms from the world of industrial control systems to distinguish these two types of behaviour, although the terms are not used in their strict senses in this context. We could assign the term "open-loop" to those artworks that simply perform fixed sequences and "closed-loop" to those that sense their environment and make some response based upon what is detected.

It does not matter whether the artwork is open-loop or closed-loop, the decision on how the artwork operates must remain the province of the artist. It is in realizing this that the software engineer suddenly understands that the job is not as simple as at first may have been apparent. We have already observed that the hardware is at the simple end of the spectrum of control systems, but that is possibly where simplicity ends. It is a well-established fact that many clients making use of a Software Engineer will be unaware of what they really require at the stage at which the requirements are specified. This is often due to that fact that the client does not really understand what is possible within software in general. Software engineers will often say that "anything is possible", although what they really mean is that "we can make the computer do whatever you desire, but you must know what you desire before we can start". When working with artists, it is here where the biggest challenges arise. They, quite rightly, have the creative talent and should not be expected to be familiar with the electronics and computing.

Embodying the Artist's Ideas

A simple approach to providing the software for a digital artwork would be to ask the artist to specify the sequence that is to be followed by the piece and to encode this directly within the software. Let us consider, for simplicity, an open-loop artwork and one that has a series of LEDs that can be lit independently to produce some effect or other. Early collaboration with Esther Rolinson at one of the COSTART project residency sessions concentrated on this kind of work [2]. Maybe the simplest 'sequence' that could be used is to illuminate a single random LED for a random, although within limits, time and to repeat this forever. This would have a particular level of appeal to a viewer experiencing the artwork, but that appeal may be limited, beyond the curiosity value associated with the viewer attempting to predict the next change. Such behaviour would be easy to permanently embed within the software that controls the artwork and indeed this approach would be completely justified.

If we assume, though, that the artist wishes the artwork to portray some artistic merit, beyond its basic structure, we must look towards embodying the artist's ideas with the LED sequence. The artist will sketch out the proposed sequence and pass it to the software engineer. It is the software engineer's job to encode the sequence into the software that is to control the artwork. The artist will doubtless be astounded by the ease with which the artwork follows the intended sequences, but will equally likely become bored with the repetitiveness of those very same sequences. The artist will have to go back to the Software Engineer and ask that the sequences be amended or expanded. This process could repeat itself many time over before the artist is sufficiently satisfied to allow the artwork to be seen in public or until the patience and resolve of the artist and software engineer finally expire. It is likely, then, that the artist will, at the end of this, still not be totally happy with the artwork and will be hankering after bigger and better things. Reluctance to bother the software engineer or exhaustion of the budget will then prevent enhancements from seeing the light of day. Further, experimentation with new ideas will be stifled by the same limitations. This scenario has a close parallel with that faced by businesses that took the step of utilizing computer systems many years ago. They either employed their own programmers or enlisted the help of software houses to write systems to support their business processes. They, too, had to specify the operation of the software beforehand and required changes to the software's operation had to be implemented by the same teams. Computerizing even the simplest of business processes required this sequence of events.

Increasing Flexibility

Nowadays, many of the less demanding business processes are implemented using spreadsheets or simple database systems. In this situation, the spreadsheet program has been written to allow the user to configure a spreadsheet to solve a particular business problem. When the user wishes to add an extra column of data, there is no need to consult the team who programmed the spreadsheet application. Instead, the user simply points and clicks and immediately the new column is added. Its functionality is then easy to define, perhaps with the insertion of a formula linking cells in other columns. This begs the question as to whether the creators of digital artworks should be required to behave as the clients of software houses did in the 1970s or should they now expect a more modern approach? It is only by allowing flexibility that the creative processes can be enabled. At odds with this approach is the fact that the microprocessor technology that is typically at the heart of the artwork's controller is not particularly amenable to supporting large point-and-click applications of the spreadsheet genre.

One method that can be used to provide the flexibility that the artist requires is to for the software engineer to provide a mechanism in the artwork's control software that will interpret sequences that have been specified by the artist. The software engineer in fact expends no effort on encoding sequences, but instead puts time into providing the mechanism. It has to be said that the time taken to achieve this is far in excess of the time that it would take to encode sequences directly, but the benefit to the artist is out of all proportion to the extra effort. Of added benefit is that the resulting system stands much more chance of being reusable in a future project.

Let us return to our simple example of the set of LEDs in order to illustrate the principle. Suppose that the artist wishes to illuminate a particular set of LEDs for a given time and then illuminate another set for a different time? It is a simple affair to write a sequence something like that given below.

```
TURN ON 6, 7, 8, 10, 12
WAIT FOR 10 SECONDS
TURN OFF ALL
TURN ON 3, 4, 9, 14
```

It should be obvious what this achieves, simultaneously turning on LEDs 6, 7, 8, 10 and 12, then after ten seconds, extinguishing all of them and then turning on LEDs 3, 4, 9 and 14 instead. What we see here, of course, is something very much akin to a program. In fact, given that each instruction causes exactly one thing to happen, it is in fact just like a program written for a microprocessor. It is not, though, in the microprocessor's own language, but in some kind of application-specific language and the artwork controller's software is simply executing an interpreter for that language. By including statements that allow looping and both unconditional and conditional branching, we can easily build up a powerful set of instructions for commanding our artwork controller. We could command our set of LEDs to perform the sequence given above 20 times before moving on to something else by the simple addition of two statements as shown below.

```
REPEAT 20 TIMES
TURN ON 6, 7, 8, 10, 12
WAIT FOR 10 SECONDS
TURN OFF ALL
TURN ON 3, 4, 9, 14
LOOP
```

The REPEAT instruction tells the interpreter to repeat the instructions between it and the next LOOP instruction a given number (20 in this case) of times. Loops formed by this simple construct can easily be nested so that repeated blocks may themselves be repeated. In the skeleton below, indentation has been used to illustrate this nesting.

```
REPEAT 20 TIMES
REPEAT 10 TIMES
<block A>
LOOP
REPEAT 5 TIMES
<block B>
LOOP
LOOP
```

Here we see the instructions that form <block A> repeated ten times followed by those in <block B> being repeated five times. That sequence is then repeated a further 19 times before the sequence moves on. Conditional branches (GOTOs) can be used, for example, to alter the sequences according to the time of day or in response to the presence of external stimuli, thus allowing the building of complex sequences.

The controller that is integrated into the artwork will not usually have a keyboard and screen present and so these sequences will have to be up-loaded to the controller from another computer – a PC or a Macintosh. The sequences are presented in textual form to this *host* computer where they are checked for syntactic accuracy and then translated into a form that is more economical than the textual form. This is then uploaded to the controller for storage and execution. In terms of the evolution of computing in the business environment, to which we referred earlier, the present situation is much like that at the time when SQL (Structured Query Language) was developed for manipulating databases. SQL is essentially an application-specific language that allows records to be stored in and retrieved from a database that has already been set up. Of course, SQL is a long way from the point-and-click nature of today's applications.

Visualizing the Piece: A Simulator

We will assume for the moment that the artist can master the idea of writing these sequences and examine what else the host computer can do in order to assist the artist. Before the artwork controller is installed, it is difficult for the artist to visualize the effect of the sequences that have been programmed. For that reason, it might be of great benefit to provide a simulator for the artwork. It is possible to produce an on-screen graphical representation of the artwork in two dimensions and to show them with a further representation of the elements that are to be controlled, such as the LEDs in our example. The simulator can "run" the sequence and portray the results on the image. An extension to this idea involves the artist in producing a three-dimensional representation of the artwork, in some preferred Computer-Aided Design (CAD) or other drawing package, upon which the controlled elements can be projected. Whilst working with Esther Rolinson on her project to incorporate Priva-Lite panels into glass columns, a simulator was produced for this very purpose [3]. Figure 14.1 shows a screen view of the simulator.

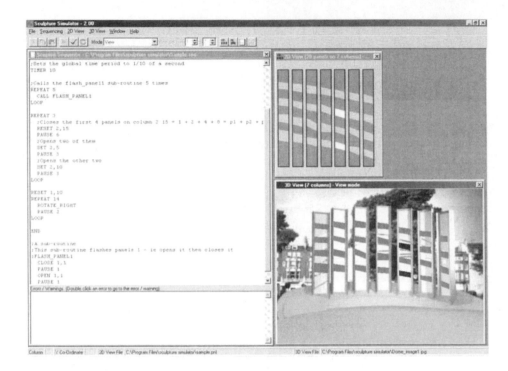

Figure 14.1 Sculpture simulator

The Priva-Lite panels are constructed as a sandwich of glass and a material that is clear until an electrical current is applied, at which point they become opaque. In this context they behave very much as shutters. What we see in the simulator is a two-dimensional representation of seven columns each with five panels of Priva-Lite, together with their projection on to the three-dimensional artist's impression of the artwork in situ. The views represent the Priva-Lite panels as coloured areas of the screen and different colours are used to distinguish open and closed shutters. A sequence to operate the artwork is shown in the window to the left and as the sequence runs, the changes in the Priva-Lite panels are reflected in the 2-D and 3-D views simultaneously.

It has been suggested that technology has an impact on artists in three distinct areas, namely in thinking, in making and in communications within the team. Furthermore, there is a likely impact on artists and technologists alike of aiding in the development of the technology: discussed earlier in Chapter 2 of this book. The simulator clearly makes a contribution to the making phase, as it allows the artist to visualize the sequences that are to be used in the artwork. It could also be said to be making a contribution to the communication aspect as it allows the artist to understand the possibilities of the piece. However, this useful tool could be used, in a different commission, to actually assist with the design and will clearly contribute to the thinking phase. The simulator in question is itself 'programmable' in terms of the numbers of columns, their spacing and the numbers and position of the panels. This simulator was designed with the particular artwork in mind, but it would not be difficult to imagine a situation where the artwork's design (the creative bit) and operation (the technical bit) are integrated into one package.

The Next Step

We have been assuming that the artist is comfortable with sequence programming, but what if it is deemed to be too complex? What is needed here is a point-and-click interface to the programming of sequences. Some of what is necessary to achieve this step is difficult, though, especially if we are looking for integration with the design process. We would first need to integrate a user interface that can capture the artist's creative processes and enable the identification of the elements to be controlled, be they LEDs, Priva-Lite panels or whatever else. We would then need to have the software be able to visualize those elements on the screen.

All of this is conceptually achievable and is indeed only a relatively small step from the existing simulator. It remains only to enable the specification of different kinds of controlled elements. There is a parallel here in the simulation of electronic circuits. Standards exist for the specification of the behaviour of components and models of each component are processed in a manner defined by a circuit.

The technology to achieve this goal exists in other related spheres. Perhaps the most difficult aspect of this step is the manner in which the required behaviour of the artwork is to be captured. We need to be able to capture the artwork's static conditions along with temporal information defining the timing of the piece. Clearly the system could enter into a dialogue with the artist, but this would serve only to restrict the flow of the creative juices.

It will be necessary to work with artists in order to determine what they desire in such a product and to attempt to identify new ways of capturing the information that is required. Active drawing surfaces have been aiding artists for some time, although there is debate about their effectiveness and whether or not the technology actually inhibits the creative process [4]. More work will be required to determine the manner in which various technologies might be integrated in order to be able to capture the creative aspects of a digital artwork.

References

1. Rolinson, E.: Shifting Spaces, Chapter 28, in this book.

2. COSTART Project Artists-in-Residence, Loughborough University, England,
    http://creative.lboro.ac.uk/costart.

3. Garton, D.: Design and Implementation of a Software System to Aid Esther
    Rolinson in Designing the Brighton Dome Sculpture, Final Year Undergraduate
    Project, Department of Computer Science, Loughborough University (2001)

4. Quantrill, M.: On the Creative Use of New Technology by Artists, Creativity
    and Cognition Research Studios, Department of Computer Science, Loughbor-
    ough University (2000)

15   Being Supportive

André Schappo

My involvement in the Creativity and Cognition Research Studios (C&CRS) artists-in-residence programme started a long time before the actual arrival of the artists for their period on site. At that time, I had a dual role in the University of Loughborough. In the academic department of Computer Science, I had been involved in various research projects over the years and had gone on to join the support services for the departmental computer systems. Later on, I also took on a campus-wide responsibility for Apple Macintosh systems support, this time in the Computing Services department. This enabled me to extend an already strong network of contacts throughout the university. This proved to be very important when I joined the COSTART project in 1998 as a technology coordinator [1].

There were several stages to the preparation of the technology at C&CRS before full-scale residencies could be run. Our objective was to create a fully integrated system of facilities comprising equipment, devices, software and networks into which additional technology could be added as required. Although considerable effort was spent in identifying the right kinds of technological facilities in advance, this was never going to be sufficient to enable us to predict everything that would be needed. It could also not prepare for the unexpected failures in those things we thought had been addressed.

The University departmental support staff played an important role in helping set up the new equipment and this was achieved in a very short space of time. Delays brought about by the tendering process and the delivery of equipment added to the problems of ensuring that everything was installed and tested by the beginning of July 1999 when the COSTART residencies were due to start. In the event, a number of devices were not fully integrated in a manner that satisfied our high usability goals: for example, initially, there was no easy to use method for artists to transfer files from the Apple Macs to the Silicon Graphics Origin computer. This meant that archiving files and freeing up space on the shared computers in the Studios was a time consuming business that not all artists could manage on their own. Time to achieve everything to our complete satisfaction was short. Having set up the basic infrastructure there was still more to be done to address the specific needs of the artists.

In order to ensure that the right facilities were in place before the artists commenced work, we held a workshop to meet the prospective resi-

dents. This was when we got down to details about their needs and expectations. Because for some, there was uncertainty about what would be
appropriate, this was very much a case of anticipating their requirements.
The artists did supply a broad-brush description of the kind of things they
wanted to do and we had to translate that into "What would we actually
need?".

Throughout all stages of the establishment of the Studios, for me personally, there was a lot of time spent exploring technologies, evaluating
technologies, making purchases and setting up equipment and software
and chasing new developments as they appeared. This involved liaison
with other project members and my network of contacts in the university. The first liaison was mainly with artists, Mike Quantrill and Dave
Everitt both of whom were accessible locally and who had had some earlier involvement via Gallery of the Future events. My role was to offer
technical advice and trouble shooting and be available for general brain
storming sessions. There was also a period of learning for me before the
residency period. I intended to become familiar with relevant technologies and software packages. Time did not permit me to become as familiar as I had hoped. I anticipated that I would not have all the relevant
skills necessary for the actual period.

The Residencies

The residencies were very challenging and interesting. It was made more
challenging by the fact that during that week I still had my departmental
and campus wide duties to attend to. There were, in effect two distinct
roles within the research project: one of general technical coordinator
and the other of technology supporter for a specific residency.

My main involvement as a technology support person was with the
artist Sarah Tierney. One aspect of Sarah's work was the requirement to
capture and edit video. This involved taking sequences of movements of
a model. I knew that given the limited amount of time available I would
not have time to learn how to do it professionally myself. This is where I
made use of the network of people I have come to know at Loughborough University over the years. I contacted Paul Wormald in the Design
and Technology department to see if he could help. He did more than
help. He actually setup the lighting and captured all the necessary video.
In the process I did also learn something.

More generally I consider that the residency went very well. There was
a good atmosphere and everyone, both artists and support staff, got on
very well together. Or to put it another way it was, "Totally cool".

Experiences from the Case Study

To give an idea of the events and the experiences as they happened, some extracts from the residency I supported are included. The labels A, T and O stand for Artist, Technologist and Observer respectively. The direct quotations come from any one of those people and are included within borders. The other text was written by the researchers who collated and analyzed the data.

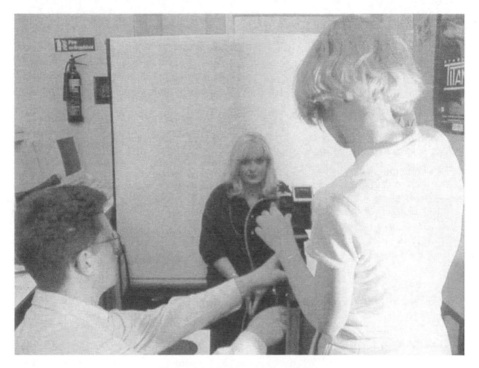

Figure 15.1 Making a Video

Figure 15.1 shows the artist, Sarah Tierney assisted by Paul Wormald, filming source material for a video work. The material took the form of a spoken narrative delivered by the actor Sarah Moffat. Close up shots of Sarah's mouth and eyes were taken. Later the source material was downloaded to an Apple Macintosh G3, and edited into a video work: see Figure 15.2 below.

Case Study: The Artist Sarah Tierney

Sarah Tierney's explorations of the effects of breaking up images are an intrinsic part of the underlying concept and exploration of her own life. She described the artistic process in terms of the relationship between the artistic ideas stored mentally and the externalization of those ideas through production. The integration of "thinking" and "doing" are particularly important to her. In respect of guiding ideas, there are two interests: one is the combining of text and visual image and the other is that of time. The importance of time within her art had increased as the technology opened up all kinds of new opportunities within this element of her work.

The thing I think about structuring is the time concept. So time is distorted, it's exaggerated and speeded up. That is connected to my interest in how long you can capture a viewer. Artist interviewed July 1999

The original proposal submitted for discussion was a project to develop a film/installation piece. The project was too large for a week's residency but in that time, the aim was to explore how to make a short film using video technology. The artist felt confident about her knowledge of Apple Mac computers and the editing application Adobe Premier and her capacity to grasp new applications provided there was someone to assist. Her expectation at the outset was that she would need to spend time exploring the software and learning as she worked. This expectation was dependent upon having adequate and appropriate expertise on call. Whilst she did not feel that she had achieved very much in terms of the production of the video itself, she did feel that substantial progress had been made in terms of developing the concept behind the piece. As she said:

In my head I have moved on a lot but out there, physically, it has not moved on a lot. But as the week has gone on and as I started formalizing more...I can see the end piece I have visualized...Artist interviewed, July 1999

The relationship between the thinking about the guiding concept and the actual visualization of an image seems to be an important element of this artist's practice. The total concept must be realized in response to the developing physical and virtual realization.

A year later, the following feedback was received from the artist commenting on her case report:

I am now in London and have been travelling quite a bit in America. I have made some good contacts with galleries and artists in New Orleans and I plan to exhibit there in 2001. The work will be photographic/digital images rather than video/film. I have evolved the work I did at Loughborough and I am using text. E-mail from Artist July 2000

The artist's goal of learning new skills during her exploration of new ideas was difficult to achieve. Problems were faced because of the lack of expertise in one critical software application. The time and effort spent on learning how to use the software from scratch required frequent referral to manuals. The situation was hindered by the difficulties experienced by the artist in adapting her knowledge from one video editing application to another which she found less transparent and more cumbersome to use. There was also much to be learnt about the use of the digital video camera but with the assistance of an experienced user, this part of the process was more successful and was one of the main achievements of the week.

Communication and Collaboration

The artist considered that communication with others, particularly fellow artists, was a fundamental part of the process of creating art. She reflected on her experience during the week and referred particularly to the issue of effective communication between artist and support person. She draws interesting parallels between the media and processes utilized, the preferred working environment and the ability to communicate your ideas with fellow artists and technical support.

It's a weird experience being observed/monitored as I work. I have always worked in an isolated way. This is especially true throughout my degree at university — the nature of photography and darkrooms reinforces a very individual work ethic...When I say it's a weird experience, it is not unpleasant or anything... I enjoy the interaction of other artists and designers. You need to be a good communicator verbally as well as visually though, to achieve a mutual understanding of the work-process-thought-idea-progressing. A's diary

Whilst there are some relationships that are successful immediately, with others, time is needed to gain confidence in that person. The artist found it easier to establish an instant rapport with one assistant over the other and this is certainly evident when listening to recordings taken during the early part of the week in terms of the nature and tone of conversations. However, she did manage to establish a good working relationship with the main contact person by the end of the week and valued the calming effect of his personality in the face of technical problems. This highlights the importance that many artists have attributed during their residencies to establishing longer-term relationships with technical assistants. This need for familiarity is evident even at the most basic level such as developing a common language (particularly when discussing technical issues) that both parties can understand and work with.

In terms of fundamental knowledge of the hardware and software, the support team was proficient:

P is definitely the star today. His knowledge of video is extensive. It would take me weeks to learn that much about video cameras. Need: more lighting and improved audio capture. Found the AGK omni-directional mike. Certainly seems to improve audio capture but Wednesday will tell. T's diary, July 1999

The artist commented on the skills of the team during an interview on the last day of her residency:

O. What do you think you got from them? Was it useful, interesting?

A. P's knowledge of video camera and his interest and T is so unflustered – a calming effect t– re horrible things with Edit DV.

O. So generally you felt they had skills you found useful and you learnt things?
A. Yes I learnt things...the video camera. Not around the computer – I am quite used to a Mac, except I am beginning to learn something about this new software package.

O. What about things that were not there in terms of support, access to people, skills?

A. It would have been brilliant if there had been someone on board who knew the software Edit DV. I think that would have speeded up the process because I have my head in the manual all the time. I learn best with someone there to give me a quick demonstration. I work better talking to someone. Artist July 1999

The preference is for access to a person who can filter the information needed according to the task needs as they arise. Does this imply the artist does not work in an anticipatory manner but in a reactive mode? What are the implications of this for advance planning for a support environment and for training?

The problems that were encountered in using Edit DV slowed down progress considerably throughout the week. A problem of an incompatibility between QuickTime Version 4 and Edit DV was identified and caused delays until later in the week when the artist found that the next version of Edit DV was available and this solved the incompatibility problem. She had been left to get on alone while support staff were otherwise engaged and during that time browsed the website of Digital Oregon in order to find a solution. The updated QuickTime 4 compatible application was available immediately and without further cost.

The artist was conscious of her personal computing limits and the impact that it had on her working practice. However, the migration to higher end technology appeared to have marginal benefits in a number of respects. This is particularly so in respect of how she envisaged her final work being displayed. The choice of video projection versus onscreen computer-based delivery would afford significant differences in the quality of the image she was striving for.

Use of the Internet

The Internet proved to be a valuable tool, not only assisting the team to identify suitable software, but also in seeking solutions to specific technical problems.

Looking at obtaining a DV-IN enabled DV camera. Quadrant video will hire one for £100 + Vat per day. Just found on the Web a DV-IN widget that will enable DV-IN on Canon Cameras. Widget for MVI due end July @ £99-00 + Vat. T's diary

Thursday late afternoon-continued working with DV Edit. Explored Web site to find answers. At least the upgrade is now available so T downloaded it. A's diary

Although exposure to high-end technology during the week of the residency had enabled the artist to develop her work much further than had previously been possible, in terms of the ideas behind the work and production techniques, this would not be realistically sustainable beyond the week. This had created an interesting situation whereby she made considerable mental leaps forward but the results of which would be almost impossible to realize without the support of C&CRS or similar facility.

End of Case Study Report Extract

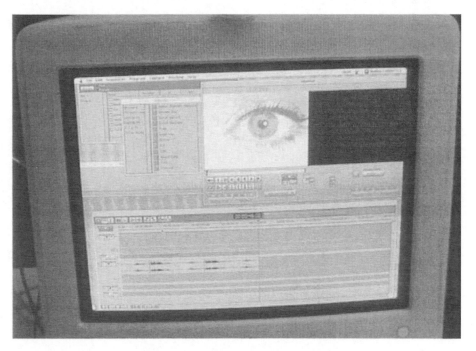

Figure 15.2: Video editing in progress

Lessons for the Future

From the COSTART experiences, there were a number of lessons learned. For me, the most significant ones are:

1. There is a need for a very wide range of skills and talents in order to support artists. A university is an ideal environment for artists

because of the skills available. Having a network of people with relevant skills is very important.

2. Because of my other commitments I only worked part time with the artists. Supporting artists is very demanding on time no matter what their level of experience or knowledge. It would have been much better if I had been full time on the residencies.

3. Most of my everyday work is on the computer systems side. Therefore my knowledge of the various packages that the artists used was minimal. I probably needed more time before the Residencies to become more familiar with the packages.

4. Having experienced one residency I am now better equipped to handle a future residency.

The COSTART residencies required considerable preparation in order to make sure that each artist had a realistic opportunity to achieve their goals. They were also intended to be a method of learning about what is needed to make art and technology collaborations successful and, in that respect, they served the purpose well.

Reference

1. COSTART 2000: http://creative/llboro.ac.uk/costart/

16   Working with Artists

Manumaya Uniyal

This chapter discusses the artist and computer technology from the perspective of a support person. A support person is comparable to a middleman who is, on the one hand trying to understand the ideas of an artist and, on the other, translating them into technical terminology so that the artist's requirements can be realized.

Working with the Technology

What a creative person wants to achieve at times does stretch the limit of available technology but it is highly important to understand the constraints of that technology. The idea is to try to push the limit but ever so gently, otherwise the bubble breaks. As much as one should recognize the creativity of an artist, the artist also needs to understand the constraints of a given technical environment. Often it is not just a question of knowing how much memory and machine speed is right for the project. Having partial knowledge can be a worse problem. I have encountered many cases in three-dimensional animation where people have made computationally heavy models without realizing that with half as many image vertices, after rendering, the difference between the two models would be negligible.

Everyone wants a bright crisp image every time they look at it. What they should ask is why do they need a high resolution? I have seen cases where an image was scanned at 2000 dpi (dots per inch) filling up the entire hard drive and reducing the system speed only to display the image at 1000 dpi and be printed at 600 dpi. In some cases, this might be justified but in most it is overkill. By not understanding the basics, too much investment in technology and time is made in order to create something that could be achieved by committing far fewer computational resources.

Every time I get a new piece of kit my father always tells me, "read the manual before you do anything". At times, the excitement takes over and we bypass that all-too-crucial stage. My father, on the other hand, has this amazing patience to go through any book, but then he is a journalist and reading comes naturally to him. The trick is to read the manual thoroughly just as you would go for a driving test before driving. Most of the people I have worked with tell me where they keep their manual and want me to read it for them. Their way of reading a manual is from the back, they read the index to work out the problem and end up getting more confused. In my opinion, that's the wrong end of the fishing rod. This way you will get yourself hurt and lose the fish. Learning to read the manual, understanding and spending time on it will give us all a long length of working enjoyment. It is important to understand the software and its functionality otherwise you will miss out those key points.

Today's creative person cannot afford to say, "I am an artist not a computer person so I will not learn this". It is of great importance to look at the past. A number of great painters spent time learning about human anatomy and they never said, "I am not anatomist". Leonardo da Vinci looked at both the art and technology and how they can positively affect each other. Whatever is tool of the day, it is good to have more than superficial knowledge of the tool and it is not just the responsibility of the artist but also the schools who should teach young artists about computing.

Working with the Artist

If a technical support person is faced with a situation posed by an artist that entails work beyond the scope of his expertise, that person should admit the limits of his knowledge, as difficult as that might be. By saying "it cannot be done", this leads to the spread of wrong information and that, in turn, leads to the artist doing things in a misguided way. Before saying no, it is better to find out if it is not possible or could be done by someone else. Recently, I worked with an artist who had to change her whole project because of totally wrong information given to her by the technical staff.

I have had my own sleepless nights but I have learnt by working with artists that the best strategy is to hear them out. Being dismissive and measuring an idea in terms of physical effort needed to do that job is nothing short of insulting to the idea of the artist, however far-fetched the idea might seem to be. Talking (and more so, listening) also allows one to get to know the person you are working with, which, in the long term, helps more than one can imagine. It is not appropriate to have a technician who does not understand the nature of the job. The difference is how one defines oneself within that relationship. Is one an outsider, a mere technician with the job of fixing loose cables, or is one someone who is sharing and understanding the idea from the inside? It is more like acting like as an adviser than a technician, in fact you have to be a in-termediary for both computer and the user. Eventually the support person becomes an integral layer between the computer and the artist. A computer is programmed to react and hence, it is a reactive device unlike humans who are interactive and proactive. Intelligence is not just being able to learn from a set of rules but being able to learn from a system where there are no rules. Most people almost bring these dead machines to life by being frustrated or angry with them.

The Residencies

The COSTART project allowed me to actively participate in the processes of creating artworks. The project entailed collaborating with two different artists by sharing my skills with them. The common feature between the artists and their artworks was the use of computers. Computers, although not central to every idea, were important in facilitating the main concept.

My own background in computer animation, as well as economics, influenced how I looked at the methods of creating artworks using computers. In any given work, I prefer to make things simple, often starting from the lowest common denominator. Simplicity is important to me for two main reasons:

- When two people start work for the first time, simple ideas are easy to communicate and help build up a rapport rather than complex ideas.
- It is easy to develop a simple idea into a complex one.

The two artists I worked with had had previous experience of using computers, one having taught Web design as well as having worked as an artist. One of the artists, seemed to be excited by the idea of learning about 3D software whereas the other artist felt that mastering the complexities of a graphics software took her away from the actual work – the animation film that she wanted to create. It must be said that both artists were keen to learn about software.

Artist One

The first artist I worked with, Beverley Hood, showed an inclination towards computers and the different software that were to be used in the project. She had earlier found three-dimensional software useful. The COSTART project gave her a chance of exploring this area further. The collaboration started with a lot of talking. We decided to explore the idea on paper before getting on the computer.

- the artist developed a rough storyboard
- the storyboard was used to examine both
- the technical issues
- the art issues

It also allowed us to be critical about the idea without affecting the actual artwork, since it had not yet been developed.

Early in the project, it had been established that certain cuts would have to be made when it came to the visual quality of the textures and model detail. This was mainly due to the short length of the project. Early discussion helped iron out a number of issues such as modelling, motion of the object etc. All through the project there was a constant flow of ideas.

Some of these idea were not as meaningful as others but as Edward De Bono puts it:

> The first idea that comes to mind may not be so interesting but the second and third that flow from it can be very interesting. [1]

The artist picked up the basics of computer modelling and animation very quickly. She meticulously took notes, at times asking the same question over and over again until she understood a given concept. Her repeatedly asking the same question helped me modify my process of mentally developing an answer. It made me realize that I had to simplify my answers without losing the meaning. I learned that the best approach was to give out specific information within a very generic overall structure.

At first, I was giving information loaded with jargon and shortcuts. I was answering two different questions without trying to make a link between them. Soon I learnt that wherever possible, it was important to think of a correlation between any two given answers, for example, the relationship between heavily detailed models, rendering time, final model quality and economics of the whole process. A lot of the work done with Beverley Hood was hands on. At times she would ask something and I had to take over the computer and do it myself. This was mainly because it was not judged possible to explain the entire background under the given constraints of time.

Early on in the project I suggested drawing a timeline so we could see our daily progress. The timeline process was a very pragmatic approach compared to the way artists like to think about artwork creation – that is, something that flows without any limits of time and even an unfinished work of art is acceptable. Without getting into a debate about different working styles, my reasons for the timeline system were:

- to see our daily progress mainly in terms of computing skills learnt

- to be able to generate something, that could be taken away after the week.

The artist could then further explore the computer and her artwork however she pleased and she agreed to the timeline approach. The timeline approach required direct intervention by me when she had a problem. Perhaps, at times, she felt that either I was doing things quickly or not explaining them appropriately. Such issues were always in the back of my mind but the time constraints forced me to overlook such issues.

The outcomes of the project were:

- a completed piece of artwork (perhaps we can call it a draft artwork)
- the artist's feeling that computers and software can be a useful tool for creating art
- an increase in the artist's understanding of three dimensional software.

I feel that at times that I was pushy but practical. However, as a collaborating partner, I had to play my role as I felt it right. In the end, it was satisfying to hear that the artist felt that she had gained something positive out of the week-long exercise.

Figure 16.1 COSTART project discussion

Artist Two

The second artist I worked with, Joan Ashworth, was an animator. She had come with an open mind to see if computers could help enhance her existing ideas. The basic concept was a short animation involving a mermaid as the lead character, set in seaside landscape with a lighthouse. Her experience with computers was similar to the first artist. The style of collaborating with Joan Ashworth was based on the pattern developed when working with Beverley Hood. However, although keen on using computers, she felt that the software applications restricted her at times. Later in the project I noticed that my timeline approach burdened her. Perhaps that system made her feel claustrophobic when it came to thinking and testing out her ideas. Although I set targets, I failed to make it clear that they were primarily there to help us manage the project. Since she works on numerous commercial projects and is well aware of deadlines, perhaps she felt the timeline approach a bit too rigid in this situation. She preferred to use the opportunity of the COSTART residency as a feasibility study in using computers to accomplish a task that was otherwise done in a traditional manner. I feel I should have modified my approach and not necessarily apply the same system that worked well in case of the first artist. From a perspective of sharing ideas, a number of things might have been left unattended, for example, some of the technical queries. This is evident from the test animations that were developed during the course of the project. I felt at the time that that a longer project would have helped us to communicate our ideas better and allowed me to share my role in the project better. In the event, we had an opportunity to follow up this work and were able to build upon our knowledge of the project. The final work turned out to be very successful.

Conclusion

The COSTART project gave me a chance to interact with the artists in a manner that would not have been possible otherwise. It was interesting to support an artist from the inside by getting involved with artwork and the artist. The project also showed that people with two different skill sets can combine their strengths and create an interesting piece of work. It is important, though, to realize that in a project like this the main job is of the artist and the technically skilled partner should stay in the background. At times, I found that it was difficult to adhere to a particular role i.e. 'artist', 'support person', whilst doing jobs that demanded something from all the areas. Perhaps more time spent talking before the actual process would have helped. We might learn from Edward De Bono when he says, "The fact that computers can handle complexity does not mean that we do not need to design for simplicity" [1].

References

1. De Bono, E.: Simplicity, Penguin Books, Harmonsworth (1999) 210. (First published by Viking, 1998)

17 Creating Graspable Water in Three-Dimensional Space

Joan Ashworth

By building characters and being inside them in a variety of invented situations I am attempting to visualize a sense of being and physicality for other people's eyes. In the Stone Mermaid project, I aim to express some of the feelings I have for the texture of stone in and out of water. The main aim of the work I have done at the Creativity and Cognition Research Studios (C&CRS) is to develop the water element of this project which must appear to have the 'graspability' of cloth as well as the movement, translucence and flow of water. I have written a narrative called *How Mermaids Breathe* which explores the fertility of stone women who live in the sea and control the waters movement from its edges. The design of the project was inspired by the chalk stones of Birling Gap beach, the sculpture of Henry Moore and Cycladic Art.

In my practice, I am attempting to communicate ideas through narrative in a three-dimensional environment. I mean to express character, feelings and emotions through moving figures and trying to inhabit their bodies to enable them to perform: expressing feelings through movement just as the human body does. I create this movement using the stop-frame technique of animation. I approach animation as a "method" animator, as I need to rehearse a movement myself before moving a puppet or model. Not that the movement needs to be hyper-realistic, but something of the movement needs to be recognizable by an audience. The movement needs to create resonances that communicate a particular feeling that can be read by the audience. Additionally, I prefer a cinematic approach to film making rather than a theatrical approach. By this I mean that I want the audience to believe that the characters on the screen are actually involved in, and reacting, to the shown actions. They are not actors in a play who are re-enacting something that has already happened in the past. I also use focus and depth of field in my work to enhance and reinforce the emotional focus of a sequence. Textures, lighting and sound are all critical in the construction of my images.

I discovered digital methods of production through making commercials, title sequences, and short graphic clips for broadcast television. After seven years of making thirty-second pieces I became frustrated with the short production and screen times involved. Just as an idea would become interesting, the project would need to be shot, delivered and on air. I then took over the running of the animation course at the Royal College of Art, London to help me focus on developing longer projects and to spark off ideas with other artists. However, because the running of the Course is very demanding, progress of my own work has been slow and not much sparking has occurred. In that context the opportunity to have time and support through my contact with C&CRS has been invaluable and given my film project the space it deserves.

Influences

The work of the choreographer Pina Bausch is very appealing to me because it takes an everyday movement and by repetition makes the mundane a celebration. According to Sanchez Colberg,

> Bausch has always been fascinated by a variety of behaviour and has developed a unique vocabulary of movement from it. Her pieces have always been geared to making her audience see what is either taken for granted or ignored [1].

The visceral and extreme movements of the dancers in Bausch's choreography is meaty and vigorous showing the characters' determination and belief in their own world. This claiming of space through movement is an element I will explore further. For additional inspiration I have looked closely at natural history footage of underwater worlds. I have a hunger for creating three-dimensional spaces and atmospheres through movement and sound. For my film, The Web [2], much inspiration came from the interiors of buildings and the narrative in Peake's Titus Groan [3, 4] gave me a thread to connect these interiors.

My current project has had a long gestation period beginning with cloth and binding. This was a development from a sequence in The Web in which a character binds his knees with cloth to stop them clicking. These sources I combined with story of The Little Mermaid, wanting to show that when the mermaid swapped her tail for legs every step she took would be like walking on sharp needles, as if her new legs were footbound. I explored these ideas for some time, but the narrative became too complicated. Eventually I stripped the story down to a mermaid in search of semen to fertilize her eggs. I liked the idea of her not being prepared to change into human form to procreate. Because of this reluctance to transform, she risks her race dying out. She has to consider the compromises and sacrifices of breeders.

The look and style of my mermaid characters evolved into ancient, long-lived creatures and eventually stones. Their texture and shape were inspired by the chalk stones on Birling Gap Beach, Sussex, which have some of the qualities of the work of Henry Moore. This, in turn, led to Cycladic Art [5] and the Bronze Age fertility idols discovered in excavated graves. Some of these figures are thought to have been carved by women and look as if they have been frequently carried around in pockets as they are worn smooth in parts. This smoothness and their association with fertility fits very well with my narrative. Also, the digital process I am using involves modelling a figure in plasticine and then scanning it three dimensionally. The process of scanning and smoothing the information softens the detail of the original sculpting and so mimics the work of seawater wearing away a pebble or the many touches of a Cycladic figure by ancient Greek hands.

Residencies

During the time I have been visiting C&CRS, I have chosen to focus on developing the look of the water for my Stone Mermaid project. I was not convinced that computers could give me the look I wanted which in my head was a mixture of cloth, ink and moiré patterns. This mixture needed to move and behave like water, but also, for narrative purposes, be graspable like the edges of a tablecloth. At this point I was still at the chalk stones stage of my character design and I wanted to put together a sequence of an animated figure moving through an inky cloth-like volume of water. I wanted to see the surface of the water and under the water to assess the combination of textures and their effect on the moving stone figure. It was also important for me to find out if I could work with the texture of the material being removed from my hands by being composited within the computer. My previous work had involved building and animating with real materials which, through touch, suggested how they should move. I relied on this contact for knowing how to perform. However, I knew that I had little choice as the water I had in my head could not be created organically.

Digital technology has enabled me to work in a more contained and less physical way. The square footage of studio space required is less. It makes me feel restricted in some ways and my hands and body get bored with doing small movements. They need bigger gestures with more physical effort required to feel satisfied. By retaining the need to sculpt the stone mermaids in clay and then scan them in three-dimensions, I am able to combine the physical and the contained ways of working. As I progress, I want to refine my methods of working and find more ways of combining the digital with the pleasures of the tactile and physical.

I visited the Studios at Loughborough several times for short periods – the longest being five days. The supportive atmosphere and practical arrangements are very productive for me. It is stimulating to be able to talk through some of the work both technically and creatively and be more reflective about the processes involved. Ironically, it is what I provide for my students but it is very hard to get that support and feedback once you cease to be a student. On my first visit, I worked closely with my technical support person and relied heavily on his skills as I was unfamiliar with the software identified as being the most appropriate. This was quite frustrating at times as it was difficult to build an understanding quickly enough and hard to work through someone else's eyes and hands in a collaborative way. In spite of the frustrations, the first residency was immensely fulfilling and enjoyable. During subsequent visits I worked with a different support person and attempted to work more independently by choosing to use software which was much easier to learn or that I was already familiar with.

The residency helped me to develop my current project and formalize my time allocation to it. Each visit offered an opportunity to discuss ideas behind the project that I found very useful. I accepted that I was too keen to keep deeper ideas hidden. It is easier for me to discuss the technical aspects of a project than to discuss the deeper meanings. Too much discussion feels too probing especially in the early stages of a project when the idea is raw and embryonic. By excavating some of these layers through reflection I was able to progress the project.

Having achieved some promising clips of graspable water I am continuing to develop the stone mermaid project. It has reassured me that working digitally is appropriate for this project. I have been learning 3D software to give me insights into some of the restrictions within the software as well as the freedom to experiment. I have been preparing myself for animating the characters I have invented by imagining their motivations. I swim to imagine their movements in water and view wildlife films to examine how difficult it is for water mammals to move on land.

The next stage is to raise finance for the production costs. When finance is found, I will put a small team together to make the film as it will require more skills than I have. I will continue to visit C&CRS to work with the support of the staff there as I refine and develop the water animation. The next challenge is to create a storm as my experiments so far have been with a relatively calm volume of water.

Art Practice with Digital Technologies

Digital technology has encouraged more and more people to work with moving images and particularly animation. The accessibility and ease of use has brought a breadth and freshness to moving image with many painters, sculptors and photographers creating time-based pieces for exhibition in galleries and public spaces. This is a challenge to more passive viewing spaces such as cinemas and family living rooms. The film industry is in a turmoil of excitement and despair as the changes in technology ravage through traditional film and video production and role definition. For a while, expert skills seemed redundant as new tools enabled one person to do everything. Gradually, the roles are separating out again, as new experts are required to push the limits of the technology. New technology has influenced the content of films with narratives being selected for their ability to show off some of the latest tricks and skills of the film-makers, for example, The Matrix and Toy Story. Is this stage coming to an end?

The role of an animator has changed and broadened over the last ten years as live-action work, feature films and commercials, rely more on frame-by-frame digital manipulation of images. As the tools have become more sophisticated, more time and budget is spent on them. Most artists find that many of these post-production tools are out of their price range but by viewing films they are influenced and given a hunger for sophisticated image manipulation. Many artists become hooked into advertising and promotional films in a symbiotic relationship which gives the advertisers a fresh look to their product and the artist access to the latest high-end equipment. I found it unfortunate that many of the experiments and artistic achievements produced for advertising are quickly archived and forgotten as the next job comes barrelling through. It is important for these production and post-production companies to take time to reflect on their strengths and areas of genuine innovation. It is also important for artists to develop continuing relationships with talented operators of these tools, to keep getting the best from the equipment and the people.

Burning Issues

There is a kind of slipperiness and insecurity about digital technology which film and film-cameras do not have. The tools for filmmaking are mechanical and reassuringly cool to the touch. Changes in design of film tools are slow which creates a feeling of stability, confidence and expertise in their users. Digital tools tend to be plastic boxes with their function more removed from their shape. The tools are found under buttons and moved around with fingertips rather than the whole body. This inevitably has an impact on how an artist's work progresses as different thoughts are triggered by different physical situations.

As an artist it is important to question whether you are putting your energy into the idea and expressing it as simply and directly as possible. It is a big investment of time to learn how to use any new tools, and digital tools can change or develop quite rapidly. Digital advisors with artistic sensibilities are needed by artists to guide them through the exciting but confusing software and hardware jungle.

Within art and design there is still snobbery about computer created art, partly because often there is more than one version of a piece which can take away its uniqueness and collectable value. Collectors of art need to be reassured of the value of digital art as art and not just technical wizardry. It is easy to be branded a technician once you admit to being able to use a machine. It is easy to get distracted and become a technician once you can use a machine.

Another reason for people's distrust of digital art is the perception of the computer, not the artist, making the art. The artist's hand and skill is not always so obvious. Unless artists learn to customize the digital tools then the work of many artists can look very similar. Getting beyond factory settings takes time and commitment. The environment at C&CRS is extremely valuable in advising artists on which tools to choose for their particular project or way of working and goes some way towards encouraging artists to being involved in creating the tools they want.

Figure 17.1 Still from the Stone Mermaid, 1999 © Joan Ashworth

References

1. Sanchez-Colberg, A.: Reflections on Meaning and Making. In Pina Bausch's Die Klage der Kaiserin (The Lament of the Empress). In Parallel Lines, Media Representations of Dance, S. Jordan and D. Allen (eds) Arts Council of G.B. (1993)

2. Ashworth, J.: The Web, a film based on Mervyn Peake's Titus Groan. Mari Kuttna Prize for Best British Animation 1987 and broadcast on Channel 4.

3. Peake, M.: 1911–1968. Peake's Progress, Gilmore, M. (ed) The Overlook Press, New York. (1981)

4. Winnington, P.:(ed) Peake Studies, 3 (3) winter (1993)

5. Fitton, L.F.: Cycladic Art, British Museum Press (1989)

18   The Artist as Digital Explorer

Dave Everitt

My art practice is primarily concerned with collecting, processing and arranging information of various kinds. It involves the combination of knowledge, issues, digital methods and performance and exhibition locations. There is no central concept. Rather, I allow connections, patterns and creative direction to emerge from multiple lines of inquiry. When a particular thread coalesces, or larger 'nodes' forms from overlapping information, I embark on the process of generating a piece of work, from which two main projects have emerged.

Although the thinking and research is often solitary, collaborations have become essential, embracing the skills and creative input of specific individuals in ways that integrate my own web of activity with more extensive networks, feeding new material back into the process. I use the term 'synthezist' to describe this activity.

Although I find some historical inspiration in those digital artists who program, I do not identify strongly with previous art movements. Instead, I use digital technology to enable me to synthesize multiple areas of inquiry into new forms that cross-disciplinary boundaries, attempting to avoid 'generalist' traps such as ignorance of existing research.

Number patterns have been a perennial source of inspiration for as long as I can remember. Certain integer patterns can be made to display rich arrays of interwoven permutations that demand fluid classification while constantly hinting at underlying structure. These suggestions of order within disorder, symmetry within asymmetry, hint at the complexity of human experience. The meaning we construct around pattern may be one reason for mathematics being a core focus in the urge to seek increasingly complex kinds of order in both the tangible and conceptual realms. Specifically, magic squares and cubes with their almost impenetrable variations have a particularly symbol-laden cultural history, from China and the Vedic mathematics of India, through Dürer's famous engraving, to an appearance on Gaudi's cathedral in Barcelona. The cultural meaning of number, combined with the abstract evasions of rigidity in something so obviously structured, fuel my interest in the subject.

Two long-term projects which serve to realize these lines of inquiry are described in the following sections.

CubeLife (www.cubeLife.org)

Figure 18.1 shows the first installation of cubeLife at the bioMatrix exhibition, Loughborough University, October 1999. The image is back-projected to a polycarbonate screen. The only input device is the heart-beat monitor clipped to the artist's little finger.

Figure 18.1 cubelife, bioMatrix exhibition, 1999 © Dave Everitt

An ongoing project, undertaken with computer scientist Greg Turner, "cubeLife" evolved from an application I wrote for drawing magic square patterns (using the power of Apple's venerable and neglected RAD HyperCard as a digital sketchpad). The process of transforming this into an exhibitable project started as a basic Java Applet written by friend and programmer Ben Daglish, using Java for its Web and cross-platform capabilities. CubeLife is an inquiry into two areas: the input of biological cycles into art, and the interface between pure mathematics and visual imagery. Exhibited, cubeLife only exists when an audience participates – mathematical entities in virtual space are created from heartbeat data, on a wall-sized screen that remains blank until the first participant creates an object. Each one leaves tracks as it moves and is associated with a unique digitally treated sound sample from a large water-filled clay bowl (prepared by collaborating musician Kate Rounding). As others add their pulse-inputs, objects and associated sounds build, interact and finally decay. Each session produces a unique combination of forms, sounds and colours. Seats are provided for people to stay and watch the image they themselves have created. The non-repeating cycles capture attention in the same way as do natural forms, or perhaps there is an unconscious unity in sharing something created by the collective heartbeat of a group of individuals.

Emergency Art Lab (www.e-artlab.com)

This project, part of a COSTART residency with Mike Quantrill, began as the commissioned work, 64 Samples, at the Wired and Dangerous digital art conference in the UK (with Greasley and Rogalsky). The e-artlab concept is to use live digital performance to make serious, yet playful, comments on the electronic gathering of private information in society. Video, audio and personal details were taken from conference delegates, scrambled, and reprocessed into a single animated virtual entity – a visually arresting but commercially useless 'database' as the antithesis of corporate data-gathering methods, appearing as a cube of 'flesh' gradually exposing 64 smaller cubes containing personal data. The 'lab' went on to perform Club confessional in the UK and Holland, playing on the collision of private and public territory that digital technology creates by setting up a 'private' booth in a night club, then feeding remixed 'confessions' and other material from club-goers back into the music mix they are dancing to. There is an element of theatre, with the artists wearing lab coats and identification badges to provoke issues around authority, privacy and information.

Residencies

In 1997, I began to synthesize creative activities with computer experience and interests in information systems, psychology, cultural issues and history, and pure mathematics. In 1998, under a Gallery of the Future bursary at Loughborough University, I began to use digital technology to handle this task, devising the bioMatrix exhibition at the School of Art and Design gallery in October 1999 [1].

Work undertaken at C&CRS has coalesced through residencies and bursaries into the above projects as vehicles for the growth of collaborative partnerships. The result has been to gradually expand my original interests and to considerably extend my knowledge of computer science.

My work with Mike Quantrill, tracking movement through the infrared sensor grid at C&CRS, was the start of an unusually complementary collaboration that has emerged in the e-artlab project.

Figure 18.2 shows the artist working on 64 Samples, the Emergency Art Lab Year of the Artist on-site commission for Wired and Dangerous, the final conference in the Eastern Touring Agency and Arts Council of England conference series on art and digital technology called Get Wired.

Figure 18.2: Emergency art lab at Wired and Dangerous, 2000

Impact of Technology on My Work

I use the computer directly as a creative medium, via programming and custom hardware. Digital technology provides multiple methods for both informing and disseminating whatever emerges from the continually developing lines of inquiry. The 'input and output' of this process, with the need to manipulate information and devise software to try out ideas, is entirely computer-dependent. This dependence has generated collaborations and partnerships in order to extend the range, strength and aims of the work, and to provide specialist expertise wherever my own (shifting) territory ends.

Personal Reflections

As an artist with no mathematical track record, I faced the formidable task of learning the essential tools to increase the depth of my inquiries (buried in the mathematical symbols of a language not usually covered by art practice). Until very recently, magic squares were a neglected or un-fashionable area of mathematics and any material beyond the obvious was initially hard to find, even in mathematical works. Fortunately, the Web's small but active interest group is a healthy mixture of profession-als and math hackers. Related sites have grown almost threefold since I first began. In addition to this, some historical source material is only available in Chinese, which necessitated learning to recognize Chinese numerals.

Where Next?

Current plans for cubeLife include the incorporation of artificial intelli-gence principles and the development of a distributed web-based 'nodes' through which participants update an exhibited version. Mathematical inquiries continue in a cubeLife spin-off called cubeEx(plorer), an intui-tive visual software tool for examining magic cube patterns. Separate work begun at C&CRS with Simon Nee on algorithms for detecting pat-tern sequences in magic squares is also in progress. Work on a sensor grid with Quantrill aims to develop a time-based "landscape of activity" by tracking and mapping movement, and to expand the possibilities of the e-artlab. Further proposed events include a touring exhibition with the five Year of the Artist [2] award winners and an e-artlab project at a con-ference on art and complexity in the USA.

New Forms of Inquiry

Together with others who use technology daily, I feel part of a new kind of human inquiry that extends the current meaning of art, or even steps outside it. Pushing technology into new adaptations, creative interests and research can cross boundaries into unnamed territories beyond the traditional artistic role. As part of this process the 'art' label, with its rich history and cultural burden of presumptions, will be expanded by the activities of those who produce the work it defines. There are many ques-tions raised by the cultural shifts driving this process. Some examples are listed next.

Do we need to further redefine art practice to recognize and actively support cross-disciplinary lines of creative inquiry more effectively? At one end of the scale, artists are 'playing with' science; at the other: an entirely new discipline is emerging where art–science partnerships are interwoven in new forms of inquiry. How might established research methods be adapted to support these new forms? How can arts-based critical languages be sustained in such a climate?

When artists working with technology refuse to accept no for an an-swer to some thorny problems, might their input be directed more widely towards teams developing new technology? Are labels redundant when artists become inventors, developers, problem solvers; and scientists utilize creativity, inspiration and intuition? Are the most striking discoveries made by those exploring territory outside their own discipline? Will the social responsibilities that emerge from this new form of inquiry be at variance with commercial and scientific ethical codes? As the critical point approaches where virtual and actual realities come to be experienced as one, will the divorce of virtual space from the physical and moral constraints of actual space raise increasingly complex issues concerning the formation of new ethical and social codes of interaction?

Artists, Interfaces and Novelty

Technology simultaneously frees artists through informational manipulation, speed of results, and freedom from traditional media restraints. It also constrains through technological limitations, stereotyped user-screen formats, expense, reliability and compatibility issues; and the need to follow new developments. These issues encourage artists – with computer gamers – as the user groups most likely to drive innovations in non-screen-based human–computer interaction. The use of biological data as an interactive element elicits an immediate involvement that bypasses the 'real-world' analogies of interface approaches to allow intuitive control and feedback. However, cultural familiarity with technology means that even those artists using the very latest technology need ideas that exceed the 'oh wow' factor. The strength of the underlying creative concept and its connection with an audience remain crucial. In other words, the irrelevance of the digital medium itself is periodically obscured by its novelties.

References

1. Personal website: www.daveeveritt.com or http://www.innotts.co.uk/~deveritt/
2. YOTA: Year of the Artist, UK Lottery Funded Scheme (2000)

19   Hybrid Invention

Beverley Hood

In my work I explore the creation of manifestations and representations of physical or emotional qualities, attempting to document and pin down elements such as intimacy, emotion and physicality. Throughout my practice, I create subtle layers of contradiction, with unexpected combinations of material and subject, in an attempt to define and quantify ephemeral qualities. In doing so I have used a wide range of media in the creation of my artwork. This has included Internet, sculpture, interactive installation, performance and digital photography. Often my work pairs traditional and non-traditional processes as I am interested in the hybrid possibilities of new combinations of materials and media. My work explores the relationships between the more traditional processes of disciplines such as sculpture and printmaking and new technologies, where they overlap and differ. These hybrid approaches offer the opportunity to combine the physical and virtual realm, both in the process of development and the presentation of final works.

I am also interested in the fabrication of emotional content, contriving intimacy from suggestion. My work has examined the balance between this constructed sense of the personal, through the use of suggestively private and intimate material, within what is traditionally perceived to be a cold and remote medium, technology. This gives my work a subversive sense of balance being both seemingly personal, physical or emotional, and simultaneously distant, due to my calculated processes of mapping and documenting these qualities.

Residencies

I was artist-in-residence at the Creativity and Cognition Research Studios (C&CRS) for the first time for one week in July 1999 as part of the CO-START research project [1]. My aim for the residency was to experiment with the potential of 3D computer animation and virtual reality, towards the development of a sculptural installation called asex [2]. This work stems from my interest in representations of the body using new technology, particularly the exaggerated and erotic nature of many of these pre-fabricated physiques, for example, within computer games. The work, asex, is a reflection upon these representations and an attempt to create a bisexual form.

The project is an example of my current hybrid approach to creating work, combining traditional processes with new technologies, exploring where they connect and differ. The installation involves three distinct sculptural processes of development (both traditional and non-traditional), individually applied to the same conceptual form. My intention was to allow each process to influence the form as it develops, creating three objects which rather than being replicas of one another are shaped by the process of their development.

The three processes are bronze casting, 3D computer animation and rapid prototyping. The 3D animation created at C&CRS was the first stage in the work to be developed, as none of the objects at that time had been realized. The residency gave me the opportunity to make substantial progress with the animation element of the installation and the work as a whole. A vital part of this opportunity was the access to equipment and software that the residency provided which had been previously unavailable to me.

Initially I had intended to work at C&CRS experimenting with Virtual Reality (VR) environments, to explore the possibilities of creating virtual, malleable objects. Although this is still of interest to me, soon after I began working on the residency I realized that a VR environment was not appropriate for the installation. This was due to the specific presentation requirements of VR, which being an immersive and contained environment would interrupt the physical relationship between the objects within the installation. I therefore decided to re-direct my attention to the potential of 3D animation, which would be a more cohesive element.

As part of the COSTART project residency I worked with Manumaya Uniyal, a specialist in 3D animation and VR. This was a great opportunity for me to work with someone more experienced in this area, enabling the work to develop more quickly and for myself to gain some fundamental skills. An interesting experience, it was challenging to develop a working relationship in such an intensive period and was a demanding situation, requiring much flexibility and communication. I find such situations can be very dynamic and hugely beneficial in the creation of work, as the situation was at C&CRS. To develop and experiment with ideas required many discussions to establish aims and technicalities. Such communication is integral to the process of development for my work, and highly influential in establishing a level of technical and conceptual understanding.

A great deal was achieved in the week and I developed a sequence of wire-frame animations. The use of wire-frames rather than maps around the objects was a decision that evolved through the process of development and such decision making was totally facilitated by the residency. Without the means to try out the various options I was considering, I was in no position to come to such integral but fairly straightforward conclusions.

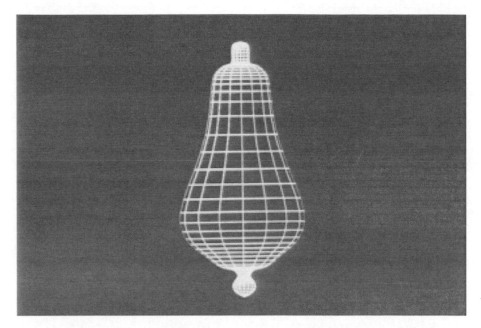

Figure 19.1: asex 1999 3D animation test model © Beverley Hood

After leaving C&CRS, I compiled these animated sequences into a single animated movie and from this I later developed an animated screensaver. I am interested in the potential of creating work, which lends itself to distribution and have also developed artist books, multiples and recently a postcard series. The 3D animation transferred perfectly to this media.

The asex screensaver has been exhibited independently from the larger installation work in the following exhibitions: Sum of Parts, Fruit Market Gallery, Edinburgh (2000/01), Infinitude, Gallery of Modern Art, Glasgow, (2000) Jesus, Mary and Joseph, Stills Gallery, Edinburgh and 114 Byres Road, Glasgow (1999/2000). A view of the rendered image appears in the colour section as Plate 7.

AA2A and "in conversation"

I continued my work at C&CRS as part of the Artist's Access to Art Colleges (AA2A) scheme and in October 2000 returned to Loughborough, again working with 3D animation. The resulting work, In Conversation, examines the nature of communication within networked technologies, specifically the Internet and email. I am interested in how these networks are constantly transferring private and intimate material, although our perception of computers is rational and unemotional.

In Conversation is an installation using projected 3D computer generated animation, based on a series of emails, which make up a three-month conversation between two individuals. Each email message was added and animated as a separate layer in 3D, to build up a dense and visually complex mass of moving text. In the installation, there are two animations, one for each individual's 'half' of the conversation, which are presented as large-scale projections, placed opposite one another. The work is sculptural in that the projected image takes on a physical three-dimensional presence but at the same time has a painterly surface quality, which is apparent in close up.

The work featured in the 7th International Computer Art Festival, Maribor, Slovenia in May 2001 and in the Festival Show, Edinburgh College of Art, August 2001, marking the end of my post as John Florent Stone Fellow in the School of Drawing and Painting.

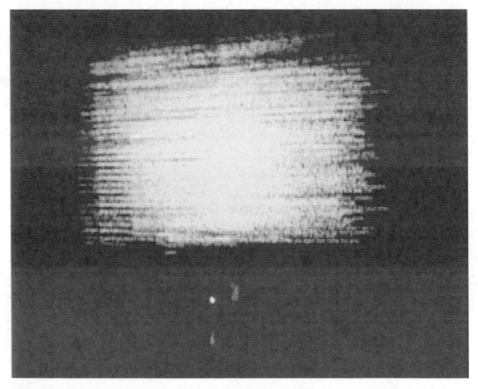

Figure 19.2 in conversation 2001, Installation Edinburgh College of Art from a photograph by John MacGregor

Reflections

There are key issues to consider regarding the potential of digital technologies as a medium for the development of art work, as this is dependent on factors such as access to equipment, technical knowledge, means of presentation and funding. Digital technology, as with previous developments, such as video and photography, opens up an array of new possibilities. It can be used as production tools that assist in the creation of work and an entirely new medium within which to create and present work. In my own practice, there are ways different technologies allow me to work which are not possible in other media, for example, when working within and referencing, aspects of the Internet. Such an approach also requires an understanding of the medium, its standards and idiosyncrasies.

Access to equipment is a fundamental issue in encouraging and supporting artists wishing to create their work using digital technology. Many artists now have their own facilities where often it is vital to their working practice. However, many do not have the financial resources or the confidence with such equipment to be able to work with it within a studio situation, which could often be isolated from any potential support.

Those artists who do have access to their own equipment are generally limited in what software they can afford to buy. This is an interesting and also frustrating situation, whereby generally the hardware (as in a basic computer) is more accessible in price than much of the software necessary to develop creative work. There are also many hardware extensions to the standard PC or Apple Macintosh such as CD writers, scanners, printers all of which can be costly.

Access to equipment, via academic institutions, media labs, resource centers, etc., supports artists in a number of ways. An artist, with equipment of their own, may require access to hardware out-with their own facilities. Similarly access to software can provide artists with opportunities to develop work in high-end programs inaccessible to them financially for use on their own equipment. Such software may allow them greater freedom in how they work and sometimes simply enable them to realize their ideas. Examples are 3D animation and multimedia software, which are both cost prohibitive to a non-commercial, individual user.

For an artist who has no equipment of their own, and artists who are not computer literate but interested in the potential of digital media, access to equipment is vital, as are workshops and courses, which can build confidence and knowledge. This is very important in allowing artists who may be intimidated by technology to demystify the processes and be able to make choices about whether digital technologies are appropriate to their working practice, rather than being restricted through lack of knowledge and accessibility.

Alongside equipment, technical support is vital. As previously mentioned, workshops can be an invaluable introduction to software, processes and means of artistic production. In organizations and institutions, which provide access to equipment for artists, it is vital to have technical support at hand. This can often be needed most on an everyday level, to provide advice on simple issues, which without instruction on how to resolve can become magnified and inhibit progress.

Another means of technical support is for artists to collaborate with more specialized programmers and developers. Such support allows artists to develop projects requiring more complex programming, for example, than the artist himself or herself is capable of. Institutions such as C&CRS, offering this level of support, provide challenging opportunities for both artists and developers.

The issue of funding is equally important. The prohibitive aspect of new technology, besides unfamiliarity with equipment, is often expense, whether buying hardware, software or paying for technical support time. Although organizations, such as digital resources and media centres, often need to charge some costs for use of facilities to cover their own running costs it is important to establish a balance whereby the fees set for access and workshops are not prohibitively expensive. An issue amongst funding bodies is to ensure, where their funding criteria is appropriate and can include work within digital technologies, that they can adequately assess the work being presented, sometimes as simple a point as ensuring a computer can be available to view work.

Digital technologies also carry specific difficulties in presentation, particularly within the traditional gallery context. These issues are varied, for example, power and networking requirements for an interactive installation may be beyond the capabilities of numerous galleries. Many could not provide any technical equipment, insurance for such if brought in by the artist, and there also may not be any level of technical support within the gallery space to facilitate the presentation of the work on a day-to-day basis. It is, however, vital that the presentation and therefore visibility of digital work is supported with consideration. Digital technologies are fast becoming a standard tool in art production, used in a variety of ways, from the means of production and presentation, to a facility for documentation, research and planning. Beyond this there is also the global environment of the Internet, not only influential as a medium within which to create and present work but also offering vast opportunities for new networks between international artists and organizations.

References

1. COSTART Project: http://www.creative.lboro.ac.uk/costart
2. Hood, B.: asex 2000-installation: http://www.bhood.co.uk

20   Contemporary Totemism

Jean-Pierre Husquinet

My artwork has developed over many years and has been guided mainly by the use of symmetry and asymmetry. It is also influenced by the use of a 'system' of an association of the twelve notes of the chromatic scale with the twelve colours of the chromatic circle. This research aims to create 'parallel' harmonic musical and plastic structures. To that end, the phases undergo successive restructuring and different types of material are used.

The main idea behind my work is the relationship between colour and the structure of those colours together with music and also the structure of the music you create. I am trying to create a code or language that has a relationship: this means that I am not working with musical theory but with visual images in the form of colour structures.

Correspondences between Colour Structures and Music

There are many aspects of those two worlds that are very different. You cannot structure music and visual art in the same way. But there are some rules that you cannot avoid. The main goals are to respect the known rules and to try to match the relationship between the colour structures and create music out of them. For the time being, it is mainly the visual work that is driving the music and not the opposite. I am not actually trying to put into images a particular kind of music but instead trying to build a logical system and construct a visual world of interest to me.

In respect of the structures underlying the artworks, the visual images drive the music: therefore, the structuring takes place in the visual domain rather than in the musical. I work with professional musicians and the main idea is not to write either music that changes into images or to make images that change into music, but to try to build an entire world. This means that, ideally, all the elements should be interrelated from the beginning.

The way we have worked is that I use musical chords and notes which are given to me by one of the musicians. All the notes are related to one another which I have to use in that section, so I do not use another colour which is not included in that chord and the way I am using them gives like a rhythm and the melody and it is the interaction of those voices working with the colours which re-creates all the melody. The best word

for this is 'structure' because it is built either visually or musically in
structures – that's the goal.

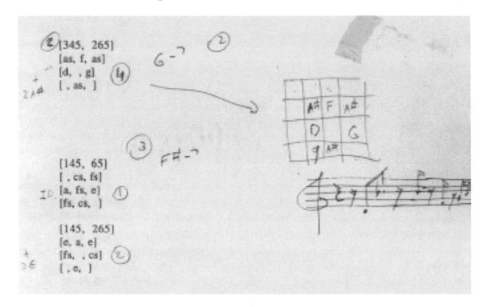

Figure 20.1 Notes for Crinan 1 © Ernest Edmonds

Figure 20.1 shows notes for a work called Crinan 1, made with my
collaborator, Ernest Edmonds. On the left are the schematics that represent images to be projected in sequence. The note was produced during a
debate about the correspondence between the music and the sequence of
images. It illustrates how we explored a way of mapping inter-
connections between the image structures and the musical notations.

The evolution of my work has progressed by successive steps: from
the two-dimensional picture to the third-dimensional material (e.g. wood,
metal). One of the first phases was the assembling of coloured cubes, then
by assembling tubular structures, this paved the way to discovering the
material which has really allowed me to evolve and access other plastic
aspects... the rope!

Rope Works

In the early stages of its use, the rope material was painted according to
sections of different lengths, each section having a numeric value in relation to the value of a musical note, that note being shown by its colour,
one of the twelve colours of the chromatic range.

I use three different methods: the first, for me the more interactive
one, is three-dimensional work using rope. This allows me a lot of flexi-

bility and the material is cheap and easy to paint. The rope works can be developed in a space and attached to some existing elements, such as trees. This allows me to visualize the world in three dimensions. This is, however, constructed first in two dimensions because the colours which are painted on the rope determine the musical beat. The rope in the space is not properly the music but it is the rope in itself which provides a reference for the music.

The second medium of the music is two-dimensional – painting, wood, canvas more in a classical way – and the third one is a line-based system. I have been developing line-based images, which are very interesting in the sense that music cannot be reduced to one surface, either two-dimensional or three-dimensional. Line-based parts are much more interesting because they can develop a system which allows you to visualize the notes at the same time as you are hearing them. The people who are seeing and hearing it can appreciate and understand the work much better that way.

The ropes were hung in space by the use of anchor points or existing intersections. At that stage of the research, I started to be interested in the intersections of the ropes and to realize a series of paintings in the form of a cross. This has naturally led me to explore the problem of the knot [1]. Because I knew nothing about them, it took me two years to learn how to manipulate them, patiently...

That inquiry has led my thoughts on to unexpected, experimental ways and also to some fascinating reading matter. The further I go on, the more I become interested in the relationship between what we call 'shamanism', in terms of communication, empirical, and the rationality of sciences.

In the past, knots were of great interest only to biologists, chemists and physicians at first. Then, a first attempt in mathematics on the use of knot was done by Vandermonde during the seventeenth century. His efforts led to failure and we had to wait until the twentieth century to see mathematicians work at it again. Among these searches, we can mention the mathematicians John Conway and Vaughan Jones who discovered the polynome of the same name, which restarted the studies of knots invariants. The research on knots theory is described in the excellent book by Sossinsky [2].

A common point seems to exist between scientific objectivity, using rationalistic methods, and artistic empiricism, using intuitive methods: it is that each one is looking for a form of purity, a truth which would be their own, to discover the unexpected and to discover the harmony which is hidden behind "disorganized" appearances. Poincaré wrote: "It is the search for that special beauty, the sense of harmony of the world, that makes us seek the facts to contribute to that harmony" [3,4].

Residencies

When, in January 1996, I received the invitation to participate in an artist's residency with the theme "the artist and the computer" at C&CRS, Loughborough University, I was persuaded that the computer could have an answer to the questions I had in mind since I thought those questions were perfectly rational and purely logical. I was rather disappointed when I saw that these things were not as simple as I had imagined. In the residency, I had access to the skills of a software engineer. For a week, we tried to solve a concrete problem about the focusing of a knot network, tightened in space which had to be of a scheduled length and on which different sections of colours were applied.

Working Collaboratively

To build a computer model of a net of ropes of different colours and precise lengths, we had to call on the expertise of Rob Doyle, without whom nothing would have been possible. A close collaboration between us was quickly established and finished with concrete results. The graphics program used was so complex that I was unable even to draw a single line However, with this collaboration, it was possible to make computer models of my ropes in specific proposed spaces as shown in Figure 20.2 below.

At the beginning it was strange to work with somebody you had never seen before and to explain to him precisely what you were trying to do. In his efforts to help me, he tried to find some solutions to my problems while I was not there, which did not work for me. The problem is that working with the particular program was quite a slow process so it took some time before we could actually see something on the screen that looked like what I was hoping to see. It was strange to see somebody actually doing the work for me because, as an artist I am used to doing it myself. This was interesting in itself because having it done by somebody else you have some answers to your questions, by way of a person and not through the computer. You have somebody who mediates between you and the computer who tries to explain to you what is possible and what is not possible.

Unfortunately, after much effort, the week was soon behind us. It was a week full of numerous discoveries and friendships, benevolent collaborations and mutual comprehension, which, to me, have allowed all of us to understand more about our respective disciplines and have created the need and wish to see each other again in order to go even further. I came with lot of expectations and five days was too short a time. I was surprised to have discovered there was no software that exactly served my purposes, and, for the other three resident artists as well.

Figure 20.2: Rope Works 1996, computer print © Jean-Pierre Husquinet

There were many unresolved questions and needs that could not be achieved for the time being because the software did not exist. I had been under the illusion at that time that all software was so sophisticated that it could do almost anything.

I was very pleased to work with the computer and I gained a very good idea of what computers could provide in the future. I did not think the computer could influence my work in terms of art but the time available was too short to really accomplish much. I needed to think about it more. There are other aspects of art practice which the computer will never give to anybody in the sense that if you are working with the material you have it in your hands. It could be anything. It could be metal or wood or earth or whatever you use, it doesn't matter. The contact with that material and what you do with it, opens some fields that the computer will not open, although it will open other fields, of course.

There are a number of improvements in computers that I would like to see in the future. For example, the textures you are provided with are not the kind that artists work with but rather are more dedicated to graphic art. You can actually probe one single joint on a surface, but it is very difficult when you want to take that drawing and put it into another space. With the software I have been using, it is possible to draw a house or a roof or whatever but once you want to put some particular structures into that house which are not architectural it is more difficult: it takes more time to put ropes inside the virtual space than to actually build the house.

Reflections

There are two things which are interesting in being an artist: one is the process of the development of the ideas and the other is the artifact that is generated – the work. As far as I am concerned the process is much more important than the work itself: for example with the Rope Works, these are never permanent objects because they can be re-used in a different context. Once the installation is in place it stays there two or three weeks and then can be brought down. If it is still in one piece, I can reinstall that piece somewhere else perhaps with significant changes in the environment and the configuration. The artifact has no value as a material object. Its value lies in the concepts underlying the work and its importance in helping me move my ideas forward. That is why I don't really mind if old pieces are destroyed. You can probably relate that to having a musical score that you have written: in this case it is a visual score which I have painted and every time you develop that space, you are rebuilding another structure. If you think of it in musical terms, it is as if you were thinking of a musical score again, and playing it again but differently, rather like playing jazz.

Working with Ernest Edmonds on the correspondences between colour structures and musical theory provided me with the opportunity to develop ideas in common. The links between the relation of a musical structure and a visual structure is very difficult to handle and requires collaboration between people of different skills and knowledge. The more I advance, the more I need the help of technology such as the software AVID for the images and Pro Tools for treating music. However, these programs are not dedicated to my purpose and I really would need a particular program, suited to my needs and thoughts.

For the time being, technology is already helpful to my work and would probably be even more helpful if I was involved more closely in workshops or residencies such as those at C&CRS in a regular manner. This brings me to think that residencies ought probably be done over different periods of time in order to understand the partnership better.

References

1. Husquinet, J-P.: Catalogue Notes: Knots. Installation in the C.H.U hospital, texts by Pierre Henrion, Sart Tilman (1999-2000)
2. Sossinsky, A.: NOEUDS- génèse d'une théorie mathématique. Seuil Science ouverte. February (1999)
3. Thuillier, P.: La revanche des sorcières. L'irrationnel et la pensée scientifique. Belin (1997)
4. Asher, M.: Ethnomathematics, Chapman and Hall, London (1991)

21 The Illusion and Simulation of Complex Motion

Fré Ilgen

I am a human being who tries to understand the nature of being human. What seems to match my own person best is creating art and exploring knowledge. Because creating art and exploring knowledge has led me to focus on the approach, process, contents and communication, the medium in which I create is the least important, although every chosen medium is taken quite seriously. In summary, I am an artist creating paintings and sculptures, suspended, on the wall and free standing and, sometimes, I experiment with a computer.

In my current art practice, I am intrigued by creating visual appearances or entities that emerge in certain clusterings of coloured, curved and rectilinear shapes and forms. These are always juxtaposed into compositions that suggest (simulate) a high order of complex motions. When I start a new piece, I have no precise idea how it will look or what it should look like. While making it I have to figure out its own 'logic'. A work of art is recognized as such by me and I call it finished at the moment when I have found its logic. This emerges out of my interaction, combining thought and bodily action, with the chosen material and an immediate and intense reflection on reality, as I understand it. Creating a work of art is an intense experience of life itself. Creating complex clusters of shapes and colours that are just individually different and in their context seem to make sense but that cannot be described exactly in words, seems a close simulation of life itself.

My artistic development started with surrealist painting, later developing a gradual interest in geometric compositions and discovering the art and theory of constructivism.[1] Slowly I reached beyond constructivism through an emerging interest in the interrelations between object and self, between perception, action and thinking, and, finally, evolving a serious interest in possible reasons for our desire to create and admire art and our desire for beauty.

Discovering, studying and exploring the analogies between art, science and philosophy have proved to be rewarding and have become as important to me as creating works of art. Exhibitions, learning people's response and experiencing how people handle my works of art in their own environments had a tremendous influence on my thinking. After many years of working, exploring and travelling in and through a variety of

countries in Europe, Asia and North America, I have noticed the importance of being exposed to a variety of different cultural influences – both
historical and contemporary. It certainly helps you to put one's own
thinking in a larger perspective.

Residencies

The artist-in-residency I participated in at C&CRS in 1996 was an exciting experience that led to a crucial turning point in my artistic work.
Because, in my sculptural work, I present a simulation of motions to the
viewer, I was invited to experiment with a Virtual Reality (VR) system in
which I could create actual motion in a computer-simulation. The experiences and results of my participation have been described before [1, 2, 3].
I was teamed up with Roy Kalawsky and his assistant who were experts in
the VR technology available at Loughborough.

Although I had never worked with VR before, I had some ideas about
the kind of motion and basic geometrical shapes I wished to explore. As
could be expected, we initially lost some time because of difficulties in
communication due to the differences in vernacular and viewpoints of the
different professions, Roy being a technical scientist and me an artist. For
instance, I preferred to start working in a non-referential black VR space
and Roy tried to convince me of the need to have a space with a floor,
walls and a ceiling. After evaluating the process, we decided that I relatively quickly learned how to handle the VR joystick, because of my experience as a sculptor in manually handling forms and shapes every day.

If a suggestion might be made for an improvement in this kind of artist-in-residencies, it would be that there should be more time for the artists to work with the support staff as well as the computer. The sorting
out of technicalities seems to absorb quite some time, leaving relatively
little time for actual creative work.

The impact on my own work since then has been quite clear. First, it
started me thinking a lot about the very new perspective a computer
simulation (especially in immersive VR) provides on visual illusion. It
also brought me to really consider the importance of manual handling as
an essential aspect of our creative process and as a thought-enhancing
activity. Secondly, it led me to start exploring both these aspects in new
works. I developed paintings directly derived from the VR experiment,
showing tremendous coloured space with only one or a few floating coloured bars. I called these 'virtual paintings'. Later this concept became
unified with my sculptural concepts, leading to reliefs with real and with
'virtual' shapes. These I call "augmented reliefs". The most recent step
has been to unify this relief-concept with my more calligraphic and spontaneous studies of colour splashes on paper. It should be added that the
short and intense experience with VR also led me to develop much more

complex simulations of space and motion than I ever did before. It has that much changed my perception that since then I also perceive paintings of other artists in a different way. I view the canvas of a painting not so much as a flat surface anymore, but as a window into infinity comparable to a computer monitor equipped with a three-dimensional program.

Figure 21.1 Hey Joe, 1997 virtual painting © Fré Ilgen

Reflections

Of course, it is impossible to predict where I will go next, I only suspect my works of art will become even more complex and hopefully, as such, to become even closer to life and the essence of ourselves. It is quite interesting to notice that "illusion" as a concept in Occidental culture always is something to avoid at all costs, but since computer-technology has introduced the notion of 'simulation' this was immediately accepted as a positive concept. This change of words for in fact the same phenomenon certainly allows us to understand the importance of illusion/simulation in our everyday perception: for example, the illusion/simulation of change, space or motion. This is something an artist like Wassily Kandinsky was aware of with his concept of creating space in our perception in front of the painting, or as Frank Stella explored in his similar concept of a 'working-space' of a work of art, enveloping the observer.

It is my conviction that digital technologies are very important for any art practice. However, unfortunately people always tend to polarize and exaggerate. I of course mean that fanatic believers in digital technologies propagate that these new media just replace any traditional means of creating art. The 150 years old history of the medium of photography has shown that a new technology may add important creative possibilities without ever really excluding painting or sculpture. It will take a few years more before the artificial hype about the proclaimed new media will abate and when notions like computer-artist or video-artist will be abandoned as labels altogether. It is the same as using labels like oil-painter or stone-sculptor in modern art. Although such specialization does exist, the contemporary artist chooses any medium and material that fits the concepts he or she wishes to explore. Because, for the average artist, it is difficult to have access to the right equipment and professional support, it is necessary that there are institutions that can provide both. It is important that these institutions stimulate a great variety of artists to explore and experiment with digital technologies, even though their normal practice does not necessarily seem to demand this.

Figure 21.2 No Quarter, 1996, suspended sculpture © Fré Ilgen

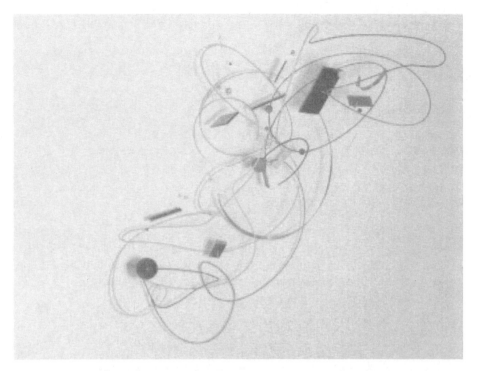

Figure 21.3 Rave-On, 2000, wall sculpture © Fré Ilgen

Because many professional artists do know what they do and what they would like to explore with digital technologies, and do not always have much time available, it will be important to develop an efficient and effective setup procedure. Much time is lost on preparing the technical equipment while the artist is present. This kind of talk should be done prior to the artists' visit. The artist is, for instance, present for a period of only three days, during which time he can work intensely with a good technical staff and hardly any preparatory discussions. One could imagine that artists will be approached on a regular basis by, for instance C&CRS, based on this institute's assumption that the interest of such an artist in digital technologies could exist. This implies reaching out, doing some active acquisition, instead of waiting for people to apply to come. At the same time, of course, it should be possible for artists to approach the institute directly to work with digital technologies.

For the future, I think it would be a very good idea if institutions like C&CRS could arrange for the leasing of equipment and technical support to artists, both for work in their own studios as well as for exhibition purposes. It is my conviction that it will become even more important in the near future to provide essential and realistic information about the opportunities and restrictions implicd by using current digital technology and what will become available in the immediate future. The sooner one can overcome the hyperbole the more interested artists will be in digital technologies.

Notes

1. *Constructivism* is a direction in abstract art started in early twentieth century by artists like Malevitch, Mondriaan, Gabo, etc., which views the world as constructed of certain universal and elementary units that function as building blocks for the perceptible world. It is a artistic development arising from nineteenth century knowledge in science and philosophy, such as Non-Euclidian geometry, Schopenhauer's ideas on the will and nature of things, colour theories, metaphysical interests in other cultures (esp. Hinduism and Buddhism) and the emerging importance of particle physics ideas on space/time.

References

1. Ilgen, F.: Virtual in Reality – Real in Virtuality, Proceedings 2nd International Symposium Creativity and Cognition, Loughborough, England (1996) 278-279

2. Ilgen, F.: Design as Connection between Thinking and Acting, Proceedings 2nd International Symposium Creativity and Cognition,, Loughborough, England (1993) 211-214

3. Ilgen. F.: CRAVE – Creative Artistic Virtual Environment – Bedeutung der direkten Manipulation, on CD-Rom "Texte zur virtuellen Ästhetik in Kunst und Kultur herausgegeben von Kai-Uwe Hemken" (1997). Arthistorical Institute of the Ruhr University Bochum and the VDG-Verlag und Datenbank für Geisteswissenschaften, Germany

4. Edmonds, E.A. and Candy, L.: Computation, Interaction and Imagination: Into Virtual Space and Back to Reality. In J. Gero and M-L Maher (eds), Proceedings 4th International Roundtable Conference on Computational Models of Creative Design (1999) 19-31

5. Bann, S.: The Tradition of Constructivism, Thames and Hudson, London (1974)

6. Rickey, G.: Constructivism: Origins and Evolution George Braziller, New York (1967)

22   The Computer: An Intrusive Influence

Michael Kidner

I am writing the following article from the point of view of a painter with no training in the fields of science or technology. Nevertheless, in the course of a long career, I have come to realize the inescapable value that the computer has to offer. As it is, I rely on the research of others for the raw materials of my own project which, in short, concerns patterns of space in the mind.

I began life as a painter in the 1950s. Painterly gestures, made from the stomach while denying the head, were typical of the strategy adopted by the avant-garde at the time. "A painting was finished if it worked" was a popular but unsatisfactory measure by which to proceed. It was not that I was scared to make intuitive gestures, I tried, but the intuitive gesture offers no satisfactory ground for dialogue – only inspiration via imitation. I chose instead to explore the interaction of colour where there was a clear measure by which to judge the effect of the experiments I was making.

I felt vindicated in following this independent approach when the Tate Gallery, London bought one of my paintings in 1962. However, colour needs form to articulate it (how big is red?) and I soon found myself more interested in form than in colour. I took a piece of bent wire and rotated it ten degrees at a time. As the form changed I noted the points where the wire profile crossed a vertical line held behind it and in this way produced a topographical map of the bent wire.

As the 1960s rolled on, cybernetics became a topic of hot debate among painters much as photography had been in the previous century. I took the view that the computer was an unwelcome competitor and I tried to imagine problems that would confound what I then regarded as an inhuman and unwieldy monster. I took a strip of paper and folded it at an angle of forty degrees but left the end sticking up at an angle of eighty degrees then repeated the operation several times keeping the sides equal in length. I aimed to come back to the starting point but for me it was a trial and error situation which made me wonder whether the computer would offer a better solution. I was afraid it could.

So then I tried to by-pass the computer altogether by stretching elasticized cloth between two wooden battens. By moving the battens I could distort an image drawn on the elastic through several repetitive stages and I devised top-down programs accordingly. However, the process was lim-

ited by the fact that the elasticized cloth would stretch in only one direction at a time.

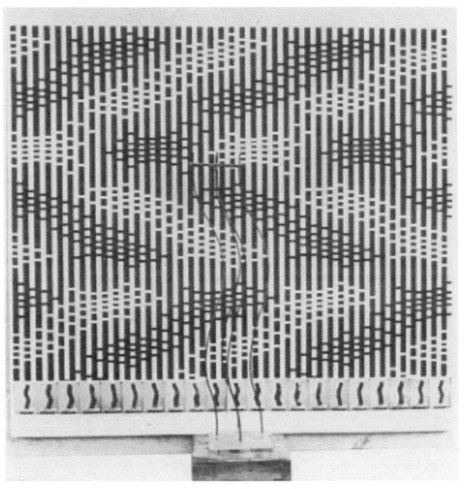

Figure 22.1: Column No. 1 in front of its own image, 1970 © Michael Kidner

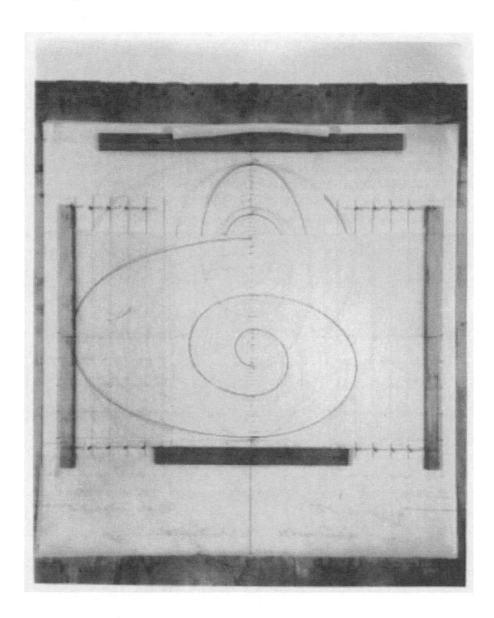

Figure 22.2 Looped circle, 1978 © Michael Kidner

Residencies

I was still trying to extend the application of this analogue device when I received an invitation to take part in the 1996 Creativity and Cognition Conference in Loughborough, England.

What amazed me here was the incredible range and diversity of the problems which engaged the other participants at the conference as though the horizon of their imagination had suddenly been exploded. At the same time I found it hard to relate to the results of their work partly no doubt because I was unfamiliar with the technology.

Shortly after this Professor Ernest Edmonds invited four of us to Loughborough to pursue whatever interests were uppermost in our minds. We were offered the assistance of experts from the university faculty which Professor Edmonds arranged to suit our different needs. It was such a generous offer that it proved difficult to make an adequate response.

Boolean nets was my problem but despite several patient sessions with a mathematician the mathematics defeated me. In the end my advisor produced a video of Conway's The Game of Life, a fascinating pro-gramme, but because it was time-based I felt, as a painter, that it was not for me. Happily this was not all the week had to offer since we all four benefited from each other's experience. See extracts from a conversation with Ernest Edmonds at the end of this article.

A visiting artist from Germany brought a drawing which she wanted to realize in print. I was surprised since her problem did not seem to relate to the computer until I realized that transposing a drawing on the moni-tor into a finished product was not as straightforward as I had assumed and a vital extension of the technology. Another visitor from Holland wanted to experience 'virtual reality' and we were all offered a brief but astonishing turn with the helmet. Back home this visitor made impressive paintings based on his experience of 'virtual reality'.

Reflections

I was still suspicious. I did not want answers that might show up on the monitor seemingly by magic. The computer could be a seductive toy of-fering only a superficial understanding but the prospect of going deeper into the technology was disconcerting. It was not only that I begrudged the time but more that I was afraid of losing sight of the purpose while acquiring the necessary skills. There had to be another way.

Fortunately I came across an a-periodic pattern by Roger Penrose. It was a highly sophisticated computer-generated drawing that seemed to answer my problem. What I saw in Penrose's pattern was a tiny fraction of space like a seed that grows in time. It reminded me of water broken by whirlpools which disappear only to reform elsewhere in an expanding space, or again like a Mondrian painting without the neo-Platonic ideal which inspired it. Indeed it was a pattern with many contending centres and no certain outcome, like the evolution of life itself.

But what in particular caught my attention was the pentagonal organi-zation of space instead of the rectangular convention which is the more generally accepted. The latter, adopted by Mondrian with his finely balanced verticals and horizontals, reflects stability whereas the former is more like the space I experience in an expanding/contracting world view.

However my response had nothing to do with the problem that confronted Penrose. His concern was to tile the plane with the fewest possible number of shapes, a well-defined mathematical problem. Whereas my concern is to define the many associations his pattern inspired. If I could reduce the number of associations to one I thought the computer would quickly resolve the problem but because I have not been able to do this I believe the computer will offer as many, if not more solutions than I have associations. I foresee that it could divert me from my present objective by suggesting new ones, and ones that would be better aligned to its own way of operating. On the other hand I recently saw, in the exhibition, Apocalypse, at the Royal Academy, London, a sculpture of the Pope being knocked down by a meteorite. It seemed obliquely close to the kind of expression I was myself seeking but I could find no logical way to connect it to my own project. In fact, I wondered what sort of logical explanation could possibly account for it?

I do not pretend to understand the mathematics behind Penrose's argument against artificial intelligence, but feel satisfied that he can make it. I like a world in which the personification of the truth we believe in transforms itself as we approach. Instead of imposing reason on feeling, I try, as a painter, to impose my feeling on reason.

Michael Kidner: From a Conversation with Ernest Edmonds

E: I would like to start by asking you to say some things about your work.

M: Around about 1970 I read a book by Dancy called the number of the language of science and it was really the history of the number theory. I was so impressed with the way number was describing or the way Dancy described number as describing life, and it made a lot of sense to me and since then I have always felt that number did account for existence, if you like, in a way that enormously impressed me. So that, number has been very important in my thinking, and when it comes to numbers like imaginary numbers or complex numbers of things like that, I am very interested to try and understand what that means just as the interval between one and two means something that is easy to understand.

One of the things about the book that impressed me was the interval between numbers was crude as long we only had one to two, three four and gradually that interval, the interval you could say in time has been shortened to the point where it becomes continuous, and what I was feeling was that experience is continuous but our description of it is always cutting it up into pieces, so that it does not correspond to experience, but number has constantly tried to fill in that gap.

E: So just to take that a step further if number is at the centre, or number systems perhaps is at the center, that presumably implies that the work is quite concerned with structure.

M: Yes...with measurement... Is structure synonymous with measurement?

E: No not exactly, so by structure I mean relationships between elements. So that, for example, a measurement can be a single entity, I could say this is eight centimetres long .. but there is no structure... so it might be that the relationship between the length and the height of this is something like a golden mean, now we are talking about structure. But there are all kinds of structure that could be (say), there are two curves that are related to one another in some way, like different segments of the same.

M: Yes that's right. You see if you are talking about the proportion of the table or door or room being right, it is a little like talking about composition. I have never had a lot of time for composition really and so I suppose, in a sense, if you are not composing you are structuring. I mean that structure becomes the nature of the composition. There was a lot of discussion I think with the Russian constructivists around 1920 as to the difference between composition and construction. And they were all trying to do structures and criticizing composition. I would side very much with this.

E: I wonder if you could try to summarize what you have done in relation to things that are valuable to your work or your thinking...

M: (Referring to problems solved) I think both of them have been resolved to my satisfaction and they didn't actually get on to computers, we resolved it mathematically. The first, the one with folding the pentagon from a strip of paper, Helmut resolved it beautifully, not even mathematically, he just folded it with the paper strip then he just pulled out the paper and found the angle that way which thrilled me greatly.

It was a very nice solution...I suppose I could have resolved that cube one, if I had had a bit more skill. but – one of the problems with the model I brought was it was a millimetre or two out in terms of making a physical square so that's not very good.....and certainly the computer does it very precisely. We did that in another department, we used a different bit of software. I didn't realize it would be so difficult to find the right software...

And I would say another thing which is almost as valuable, is for example, Helmut was able to get hold of the whole list of reading that I could browse through, which I wouldn't have been able to do at home. The thing that most interested me was that this was made possible by accessing articles, then going to the library, being able to get them out and read them.

E: Because the access was through computers.

M: It was entirely through computers, absolutely, and I mean there was a whole list that long, I only just selected one. It was really quite a basic article on how to construct the Boolean net. And then going through it with Helmut after that yesterday afternoon it became something I could in fact envisage doing with an exercise book at home.

E: Have you made an advance in that respect?

M: Very definite advance and I think if I see you this afternoon I will clear up some of the points, I went through it last night in my head, what we have done and then I realized some of the missing bits.

E: So how did it seem working with an expert like Helmut?

M: When I gave him this optical like a cube in three planes intercepting, he seemed to take a long time to realize the problem, but he was approaching it not very visually at all, I mean he was measuring proportions, what's the measure of that, what's this, he reduced the whole thing to a series of numbers and then quite quickly he resolved it, but, in order to get it to that point I don't think he would have noticed the problem at all if I hadn't asked him to prove it to me, because I don't think he thinks in that visual way.

E: You said to me earlier, the other day, that number is the essence.

M: It is. That's more to do with the thinking process, yes I don't know how number and the eye relate. In the artworld, it's more to do with anyone who uses number isn't being emotional or something...

E: So, have you been able to think at all how this might move on in your work? Have you had any concrete ideas?

M: Concrete ideas really mean going home in my exercise book, experimenting with what I now can do with Booleness because there are lots of games you can play given the structure.

I can just see that it's going to be absolutely essential and that working without a computer is going to be impossible but until that, at the moment I can do quite a lot in an exercise book to satisfy myself.

E: But you can see that to progress this as far as you would like, some software would be a positive help. Do you have a computer?

M: No, I don't. I've never even invented in the computer. But after this week I am not so concerned about the computer I am much more concerned about the software.

Date of Interview January 1996

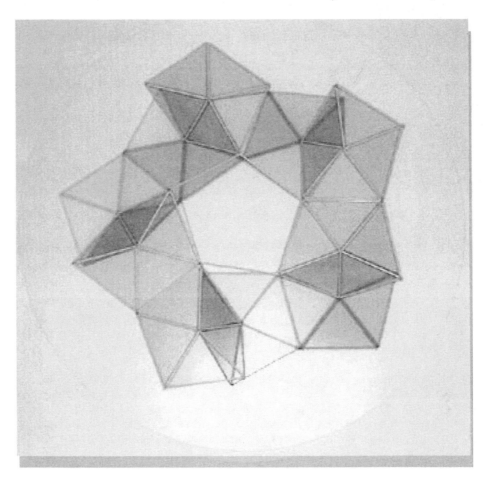

Figure 22.3 Wall Net, 1998 © Michael Kidner

References

1.   Penrose, R.: The Emperor's New Mind: Concerning Computers. Minds and the Laws of Physics. Penguin, New York (1991)

2.   Prigogine, I.: Order out of Chaos. Heinemann Ltd, London (1984)

3.   Langer, S.K.: Feeling and Form: A Theory of Art. Charles Scribner, New York (1953)

23   Switched On

Marlena Novak

To varying degrees, both my digital and encaustic[1] works address situations where cognition conditions conceptualization, and where a priori concepts influence the accuracy of our cognition. I am interested in the social and philosophical implications that exist when one realizes that 'seeing is not believing'. My geometrical abstraction and colour-based work has long been concerned with the awareness of intangible thresholds through the exploration of visual perception. It addresses the rigorous and playful exploration of Dadaist deference to the law of chance and constructivism's[2] rationally-motivated actions. [1].

Before digital technology was established in the university programme for visual art, I attended Carnegie-Mellon University for the acquisition of traditional skills in painting and drawing. This education emphasized a stringent inquiry into the structure of the form rather than, or prior to, the beautification of the surface. Having access to a medical laboratory, students could observe human dissections and make informed studies from a wide range of formaldehyde-preserved specimens of human body parts.

In my painting studio I began to experiment with the use of encaustic. As information on this first century AD technique was unavailable at that time, I developed my own working methods, tested various types of wax for melting and archival properties, and designed an encaustic workstation that I would improve upon over the next twenty years. This approach was simultaneously amplified by intensive painting study under Henry Hensche,[3] a colour-master based in Provincetown, Massachusetts; I attribute this experience to initiating what was to become a life-long personal quest into the nature of colour-theory and visual perception.

Through friendships with researchers at Carnegie-Mellon in the fields of robotics and artificial intelligence, I realized that a pure artistic endeavour could parallel a scientific approach and the reverse would also apply.

My involvement with science was intellectual rather than experiential. In other words, my time was completely committed to a disciplined training in the arts and not in the sciences. However, I was magnetized by the immediate issues addressed by these friends and a number of the topics fuelled the content of my paintings. As a film student in 1981, I developed a project to make a film of T-3 (an industrial robot) choreographed to move to Shostakovich's 8th String Quartet. However, after shooting preliminary footage of the robot I was informed that legal problems concerning insurance within the university forbid the project from advancing further. The cross-disciplinary dialogue also sparked the subject of my senior thesis exhibition, "This is no dress rehearsal". I began to exhibit my work in galleries in New York, Provincetown, and Pittsburgh.

A diversion that was to determine a significant direction in my art practice found me living at sea in 1983 as one of seven crew members aboard a 120-foot sail cargo ketch. A cargo project took me into Costa Rican villages, rainforests and jungles while working with the natives of the country to purchase goods for export to Polynesia. Multiple experiences throughout this journey – including 30 days under sail without sight of land (and surviving two life-or-death situations) – instilled in me a deep respect for the environment and a private commitment to addressing global concerns in my work.

Combining natural materials with industrially produced objets trouvés in my paintings functioned as a process to discover the intrinsic potentialities of the materials and, through that search, to expose and explore primal forces of growth and transformation. The 'found objects' became points of departure, suggesting a passage from tangible materiality to an intangible sphere of ideas and content. For me, painting was no longer a copy of the material world. My encaustic work developed a national and international audience including exhibits in Berlin, Stuttgart, Budapest, Amsterdam, Chicago, New York and Boston. The technique became the subject of a documentary film, Surfaces in Transition.[4]

Attempting to locate that which was most essential in my work I began to eliminate all that was not. This analysis revealed Golden Section (and other mathematical) relationships within the work. I decided to explore the use of these proportions so that the formal aspects of the constructions interfaced with their content. The encaustic material itself is applied in a fashion which reflects a fundamentally meditative approach, seeking to investigate and reveal the essence of the substance. What begins at first as sensory activity – olfactory in those pieces using beeswax, optical and tactile in each of them – is gradually transformed into a dialogue between modes of perception. Technically, a 'play' on the clarity of appearances develops from optical and neurological effects created by the juxtaposition and variation of colour, texture, dimension and scale. The particular location and combination of colours and textures create an awareness of visual and perceptual boundaries, affecting one's spatial and temporal experience. The presentation of some works as independent but also interdependent modular units again embodies pictorial as well as theoretical concerns.

The Impact of Digital Technology

The use of computer-based technology in my work is the most recent medium in my ongoing exploration of visual culture and therefore my observations are experientially limited to the past several years. A grant from the Center for Interdisciplinary Research in the Arts at Northwestern University provided the first opportunity for me to experiment with digital technology. My proposal involved a live collaborative performance with a poet, cellist and digital-video installation.

Although I found that many of the aesthetic and conceptual issues I had previously been concerned with in my practice using physical media could be mapped onto my digital work, I also encountered new ways of addressing those issues that were more suitable to the technology. More importantly, I discovered new aspects of art making that I could not have formerly anticipated as these elements were specific to employing the computer exclusively as a tool. The technology permits me to maintain complete control over the imagery that I use as I can draw and design directly into the software programs. A new and crucial aspect in my work, which has resulted from the use of digital technology, is the application of time and movement to the visual images that I have created.

Prior to my use of the computer as an art tool I was restricted in my working methods to making non time-based objects; these were stationary constructions and could only exist in one space at any given time. The technique of digitally animating my images introduces opportunities for added depth and content due to the temporal qualities inherent in the fourth dimension. Motion, speed and sound can be used as additional layers of content which can amplify or challenge the concepts embodied in the visual material.

Since the work exists in digital format it can be reproduced and presented in several locations simultaneously; in that way the work can be made more accessible to multiple audiences as opposed to the exclusionary situation of exhibiting a solitary physical piece. From my initial experience with digital technology, it is safe to conclude that as I continue to explore its use in my work, I am certain to encounter yet uncharted aspects of the tool that will serve to both question and fulfill my artistic endeavours.

Recent Works

Assisted by the YOTA programme at C&CRS, my current project is *Dancing Cranes,* a digitally created animated video with an original music score by Jay Alan Yim.[5] The piece, with a duration of five minutes and thirty-three seconds, is projected at high resolution onto a large screen in a space that is acoustically isolated with 100 per cent blackout. The music is meant to be experienced both aurally as well as physically through the resonance of the bass frequencies and therefore the volume levels are high. Speakers, cabling and all other audio equipment are mounted unobtrusively. When the projection reaches the end of the piece it loops continually.

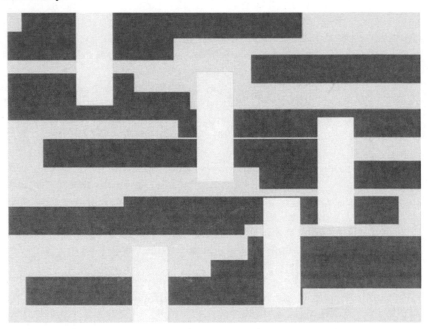

Figure 23.1 Dancing Cranes: black and white still from colour computer-generated video © Marlena Novak

The imagery and title of the piece were originally intended for a series of vertically proportioned encaustic works on wood. However, I wanted the forms to embody movement, rather than to exist in a static state; this led to the decision to execute the concept as a digital video instead of a series of paintings. In order to expand the expressive dimension of Dancing Cranes, I invited a composer to collaborate with me in creating a structure for the overall piece that would serve as an armature for both the score he would write as well as for the animation I would create. We agreed on the duration based on 10,000 frames to coincide with the inspiration for the video, which was to create 10,000 cranes for peace. This idea was a direct response to the viewing of Sorious Samura's[6] shocking documentary, Cry Freetown, and contributed to the content of the piece. Our intention was to create an experience which would move forward from confrontation and recrimination, and suggest hope and optimism.

The form of the work was arrived at collaboratively through discussion; as we both utilize Golden Proportions and Fibonacci numbers in our solo work, we chose to develop the structure and the working process based on these systems. This would allow us to fuse our subjective aesthetic decision-making with a rationalized set of proportions. Although our areas of expertise are specifically different from each other, our general approach and concerns share conceptual commonalities. This creates a working environment in which we are able to offer critical feedback to each other as we analyze the completed portions and discuss directions in each other's process that would be applicable to the outcome of the piece. I have found that a successful collaboration relies on shared intentions and responsibilities, respect for individual working processes, and communication skills that incorporate attentive listening. In addition, working collaboratively can force each party to evaluate and further develop their position or intention in a way that solitary work may not. The energy created by multiple creative minds can produce unexpected perspectives on the work resulting in more richness and depth in the outcome than that of one person alone.

Reflections

The constructivist-based notion that an artist whose work is worthy of critical attention should be 'of one's time' assumes not only the artist's awareness of contemporary issues along with the relevant developments in their specific discipline but also a willingness and a commitment to utilize the tools of the present. This does not mean turning one's back on tradition but rather extending it forward so that tradition comes to embrace the materials of the moment.

The view of a technological laboratory as an inimical environment for art making is not only an outdated position but a counterproductive concept that inhibits the potential for significant progress in the arts. My personal experience suggests to me that the most exciting contribution to the future history of art would lie in the use of technology to implement advanced modes of expression that have their origin in the union of art and technology. To arrive at this, one should be careful not to employ technology merely as a facile supplement to conventional art-making methods; in fact, it necessitates the complete abandonment of 'carry-over' techniques. If one is only interested in the technical accommodation of previous studio practice then the opportunity to create a truly innovative art form will be missed.

The potential for unexpected and relevant discoveries of historical significance is clearly inherent in an environment where one can combine the knowledge and skills of trained art practitioners with those of computer scientists. Currently available technology has the ability to incorporate multiple layers of sound, visual elements, and text with utmost precision. I believe that a digital artist with the right synthesis of inspired creativity and technical skills could produce a work with the capacity for aesthetic richness that formerly one could have only experienced in the operatic medium. A socially beneficial situation could evolve within the academic community by developing requirements for cross-disciplinary courses. The student programmer would encounter the basic cognitive and technical methods of the student artist and the reverse would occur as the art student would be exposed to similar aspects of training in computer-science and technology. The dialogue that would develop among the in-structors could be a useful barometer of their own cognizance of the needs and issues of the collaboration. Similar courses do exist at some institu-tions as electives or within a specific Art and Technology curriculum; however, I suggest that the courses be required in both artistic and scien-tific disciplines. Essential to the course would be discussions and reflec-tions on the ethical responsibility of the digital practitioner.

I am optimistic that the current debate concerning the exclusionary situation that results from the employment of high-end technology will eventually produce a variety of positive solutions; this would of course require the cooperation of technology manufacturers, governments, and educational institutions to work together to raise the standard of accessi-bility. Ultimately, I intend the social impact of my work to be felt through its induction of subtly destabilizing our perceptual complacence since it is within the boundaries of our perceptual framework that we interpret and act within the world.

Notes

1 Encaustic refers to a painting technique which combines paint or pigment with mol-ten wax. The earliest encaustic paintings were made by Greek artists working in Egypt in the 1st Century AD.
2 Constructivism \ken-'strek-ti-vi-zem\ n: a non-objective art movement originating in Russia and concerned with formal organization of planes and expression of volume in terms of modern industrial materials (as glass and plastic) Webster's Dictionary.
3 Henry Hensche was instructor of the Cape School of Art, Provincetown, MA; he opened the school in 1935 and taught until his death in 1992. The focus of his teach-ing was the perception of light and colour as experienced in nature. Please see: A Painter's Painter: Charles Webster Hawthorne and George T. Thurmond by Lauren Rogers Museum of Art: http://www.tfaoi.com/newsm1/n1m288.htm
4 Documentary film featuring the encaustic technique of Marlena Novak; Ground Zero Productions, directed by Michael Hoffman, Hawaii, USA
5 New Grove Dictionary of Music and Musicians, 2nd Edition, UK: http://www.grovemusic.com/grovemusic/home/index.html
6 Sorious Samura won the Rory Peck Award and the Mohammed Amin Award for his documentary film "Cry Freetown": it presents events that took place in Freetown, Si-erra Leone in January 1999: see http://www.cryfreetown.org/.

References

1. Novak, M.: Artist's Statement. C&CRS-YOTA Gallery (2000), http://www.creativityandcognition.com

24   The Color Organ and Collaboration

Jack Ox

For over twenty years I have been occupied with the translation of music into sets of visual languages. This continuing evolution of language systems was needed in order to express the growing number of sound situations created by composers in the twentieth century. The latter part of that century demanded a flexible expansion of parameters because of increasingly complex patterns. It was natural that I would find myself wanting to move from two dimensions into three because this move carried an exponential increase in the number of systems available for possible manipulation while translating the different structural elements within a musical performance.

The Color Organ

The 21st Century Virtual Color Organ is a computational system for translating musical compositions into visual performance.[1] An instrument, like a musical instrument, it uses supercomputing power to produce 3D visual images and sound from MIDI files, and can play a variety of compositions. Performances take place in interactive, immersive, virtual reality environments such as the CAVE (Cave Automatic Virtual Environment),[2] and VisionDome.[3]

Because it is a 3D immersive world the Color Organ is also a place – that is, a performance space. This interactive instrument consists of three basic parts:

1. A set of systems or syntax that provides logarithmic transformations from an aural vocabulary to a visual one. This includes different colour systems which correspond to elements within musical syntax.

2. A 3D visual environment that serves as performance space and the visual vocabulary from which the 3D environment was modelled. This visual vocabulary consists of landscape and/or architectural images and provides the objects on which the syntax acts.

3. A programming environment that serves as the engine of interaction for the first two parts. This part of the Color Organ is being created by David Britton.[4]

Collection of Data: Analysis of Music

The first part of the analysis task is to determine what are the structural parameters of the piece of music to be visualized, or in other words, what are the operating principles and which data sets should be collected? Does the composition exist within a diatonic/chromatic harmonic framework, or is it composed from layers of carefully chosen timbres? These two approaches mean very different things and are therefore visually depicted with completely different colour systems.

There are data sets that are contained in all of the compositions I had worked with until now with the soon to be discussed Gridjam. They include patterns of rising and falling melodic lines, changes in dynamics (loudness), and also the rhythmic units and patterns including the initial 'attack' of the notes and their articulations. This information is encoded in MIDI files in the Color Organ.

Creation of Corresponding Data Sets: Visual Vocabularies

Appropriate visual vocabularies must be found to express attributes of the music. This means that there is a metaphorical or structural relationship between the music and the images. Images are gathered by making very high resolution photographs on location and then detailed pencil drawings in the studio, often combining three or four photographs into one large view. It is important to make information rich, well-rendered drawings so that during the extensive processing to come they will hold their character and be recognizable.

The original two-dimensional, hand-drawn images are used by the 3D modeller, along with the original photographs, in order to re-create them in three dimensions. The entire first organ stop was modelled by Richard Rodriguez.[5] I drew the texture maps with a real pencil at a large-scale which then were scanned into the computer in pieces, reassembled electronically, and applied to the surfaces of the models.

Currently in the Color Organ there is one visual environment and vocabulary which corresponds to the idea of a 'stop' in a traditional organ. An organ stop is a particular voice in sound. In the future other artists will be invited to contribute to a collection of visual organ stops. For this first stop there are eight different desert landscapes gathered from real places in California and Arizona. Each one is connected to a particular family of instruments because the structure of the earth and rocks somehow mimics their sound production. Each image is itself a collection of data, containing content in both patterns of lines and colours and also the metaphorical connection to the instrument family.

Transparent Colour Systems

The second part of the visual vocabulary developed is based in the application of a transparent layer of colour over the landscape image embedded polygons which are created over the virtual desert by the playing of MIDI (Musical Instrument Digital Interface) files. The information that these overlaid colour systems expresses is determined early on.

The most recently created colour system is based on timbre, literally meaning the colour of sound. A vital component of music structured on timbre is the combination of specific, differentiated sounds, much like a painter can choose to use colour. Whereas the colour system I made which is based on the Circle of Fifths maps harmonic movement and quality in music which takes its structure from these concepts, the later system is effective with music whose actual sounds form the structure. I created a list of over 130 mixtures of RGB hues where families of instruments are represented by sets of colours in a graduated series, further modified by different mutes' and/or playing techniques' visual equivalences. In order to visually equate timbre changes in the human voice instrument I created a vowel/colour system which describes timbre changes for vocal lines through an analysis of how and where vowels are made in the vocal tract. Timbre for a singer is altered by changes in the vocal tract shape which come about through changes in the vowel sounds.

The Viewer's Experience in the Color Organ

When the performance begins the viewer/listeners are in a world of hand drawn landscapes which have been modelled into 3D. All of the landscapes are in black and white with the sky completely black. As the music plays a three-dimensional coloured and image-embedded geometric structure takes shape in the space over the landscape. This is constructed from flat pictures of the landscape images representing the instrument families which produced them. They are coloured a specific hue, based on a timbre analysis of which instrument is being played and what the particular playing technique is at that moment. The saturation of the colour reflects changing dynamics (loud and soft). These flat strips of landscape are placed up and down in vertical space by their pitch. A higher pitch will be higher in space and a low pitch will be placed closer to the landscape below. The width of the strips is controlled by the volume (attack) of the signal. After the music has been played there remains a complete sculpture which can be further explored in an interactive way. The viewer can move at will through the space and touch elements of the sculpture and hear the sound which originally produced it.

Collaboration

Why is collaboration such an important part of the new century? With increased use of more and more specialized, complicated technology it is far less productive to be an artist delivering a monologue alone in the studio. We need each other in many different ways, and the reasons to work together are often the result of collaborative energy. When working together in the same physical lab or space with other artists, ideas spring up like seedlings and all work seems to send out projectiles of collaborative antennae.

Before I came to C&CRS at Loughborough, I had realized that my time of production using only studio assistants had come to an end. In the beginning, the Color Organ project was named after Quanta and Hymn to Matter, which was also the name of the music that I was planning to produce in the CAVE. The programmer, David Britton, who turned out to be my first major collaborator, was programming our project to perform only Quanta. It took the necessary, unexpected dropping of the first piece of music, and then plugging in of other MIDI encoded music in order to realize that what Britton and I were creating was a musical instrument which should be played by many composers/performers. I also realized that Britton was my most important partner, far more essential than any one particular composer with whom I would be working. Of course new scientific collaborations keep appearing as we work, to fill in the gaps of smooth operational procedure.

MIDI music is a very accurate way to encode multiple aspects of musical sound and it operates inside the same style of systematic analysis that I have always relied upon. I map very specific values to other specific values created in the language of translation, which should have some kind of connection with the original, metaphorical or structural. I am, however, disturbed by the great missing element of MIDI, that of timbre or Klangfarben in German. The 'colour of sound' can be read as formants in auditory analysis. Clarence Barlow, an internationally known computer composer, and current composer project in the Color Organ, has made acoustic orchestras actually speak in human terms, by determining the amounts of tuning and which notes to play through computer formant analysis.

By adapting current techniques of speech analysis to timbre analysis, especially with vocal parts, I believe the Organ will achieve a giant leap in functionality. This idea originally came up when I was engaged in intense conversation with Pip Greasely at the Creativity and Cognition Research Studios (C&CRS) who pointed out that a fair amount of research had happened at Loughborough. This thought has become a focus of intent for me. I very much want to return to Loughborough to try and install speech recognition capabilities into the Organ in such a way as to signal the Virtual Reality (VR) graphics programming to the correct hue of the visual structure which is created by the MIDI information.

There are other pressing reasons to return to Loughborough. Greasely became intrigued with the colour system I created as an equivalent system to timbre changes. He wants to compose a piece of music using this colour system as the vocabulary. I would have to create, or work in another collaboration with an architect, a new Organ 'stop'. This VR architectural environment would serve as the visual vocabulary and 3D performance space for Greasely's musical composition.

Performing collaboration possibilities

Plans are currently being worked on to realize an improvised musical jam by players located at different geographical points on the AccessGrid in the US, with both the MIDI controlled 3D visualizations and synthesized sound files coming together in any connected immersive interactive environments, such as the CAVE, VisionDome, or Immersadesk, that are also connected by the Grid. This experiment will be called GridJam. At the present moment Boston University and the High Performance Computing Center at the University of New Mexico are in the future plans. There has been a lot of development on Internet2 for the sending of real-time video and many conferences, such as the Chautauqua series from the National Computational Science Alliance in the US, have become normal. However, it is much more difficult to send 3D graphic and 3D sound files in real-time. We believe that the Color Organ offers a unique application with which to develop the communicative capabilities of Internet2. SuperJANET4 is the British equivalent of the AccessGrid and both are connected through Leeds University and the University of Illinois, Chicago. This means that we are able to pursue GridJam between the UK and USA.

Internet stillshot.net project

I have been working during the last six months on an Internet project which is designed to help support complicated computer/electronic projects that are expensive to do and with which it is difficult to earn money. Unless these projects are heavily supported through grants and institutions it can be challenging to find the necessary resources.

My own history of making large projects has included the selling of material objects such as prints, drawings and collage/paintings. I have also developed various methods of print making which are well integrated into the actual production of the finished electronic project, or come directly from it in the form of still-shots. This is a wonderful way to support the work. It actually finds and nurtures supporters when they can acquire and live with pieces of something bigger and more complicated. It also provides a way to exhibit very technical art works in non-technical environments.

Multiples are not very useful without a way to sell them. I have been exhibiting in commercial galleries for many years and have found them increasingly useless in most things that an artist would need, not the least of which is selling. I know that the Web should be able to gather collectors and supporters together, without the limited value of a real gallery space that can only be in one particular city in the world.

It seems as if the power of the Internet could be used to market a very special, small corner of the art world to a large geographical area. There have certainly been many attempts to market art works, especially prints, on the Internet. However, the online galleries I have seen were trying to sell a wide variety of work to the general public. I want to find and become a point of interest for collectors who are interested in a much bigger picture than a small artwork on their wall. These people should have the kind of passion for contemporary art that they would derive added pleasure from having their purchases support something which has a greater importance.

The site which I hope will solve some of these problems is called still-shot.net and is currently under construction. Each artist represented on the site will have to provide a web version demo of their multimedia-electronic project as a link to their own site. This site will show art that is meant to be seen on the Web with still-shots from that particular project for sale as printed multiples. Because the pitch of the site emphasizes the added benefit of supporting an artwork that you believe in while enjoying a piece of it on your own wall, we will even invite them to pay more than the offered price as added support. Thus, in the US at least, we will be able to give them a tax deduction because the site is located on a server belonging to the non-profit organization, New American Radio.

I am speaking about stillshot.net here because this too is a point of collaboration with the YOTA grant winners because I have found at least three possible participants. These artists are Ernest Edmonds, Mike Quantrill, and Dave Everitt.

Reflections

In order for an artist to get access to the kinds of supercomputing technology needed in order to work in the immersive environment of the CAVE it is necessary to convince the scientists who have these machines that your creative project will somehow push forward the research envelope. When Dr Larry Smarr[6] visited my New York City loft and invited me to come and work in the CAVE at The University of Illinois at Urbana-Champaign, he said that he was interested in "bottom feeding" and when things became easy to do he would move on. I believe that he gave his very generous support to the Color Organ because we were trying to do difficult things and in solving these problems, the technology would move forward.[7]

I think that artists do have a lot to offer scientists when they are collaborating with them because, for instance, artists are trained to think in metaphoric languages. The discipline of scientific visualization is fast growing. It is not so difficult to connect one database to another in a computer, but knowing which value corresponds to what is where artists can be very helpful. I have seen many computer programs at SIG-GRAPH[8] attempting to translate musical information into visual images which basically gave one very little sense of the structure or meaning of the sounds. The realm of metaphor is a subjective world and science is not so practiced in using it to carry meaning, however effectively it can work within the human conscious. I suspect that the systematic use of poetic metaphor is one of the strengths of the Color Organ.

Figure 24.1 The Color Organ: Strings landscape © Jack Ox

The image in Figure 24.1 is a view from Fonts Point, Borego Springs near San Diego, California. These hills represent the family of strings because if one were to track the motion of the bow over the strings the mapping would look similar to these low desert hills.

Figure 24.2 The Color Organ Inside Strings landscape © Jack Ox

Figure 24.2 is a still-shot from down inside the strings landscape, looking towards piano ridge and woodwinds with vocals behind. Here the music has not yet started to play or be visualized over the black and white three-dimensional landscape drawings.

Notes

1. Ox, J., Britton, D.: The 21st Century Virtual Reality Color Organ", (2000) IEEE July-September. http://www.computer.org/multimedia/mu2000/u3toc.htm
2. http://www.evl.uic.edu/EVL/VR/systems.shtml
3. http://www.elumens.com/products/visiondome.html
4. David Britton is Chief Technical Officer of Sputnik7 and co-creator of the Color Organ.
5. Richard Rodriguez is a programmer at Sputnik7 and 3D modeller for the Color Organ.
6. Larry Smarr is first director of the California Institute for Telecommunications and Information Technology in San Diego, California: http://www.calit2.net/index.html
7. Robert Punam from Boston University: http://scv.bu.edu/SCV/scv-brochure.html was able to come on board to do the Color Organ's 3D programming and also as a collaborator with "Gridjams" because of Dr Smarr's support.
8. The international conference of graphic arts and design:http://www.siggraph.org/

25   Digital Spirituality

Anthony Padgett

I am an artist and philosopher who has worked on restoring monuments in the Holy Land and teaching comparative religion. I explore the link between mystical non-dualism – that is, experiencing everything as one and moral dualism – that is, the conflict between opposites: good and evil. I attribute abstract process to the non-dual (the universal, aesthetic, energy and flux) and figurative product to the dual (searching for a fixed, human-based, form and meaning).

Two views of nature are given in my work. The non-dual has no distinction between the natural and the technological. All is One in our inner nature, before we divide it by focusing on concepts. The dual has a subject–object relationship to figurative representations of a nature that is in contrast with technology.

I seek to artistically link the dual and non-dual in order to express that we move between the perspectives – the human condition. My theory is that primitive creativity was non-dual. It was an aesthetic, environmental, process: for example, design, music, dance and building dwelling places. Dualistic, figurative art emerged as part of a search for a fixed meaningful product. The figurative representation gave a dualistic, subject–object relationship. Faith in the dualistic product (the Gods) was established but it became apparent that this was not enough and a move was made to link back to the original process. Throughout history the psyche has unconsciously tried to balance the dual and the non-dual, the figurative and the abstract.[1]

My overall work joins traditional and futuristic technologies. My work was originally 'dualistic'. It was sculptural and expressed my ideas and experiences in a narrative, meaningful, sculptural diary. After I had a mystical experience I found I could not adequately express myself through sculpture. I began to have another form of work in abstract expressionist paintings. These were an attempt to link back to the non-dual, aesthetic activity. By stilling the mind in meditation the pen dances and the forms produced gravitate towards innate, natural forms.

These abstract expressionist drawings were to look for universal forms of design. The works were intended to reach a very natural aesthetic level. The idea was to draw without imposing any ideas of shape, colour or composition in order to see what natural forms arose from the unconscious mind. This was not automatic drawing as the artists were still wilfully creative. This abstract non-dualism was taken further in the sensor work described later. This is physically interactive and blurs the sub-ject/object dualism. You are the work that you produce in this aesthetic and rhythmic experience.

Residencies

I took part in two C&CRS residencies at Loughborough University, one as part of the COSTART Project funded by the UK EPSRC Research Council, the other, AA2A (Artists Access to Art) supported by the Arts Council of England. In the AA2A project, four artists took part, two male and two female: Marianne Davis, Mike Harte, Sarah Pace and my-self.

Figure 25.1 Drawing with the Soft-board

Abstract Expressionist Experiment

The experiment served as an idea for a larger experiment. Drawings were made with felt-tip pens on a computer drawing board. Each one was made after a period of meditation. They were recorded in real time and can be played back at different speeds in separate colours. The males covered the board and the females worked in smaller areas. One person noted that this was like when boys play over the whole playground and girls play in just one corner. The four drawing sequences began with different activities, for example: scribbles, arcs and borders, and ended with the aspects linked together. All the participants took Eysenck psychology tests [1] in order to see if personality affected drawing style. These tests gave similar readings.

The Sensor Design and the Virtual Reality Performance

The first phase of my work using the Sensor System was a C&CRS project at Loughborough University under the COSTART project residency scheme [2]. Mike Quantrill wrote the software for the system and programmed the work. In the second project, the Virtual Reality Performance, Simon Nee gave technical support for my work which was also supported by Arts Council of England Lottery funding.

Sensor beams are located on each side of an ankle high frame. The frame is in front of a large screen, onto which the sensor design – a basic shape – is projected. One person walks to one of four directions in the frame and extrudes smaller basic shapes (up/down and left/right) on the screen. Another person rotates the shape whilst small shapes are added by the walking person.

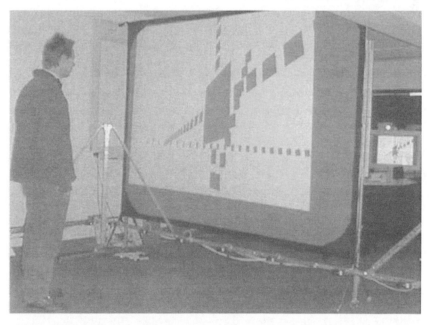

Figure 25.2 Sensor System: position and sound sensing grid

The Sensor System uses primary shapes, colours and actions in a complex design system that raises a natural aesthetic response. The work is geometric but is also very free. It is a communal aesthetic creativity that uses two-dimensional shapes in three-dimensional space. These results could not be visualized and were unexpected.

In a natural way the participant does not interpret the creative process. You use your whole being in the system. It is a very immediate experience as you are within your creation. The work is a non-dual, aesthetic activity that does not need an end product but can be used to produce an artistic image. The interface between subject and object is blurred, as is the idea of process and final product.

The "Virtual Reality performance" involved participants and a system of sensors that record their movements and then reacts visually and with music. The animated sequence was constructed but the sensors were not programmed. Using the systems video projector, a performance was made of how, ideally, the system would work. The experience begins with a 2D/3D monochrome sea. We symbolically move between the dual sky and the non-dual sea. Technology joins nature, in this sunset.

If the participants remain still they sink into a sea of non-duality and colourful 2D Jungian mandalas [3] emerge to musical harmonies. Through meditation you internally connect back to the abstract non-duality. As soon as someone moves then the shapes will go and the sea will reappear.

If the participants move then they will build a monochrome 3D Freudian tree of duality (adapted from 3Dcafe.com) that reaches a stasis to ascending notes of music (Becoming of Being). This is technology/morality seeking an end product. The tree will decay back to the sea if the people do not move, so they must continually move to stay at the highest point of duality. This is like life and death.

The overall experience expresses the movement between the non-dual (eternal) and the dual (temporal). This transition is the closest that we can get to the One. It is 2D/3D, abstract/figurative, aesthetic/symbolic, process/product.

The Sensor Theism links non-dual and dual in the transition between process and product. The participants' movement generates a meaningful object. By being still the mind connects back to the universal, abstract process. This aesthetic link contrasts with the historical narrative link that I made on Millennium Eve at the Golden Gate, Jerusalem – where the Messiah is supposed to arrive. The permanent object produced there is also very fragile – like the transition point between the dual and the non-dual.

Since that work I now think that the non-dual links to 3D interiors and the dual links to 3D exteriors. This means that the non-dual is an interior spirituality (internal space) and the dual is an exterior spirituality (external space). The C&CRS residencies broadened my practice so that I could contrast interactive technologies (internal space) with static computer manufacture (external space).

Spiritual coincidences occurred in the work. I meditated before making each whiteboard drawing. In the first meditation I had a vision of the head of Apollo (God of Prophecy and the Arts).

In the theism sensor conclusion I was looking for universal forms of design. Unintentionally, I produced swastikas and mandalas, which are mystical Hindu and Jungian symbols. After seeing these appear, then I began to have telepathic experiences. In the interactive sensor design the basic shape in the centre of the screen corresponded to the basic circle in the centre of my abstract expressionist work. This gave a link at a deep psychological level.

In the future, I would like to make performances where the audience participates to produce permanent forms and temporary experiences. Abstract aesthetics would intertwine with figurative, meanings. I would like to use technology in natural settings to break down distinctions whilst simultaneously showing them to be there.

Reflections

Digital technology can blur the distinction between the artist and the computer program. A conflict occurs between the free will of the artist and the following of a program's laws. Does the experience of artistic freedom belong to the programmer or the participant within the program? This conflict links to fundamental spiritual perspectives, where dualism is free human choice and non-dualism is Karmic Law.

Environments for Digital Art Practice

Either the use of art-creating systems will diminish the uniqueness of art creations or the computer options will be so great that there will be a need to find the most satisfying aesthetic experiences and artistic meanings.

Teams of artists and technicians will work like film crews (like the games industry) to develop projects of use in industry or of marketing value to industry. The situation will give a division similar to that between commercial cinema and art cinema.

Ultimately digital art will be aesthetic and the meaningful use of digital systems will be in developing bio-medicine, vehicle design, simulation, etc. The way for art to link to meaningful products is if the aesthetic systems also have practical, spiritual and psychological results.

Technology Opportunities for the Future

Spiritual creativity may be a new recreation where technology can enhance spiritual understanding and experiences. Aesthetic spiritual systems, e.g. guided meditations can be made. Systems designed to encourage creativity, and mental health might be designed. Close monitoring of psychological implications would be required, as introducing explicit 'meaning' to these artworks could be a dangerous form of brainwashing. The potential for use of virtual reality in psychic development might also be harnessed.

Notes

1. Other sources are extremely diverse. These range from philosophers (Parmenides, Plato, Porphry, Kant, Hegel) through studies of religions (Hinduism, Buddhism, Zoroastrianism, Judaism, Christianity, Islam, Mysticism, Theosophy) to studies of art movements (particularly Cubism, Futurism, Vorticism, the abstract work of Mondrian, Kandinsky and the Abstract Expressionism of De Kooning and Rothko). Anthony's work is also based on his questioning the nature of his own mystical experience and although there are many books on non-dualistic experience few of them offer a good critique of the mystical. An excellent example of the division between the dual and non-dual can be seen in David K. Clark and Norman L Geisler: Apologetics in the New Age: A Christian Critique of Pantheism, Baker Books (1992)

References

1. Eysenk, H.J.: EPQ Test printed for Hodder and Stoughton Educational by ChigwelPress, 11th impression (1985)

2. COSTART Project at C&CRS: (1999) http://creative.lboro.ac.uk/costart/

3. Jung, C.J.: Collected Works, Vol. 9, part 1, The Archetypes of Collective Unconsciousness" and Vol. 13 Alchemical Studies 2nd Ed. Routledge, an imprint of Taylor & Francis Books Ltd (1968)

26   Integrating Computers as Explorers in Art Practice

Michael Quantrill

Recently I have had a number of opportunities to explain my work to others and I have been surprised by how difficult it has become to articulate it. This is an especially thorny question for me, not least because it is my struggle to communicate the meaning and motives for what I do that forms the basis of the work itself.

Communication occurs in many forms. Mostly this is translated by the mechanisms used to carry it. I refer not just to the external and observable. These mechanisms begin at the moment the desire or impulse to express something in a tangible form occurs. It has also become increasingly clear that methods exist that approach a means of communication that we cannot easily explain, but are undeniable by our experience of them. These methods include the processes of drawing and movement.

One view of the drawing process is that it is the search for meaning. A conscious investigation of a space "in between" that results in transformation and the emergence of insight. When absorbed in the drawing process, something occurs that is compulsive and intense. One response to this is to make marks on paper. However, the making of marks is simply one way to try to express the process of transformation that is occurring.

But, what is really going on here? What is this transformation? I have tried to grapple with answers to these questions for some time now. It seems quite certain that the truth will never be really known but maybe we can get close enough to make the journey worthwhile. Drawing has always proved to be such a revealing process. I have thought about what makes this so. To my mind it is the immediacy of the process that gives it the power to investigate and reveal. From the impulse to the mark there is no intermediary that actively transforms the intention. I cannot offer any explanation of why this is so, but I accept that it is so.

I have been involved in the process of drawing from as early as I can remember. It is a behaviour I have engaged in instinctively rather than analytically. It has always been a testing, groping process. This has left me with something of a dilemma as I have a strong feeling that digital technology offers possibilities for the artist that can be enlightening, but by nature it demands an algorithmic predetermined input where all variables have been considered beforehand. My desire is to reconcile these two very diverse mindsets and explore the possibilities that emerge. Reflecting on this, it seemed very appropriate to use drawing as the process with which to explore human–computer integration and to search for ways to enable the technology to be used as a medium during my residencies at the Creativity and Cognition Research Studios [1].

I believe digital technology offers new ways to translate and transform. In human terms, this involves the translation of our intentions, our goals and our state.[1] With regard to machine media, it takes the form of translation and transformation of new media and machines from a purely functional context into a context where their architecture itself is an additional contribution to creative works [2].

My approach is to use drawing as a gateway to exploring these possibilities. Specifically I am using it to explore the notion of human–computer integration. The idea is to use the properties of computing machines to enable forms of expression that are unique to a human–machine environment where the human is the focus, but the expression is a composite of both human and machine, in this case a computing machine environment.

Residencies

My connection with C&CRS has been a very fruitful period and has involved a number of residencies over the last three years. Before I go further, I will say something about my work and the motives behind it.

Drawing with The Soft-board

One of the devices I have used is called a Soft-board [2], a whiteboard (4 ft by 3 ft) connected to a computer. The whiteboard is similar in design to any conventional whiteboard except it has a laser matrix across its area. There are four colour pens as well as small and large erasers. The laser matrix enables pen and position data to be transmitted to the computer. The application program on the computer looks similar to a drawing package. There is a re-sizeable window, which maps to the physical whiteboard. The resolution is high (4000 × 3000 points approximately). Any actions made at the physical whiteboard are immediately represented in this window. Drawings are entered onto a "page" using the four pens. A page is one virtual workspace displayed on the monitor. A set of pages forms a sequence. When any mark is made it is recorded as a set of points for the current page. Both positive pen marks and eraser events are recorded. At any time a new page can be generated as a new blank canvas or inclusive of the previous page's marks. The controls for starting and stopping recording and entering new pages are situated both at the whiteboard and within the window on the computer. This enables completion of a whole sequence with pen in hand, never having to touch the computer.

The drawings are made at the whiteboard. However, due to the integration of a computing machine, the creative process is fused with a machine interpretation and so the final piece is an inseparable intertwining of human and machine processes and the works cannot meaningfully be deconstructed into the human and machine parts. Really, what is going on here is that one process is occurring in a natural, instinctive way, the conscious progression of work from sketchbooks, and another parallel process is occurring under the surface. This 'under the surface' process resulted in a time-based dimension, amongst other things, being added to the work that was not expected at the start of the process.

It is important to emphasize that the work with the Soft-board does not use an input device obviously designed for a computer, such as a graphics tablet or mouse and that complete freedom of movement is enabled in the space that the work takes place. Such freedom of movement enables a creative space to develop that allows the work to progress without an awareness of the constraints usually associated with electronic media and the need to make allowances for them. This space is a dynamic, integral part of the creative process.

Figure 26.1 Soft-board Drawing © Michael Quantrill

The Sensor Grid Interaction

In 1998 I worked with artists, Leon Palmer and Anna Heinrich to develop software for an array of infrared position sensors. Their work has
involved high-resolution data projection onto various surfaces. In this
case they wanted to back project the view of a corner of a room which is
deconstructed as people move around a space. This was exhibited at the
Under Construction exhibition held at Loughborough University [3].
    The experience of using this space coincided very well with the ideas
that were forming from the work with the Soft-Board. For this and other
reasons it was decided to build a permanent array of sensors, referred to as
the sensor grid. The area is approximately 12 ft by 12 ft and the array of
sensors is an 8×8 grid connected to a computer. A display is projected
onto a screen on one side of the sensor grid and a sound system is also
connected.
    The search now began for a process akin to drawing that could provide
the same lines of enquiry without the cognitive load imposed by a connection to a computer. The process turned out to be that of movement.
At the outset the outcome of any use of this space was not defined, as the
nature of any development and use is a product only of this environment
and to impose expectations upon it would be to defeat the purpose. The
prime concern is to create an environment where creative works can take
place as a function of a person's movement through the space. Movement was chosen because of its parallel to drawing. As children we quickly
integrate movement into our world and it becomes deeply embedded in
our being. We do not utter conscious commands to transfer the energy
needed to reposition our bodies. Our minds act by stealth. We see, we
feel, we desire and before we are aware, we move. The underlying process
of movement is often ignored and yet is an intensely informative expression. The nature of any 'drawings' reflects the interactions with the media that underpin this process.
    Focusing on movement as input means that the participant can be un-
aware of the physical connection to a computer. They move as they
wish. They go where they please within the system. However, the computer is able to record and analyze in parallel with the movement and in
reaction to it. This means that creative functions can be implemented
within the computer that are part of the overall system including the
participant but without their explicit control. The computer in effect
acts by stealth.
    From the start it seemed clear that to progress these ideas it would be
paramount to discover a language that encompasses both the individual's
role and aims as well as the system attributes, form and context. This
language will be a composite of the individual, the machine and the space.

Figure 26.2 Artwork from sensor grid © Michael Quantrill

Some first steps are a series of 'sketches', or preliminary programs, constructed to experiment with the sensor grid. To begin with, simple geometric shapes form the basis of the visual data. The workstation can produce very attractive and complex representations of real world objects but these are loaded already with metaphor. Of course, geometric shapes embody metaphor, but less so perhaps. The idea is to reduce visual complexity by using shapes, colour and lighting in ways that are not in themselves inherently complex. This allows the process of moving and sensory co-ordination to evolve simply and naturally. Some of these sketches were developed in collaboration with Dave Everitt [4]. It became clear that there are a number of ways to use the system:

- use direct and event-driven immediate feedback: e.g. a sound is triggered as a beam is crossed

- Use periodic/continual event and/or process-driven feedback: e.g. the more a person moves about, the more a certain image changes.

Time-based feedback as a function of stored and processed data: e.g. a 'landscape' or map, is built up over time from the density of movement about the space. Movement through time is thus translated and realized as a map across the space. Any or all of the feedback will be integrated within the system. This feedback will form part of a trace that cannot be reversed or erased. It will become part of the work. This trace itself may well form part of further feedback, which itself becomes part of the work. This may continue in a recursive fashion so that the work grows constantly and continually changes form. At each level the experience of the individual using the system will change as this 'landscape' changes

From the initial responses to the experience of using the Soft board, through the first experiments and sketches with the sensor grid, a path is emerging that I believe is going to be rich to explore. The prospect of human–computer integration raises many questions and we have, as yet, few answers. It is hoped that ways can be found to use the unique properties of this technology as a medium. An attempt is being made here to create an environment that is intense, dynamic and allows the technology to inform the work. The intention is to use the underlying medium (the machine) without imposing metaphors from traditional art media. This is no trivial matter and much is still to be defined and gleaned from the process. What is clear, however, is that this space has real potential to provide opportunities for artists, or any individual with intent, to find ways of expression that may be surprising and informative on whatever level they wish to permit it

Notes

1. 'State' here refers to complete our mental, physical, emotional state along with any other classification of what makes us who we are.
2. The additional contribution comes from the fact that the architecture forms part of the medium for the work. Therefore, the effect is as with any other medium, in that it acts as a carrier and the carrying process has an observable effect on the message: e.g a drawing made with a pen will emphasize different facets of the creative process to a drawing made with a soft medium such as charcoal or paint.

References

1.   Creativity and Cognition Research Studios: http://creativityandcognition.com

2.   Microfield Graphics:http://www.microfield.com

3.   Under Construction Exhibition, Loughborough University UK: http://sgi-hursk.lboro.ac.uk/~gof/gof_underconstruction.html (1999)

4.   Everitt, D.: The Artist as Digital Explorer. Chapter 18, in this book (2002)

5.   Edmonds, E.A. and Quantrill, M.P.: An Approach to Creativity as Process, Reframing Consciousness, Ascott, R. (ed), Intellect Books, Second International CAiiA Research Conference, UWCN, Wales, August (1998) 257-261

6.   Quantrill, M.P. and Edmonds, E.A.: Creativity by Stealth, Consciousness Reframed III, Ascott, R. (ed), Proceedings Third International CAiiA Research Conference, UWCN, Wales, August (2000)

7.   Quantrill, M.: Drawing as a Gateway to Computer–Human Integration, Leonardo 35 (1) February (2002)

27   Deconstructing the Norm

Juliet Robson

A main area of my art practice that interests me is the deconstruction of the 'norm'. I am concerned with how the construction of normality in society and culture affects a body that is labelled 'abnormal'. In 1998, I was artist-in-residence with The Gallery of the Future, culminating in an exhibition at the Loughborough University School of Art and Design Gallery [1]. The main criterion for the residency was to incorporate new technology into the work. For this, I made the installation I call Norman.

Norman

I wanted to make an installation that had a temporary live presence, and to create a space that, at first glance alluded to the supposedly cool universal values of aesthetic architectural judgment, but a space that did not immediately reveal its function when devoid of my presence. The piece references Le Corbusier's Modular Man, which was devised in 1947 [2]. Modular man presents the human body as singular and universal as type. In attempting to subvert this architectural standardization of the body, Norman was a space in which I determined the boundaries of what is defined as the norm.

Projected onto the back wall of the space was an animated image created by using a system normally used for medical and sports research. I wanted to explore how this technology traced the moving body by attaching sensors to myself and travelling on the floor without my wheelchair. The CODA system [3] is normally used to find out how the fine detail of someone's language of movement has changed through injury. It is also used to improve athletes' abilities by refining technique and ironing out inconsistency by standardizing and categorizing physical language.

I used CODA to map a language of movement that is seen as 'wrong', and projected the image onto the back wall. What you saw was an abstracted animated stick figure, ambiguous and difficult to immediately identify as a human body. The sensors were attached to my upper body, head, arms and hands. I created a trajectory of my walking movements, a trajectory that challenged the vertical expectations of an able-bodied audience.

Projected onto the floor were architectural plans of a higher education building that I attended as an undergraduate. These architectural plans were created in collaboration with an architect. The plans were colour-coded, dark blue to indicate the areas of the building that I could gain access to in my wheelchair, and light blue to depict the areas of exclusion. The white painted square on the floor, containing the architectural projection, was mapped by blue construction lines relating to the dimensions of the gallery and installation. As the animation continued up each storey of the building, the light blue increased more and more, my presence being defined by the areas that excluded me, rendering me socially and culturally invisible.

When moving around the space I would try to stay within the mapped out blue lines on the floor, an impossible task since they were not wide enough to contain my body. I was attempting to fit into an architectural dimension that was not designed for this type of body and movement. When the figurative projection and my attempts to stay within the mapped lines were seen together it became obvious that they were one and the same movement.

While moving around the map I started a dialogue with the audience and invited questions about the piece and what I was doing. As I moved to the centre of the space I finally became immersed in the architectural projection on the floor, at which point the 'live presence' was removed until the next designated time.

Figure 27.1: Installation Norman   **Figure 27.2 Shopping © Juliet Robson**

The installations in Figures 27.1 and 27.2 took place at Loughborough University Gallery and in Loughborough Town respectively.

Artist Residencies

I found the process of my residency with Gallery of the Future difficult but interesting and I learnt a great deal. This was my first excursion into using digital technology not just as a facilitator, but as a creative and aesthetic tool central to the work. Access to digital equipment was a huge asset. However, finding technical support was more problematic. Universities are a great resource for equipment but actual human support can be hard to come by. Everyone, particularly it seems technicians, are overworked, and my problems were exacerbated by the fact that not having used digital technology before in this way, I did not know the range of possibilities and options at my fingertips. A great deal of time was spent having an idea, then trying to find relevant people to tell me if it was realistically feasible and achievable. Often the technology needed for my idea was under development, but was not yet at a stage to be useful.

It took some time to develop the concept, and find relevant and willing people who had the time to help me realize it. Although at the time this process felt frustrating, in reality it meant that I arrived at a concept I was totally committed to, knew was realistic and achievable, and one in which the role of technology was valid and integral to the piece, rather than gratuitous. In many ways for me "Norman" was an ambitious piece in conceptual terms as well as technical ones. I felt that I was able to push forward my artistic development and create a strong basis for further work.

In 1999, I was offered a residency at C&CRS, also in Loughborough University as part of the Artists Access to Art Colleges (AA2A) Scheme [4]. There was no pressure to make a piece for exhibition so I was able to use the time to explore further ideas related to Norman and develop my practice. Although money was limited, which, because of being freelance was an issue in terms of how much time I could spare, there was a wide range of resources, and technicians were specifically allocated to the individual artists involved. This meant I was able to experiment with new ideas, and learn the basics of digital video cameras and editing applications.

Having a technician allocated to me who was enthusiastic and interested was invaluable. The residency had been structured so that the roles of everyone involved were clear. Simon Nee's role was to support me technically so that I could realize my intentions. We were both very clear about our remits, and because of this at times we were able to step outside the agreed boundaries of the formal relationship, exchange ideas, talk about the concepts behind the work and whether they were valid, without having conflict about issues such as ownership. This was particularly useful to me since other artists doing the same residency had opportunities to brainstorm with each other and exchange information. Because of limited access to wheelchair users within certain areas of the university I was based in a different department, and felt isolated from information sharing, brainstorming and slightly dislocated from the scheme in general.

I wanted to develop my exploration of 'normality' and context; to this end I decided to take the language of movement used in Norman and put it into a completely different and public space, where I relinquished

control over environment and perception. I made myself a list and went
shopping without my wheelchair chair at a local shopping mall. It took
me about two hours; my shopping list included buying a Mother's Day
card, trying on a pair of high heeled shoes and buying a cup of tea in a
cafe. Before getting out of my chair in the shopping mall, I had a moment of doubt about the position I was about to put myself in. I felt,
however, that by making myself vulnerable, my audience would be more
open to a dialogue.

The installation of a stair-lift in the Computer Science Department
means I now have access to the same areas as the other artists and university staff. This made a tremendous difference and the whole process
felt much more inclusive. I felt much more in control and autonomous.
In general, it greatly enhanced the whole experience. However, the availability of human technical support is again limited, which was an issue
because I need to work with a technician who is familiar with the software
in order to achieve professional looking interpretations of the work for
presentation and exhibition. We solved this problem by finding a 3D
designer who wanted access to equipment and programs to improve his
skills, and who wanted to expand his design portfolio by working on a
professional project. Time for this was in part paid for by the funds put
aside for studio time and in part paid in kind through access to equipment
and work experience on the project.

Reflections on Digital Technology

For me, digital technology means that ideas that previously have been
too expensive or impractical can be realized reasonably cheaply and effi-
ciently, and I can have more control over what I make. Not only that but
documenting work and administrating has become easier and more man-
ageable, the number of people and cost involved has been reduced,
through use of small scale video cameras and digital editing programs for
example.

Up until now I have used technology mainly as a facilitator to help
me achieve the required result or as an administration tool; however,
recently there have been exceptions. One of these was the animated figure in Norman where the reason the technology was developed (the standardization of physical movement) and not just the end product, was
integral to the idea and concept of the work and not solely as an aesthetic.

Since using digital media the lines between process, the work and
documentation have begun to blur. The Shopping video has been used as a
piece of documentation, and a film in its own right. The material will be
edited again and used in further installations. Distinctions between traditional mediums used for documentation in my practice and what constitutes the artwork are merging. In addition, websites have not only enabled

my work to be shown to a larger and global audience but allow me access to the work of other artists. This helps me find a context for myself. Here the line between what constitutes exhibition and documentation on the Internet begins to blur.

As an artist with a disability the relationship between technology and my work is more complex. New technology obviously helps in creating a level playing field for disabled people in areas such as communication and certain art genres. There are also advantages in areas like the Internet where you have control over your identity and how you (re)present yourself to other people. You can be defined by aspects other than your disability if you choose, and avoid misconceptions and assumptions that often label people with impairments. However, I see problems in denying aspects of yourself and creating a "normative" identity, that is, one that has been constructed because of a perceived need for an acceptance by the majority group. You can choose not to risk being defined by your impairment, the danger in that being that the cultural and social invisibility of disabled people and its effects can be perpetuated.

I am also wary of the trend from some arts organizations that implies or assumes that all disabled artists do, or in the future will, use new technology to produce some or all of their art work, indicated by the increase in schemes targeted at digital media and disabled artists. This conjures up for me the (admittedly extremist) image of artists with disabilities sitting in a room in front of a computer all day, only showing work on line, communicating with the outside world electronically.

Looking at theories on disability and technology in employment is useful in reflecting on the impact of digital technology on art practice in general. Alan Roulstone reflects that the potential of digital technology for interactive functions and rapid dissemination of information offers new working environments and opportunities for disabled people [5]. The scope for the expression of abilities that new technology permits, may in some cases allow for a redefinition of one's disability. For instance, voice-activated computers, large font text facilities, design programs, ergonomically designed equipment, editing programs and so on can allow disabled people to use their potential more fully than previously possible. Technology enables disabled people not only to perform functions but also to use abilities formerly excluded by disabling environments. However, the framing of the development of new technology up until now has come from people working in technology procurement and significantly in rehabilitation. A point to note is that very rarely, if ever, are these professionals disabled themselves. Within rehabilitation of disabled people, if the role of technology is viewed in a social vacuum, it fails to address the power politics of employment and, in some cases, issues of access to new technology. In this context, technology is seen as the technical fix, in medical model terms as a compensation for physical or sensory 'problems' of a disabled person. Alternatively, the benefit is expressed in terms of augmentation of an incomplete body. The general idea in current rehabilitation programmes is to rehabilitate the disabled person into the demands of the contemporary working domain. To correct their bodily, educational and training deficits in other words to 'normalise' the disabled person at the very least, and if possible to 'cure' them of their disability. This perception is damaging and can create a cultural limitation about the way disabled people are viewed.

Artists are in an unusual position with regard to the concept of technology as a 'technical fix' and rehabilitation tool. They have opportunities to be working with technology that is in the process of being developed. Here they are in a position to influence the way in which it is being directed and its potential use. In using these technologies as creative tools rather than 'corrective' ones they are able to question the fundamental limitations of the medical model of technology and at times take ownership of them. The system used in Norman is an example of technology that was originally developed as a tool to "normalise" the language of movement that was subverted and used as a creative medium to express ideas about normality and individuality. There is a potential role here for artists to influence the shift in thinking from the medical model of technology to a more 'social' one. While freelance artists with disabilities can to an extent control the environments they work in and choose whom to collaborate with, their potential is limited by the lack of accessible studios and environments. Without addressing social and environmental factors, disabled artists will be at a disadvantage to the rest of the cultural community. As William Gibson said:

> The future is here, it's just not equally distributed yet.

References

1. Gallery of the Future: http://creative.lboro.ac.uk/gof/
2. Imrie, R.: Corbusier's modular man – Disability and the City: International Perspectives, Paul Chapman Publishing, London (1996)
3. CODA System: Charnwood Dynamics: www.charndyn.com
4. AA2A: Artists Access to Art Colleges, National Association for Fine Art Education in collaboration with the National Arts Association
5. Roulstone, A.: Researching a Disabling Society: The Case of Employment and New Technology. In The Disability Reader, Social Science Perspectives. Edited by T. Shakespeare, Cassell (1998)

28   Shifting Spaces

Esther Rolinson

The proposals and projects I have recently produced investigate simple architectural structures, such as walls, roofs, stairs and columns. They employ building materials such as sheet glass and steel, either in an unfamiliar context such as sculptural installation, or to find a reinterpretation of the material such as perforating concrete and using it as a gauze to filter light. My intention is to subtly heighten the viewer's awareness of architectural and natural forms and patterns of human and elemental movement. Alongside structural installations, I work with light, either with architectural or theatrical lights or with projected digitally manipulated animations and images. I am interested in the idea of 'sensitizing environments' by combining responsive structural materials, such as Priva-Lite Glass (which turns from opaque to transparent on receipt of an electrical current) to create animated surfaces that can be programmed to form an evolving manipulation of light. With these materials I hope to express unseen natural events such as the impact of the wind upon physical structures.

A recently installed work is Light-Decks, a publicly sited piece that was commissioned by the holdings company, COMPCO, as part of their redevelopment of the Aquarium Terraces in Brighton, England [1]. It consists of a series of 24 simple light-boxes embedded into wooden decking in a wave formation. Each box contains fibre optics that change colour at approximately walking pace. As people promenade along the boardwalk washes of coloured light rhythmically pass under their feet. The piece utilizes the structure of the wooden decking and aims to hint at the presence of water flowing underneath it, as on a ship or pier. A feature of my practice is an interest in and, at times, requirement to collaborate with other professionals. As each project can demand new skills, it is necessary to communicate the ideas to structural engineers, programmers and lighting consultants and manufacturers. I find this process develops my practice both practically and conceptually.

I have made two collaborative works with choreographer Carol Brown. Shelf Life is a four-hour gallery installation which has toured in Britain and Europe [2]. Throughout the installation Carol is suspended on a two meter high perspex shelf with steel legs. As she moves in a meditative state, animations and light wash through the space creating a strong sense of time passing. Machine for Living is our most recent work and is a large scale performance installation constructed from a series of 13 steel panels measuring 5 metres high that, when lined up, form a 10 metre wide wall. Each panel is pushed directly backwards or forwards in a space 14 metres deep creating a multi-dimensional series of corridors, 'cells' or a steel forest inhabited by four performers. This industrial, vertical landscape is then cut horizontally with linear digital animations that distort as they wrap around the moving bodies and panels. As the performance unfolds, relationships are drawn and divided between the performers, creating a 'human architecture'. The audience is able to navigate around the performance area, moving as and when they desire, at times viewing through the perforated structure experiencing moments of both proximity and distance from the performers.

These works in part explore the relationship between the body and architectural forms, drawing attention to the extremes of scale between them, attachments to space and the memories held by architecture beyond the experience of the individual.

Figure 28.1 Shelf Life, 1998 Surrey University Art Gallery © Esther Rolinson

Recently I have chosen to work collaboratively with the landscape architects, Freemont Landscape Architects, and have aimed to site work "invisibly" within the surrounding environment. We have collaborated with the view to creating a landscape that includes unusual structures and landforms without creating a hierarchy to a specific feature. The boundary between hard and soft landscape and "artwork" has become entirely blurred, creating the potential to make a work that is a detail of the global site.

Residencies

The focus of my residency at C&CRS was "Digital Garden", a project developed at the Gallery of the Future, Loughborough [3]. It is a proposal for an externally sited structure that uses sensors to detect factors such as rain, wind or heat. This is interpreted through programming to effect a grid of light emitting diodes' (LED) output within curving glass forms. Environmental sensor information controls the output of the L.E.Ds contained inside curving glass forms. This project required research into both the programming and structural possibilities. I worked in the main part with Michael Quantrill and with Colin Machin of the Department of Computer Science at Loughborough University on the use of LEDs [4].

The work Digital Garden expresses the activities of nature that we may sense but cannot see. It makes the invisible visible. It interprets information from the elements and mimics the process of organic growth, expanding and decaying in response to the nourishment and erosion of the weather. It uses light as its cell structure and builds fluctuating patterns within its outer skin of glass.

Figure 28.2 Light Decks, 1999, Aquarium Terraces, Brighton
© **Esther Rolinson**

Programming

Rather than learning a programming language during the residency (which I have had little success with previously), my objective was to explore the project concepts in relationship to available technologies and gain a greater understanding of the information I would need to supply to a programmer. Mike Quantrill was an ideal person to discuss this with as he practices as both artist and programmer. We talked at length about the extent of control I could have over the images. I did not want to constrict the potential of the technology by defining images too specifically but, at the same time, wanted the programming to revolve only around central visual themes. The aim of the work was to have unplanned events that generated distinct pattern identities.

We decided to make a model of a panel on screen which represented the LEDs with small white squares. In preparation for this I made basic storyboards of compositions that would be formed by the illuminated LEDs, noting the possible formations of the patterns. It emerged that there would be several layers of imagery created by LEDs turning on and off. For example, branching patterns may grow over the period of a year and during that period other shapes such as trickling lines may temporarily dominate the screens. This would create slow growing imagery that would be disrupted by fleeting events. From this, Mike wrote a program that simulated an animated grid of LEDs showing a sequence that randomly accumulated a number of lights in a vertical line that slowly trickled to the bottom of the screen when it had gained sufficient 'weight'.

Structure

To make a grid of LEDs inside the curving glass forms it was necessary to research how they would be mounted. I specifically wanted a transparent backing so that natural light could still pass through the sandblasted glass. To research this, Mike and I consulted with Colin Machin who informed us that it was possible to surface mount the LEDs on a flexible transparent circuit board.

During the residency Mike, Colin and I sketched out a number of programming and structural possibilities and established a working method that illustrated how the animated screens might appear. It was useful to know that this type of project was practically possible but potentially very expensive. Since this time, I have consulted further with Colin on the use of Priva-Lite within architectural proposals.

The Digital Garden was developed significantly during the residency through the common interests in patterns occurring in natural forms held by Mike Quantrill and myself. It was particularly valuable that Mike also had a visual art practice and was willing to explore the project ideas alongside the possibilities for the technology. Our discussion raised questions around the structure and sequencing of events in the animated light panels and gradually drew the use of the technology and overall project concept closer together. In particular it was useful for Mike and I to discuss the project and then spend time individually evolving ideas through drawing and programming before bringing them back together again. In this collaborative approach to making work, I have found that the dialogue assists in developing the project well beyond the initial concept.

The incorporation of digital technologies into a physical fabrication, either as a controlling or evolving device, is an opportunity to create a layer of information that the structure alone cannot provide. The experience of the COSTART residency [5] clarified the potential role of the digital technology to expand upon the original project concept, meshing together the control and form of the work.

Reflections

The interest I have in the integration of light, structure and programming is influenced by the designs of Japanese architect Toyo Ito. His work, Tower of Winds, is a disused concrete column that he has encased in a skeleton of neon and lights. It reveals atmospheric activity through the fluctuation of electric signals: "transforming changing environmental conditions such as gusts of wind or traffic noise, into light, in real time, controlled by a computer system" [6, p. 20].

This work is very beautiful and simply captures a sense of life contained by the architectural form. By combining the structure and the programming in this way I find that it motivates a response on a physical level, illuminating the impact of sound and wind on the human body. It reveals the subtlety and organic sensitivity that digital technologies can bring to an artwork or building without being presented on-screen or becoming a dominant subject in the work.

Another use of digital technologies Ito employs is the interpretation of data mapping the flow of wind over the landscape to plot the shape of a dome: "a configuration determined on the basis of aerodynamics considering the predominant south westerly winds from Yoneshiro River" [6, p. 92]. Collecting detailed information about the environment with sensors utilizing digital technology through sensors. The result is a very successful dome that has a shell-like appearance, extending the contours of the surrounding hills and finding its place within the landscape.

I am investigating environments that offer a contemplative space to the inhabitant, faintly amplifying vital components of the atmosphere and the adjacent vista to intensify a sense of place. I am interested in developing works that perform structural roles within a building, either through manipulating or revealing an element that is already present, or by adding a work that fulfils a practical need, such as the addition of a shelter over a walkway or a wall that re-interprets the transition between two areas. I intend to work both with digital and structural materials within my proposals and aim to achieve a seamless conjunction of the two.

Toyo Ito's work has an ongoing impact on my research as it raises questions about how digital controls can affect form. Using digital technology offers the possibility for creating a different type of relationship between object and viewer, not only in terms of interacting through a keyboard or sensors but through communicating more varied types of information. In particular, it offers the potential to surround the body with a responsive and evolving environment, and to provoke a heightened sense of the viewer's own presence in relation to the work rather than solely as an observer.

References

1. Rolinson, E.: Light Decks: Light Installation, Brighton, England, (1999)

2. Rolinson, E. and Brown, C.: Shelf Life (1998–9),
    http://www.theplace.org.uk/sprload/html

3. Rolinson, E.: Digital Garden (1998), http://creative/lboro.ac.uk/gof/

4. Machin, C.: Realizing Digital Artworks, (2002) Chapter 14, in this book.

5. COSTART Project: http://www.creative.lboro.ac.uk/costart

6. Taylor, J.: Transfer of Intention: Toyo Ito and the Metaphorical Tetonic, 2G International Architecture Review (1997)

29 Going Somewhere Else

Ray Ward

The story and people are my main interest and the medium or technique is driven by my ideas and selected on how relevant it is for the content. My early career was as a painter and performance artist. I use painting to concentrate on a simple idea, portray a moment or glimpse of emotion; from here I like to develop and show the apparently simple as more complicated. In performance, the reverse is true, any ideas that are complicated or unresolved are thought through during the making and performing of the work.

An interest in wanting to work more directly with literature began with me recording eight hours of speaking from poetry workshops. From this I selected 98 phrases or sentences both from the poetry and any general conversation. This led to a public artwork in a town garden of 24 × 9 metre poles with text written down them as if on the spine of a book.

Next, I used the phrases as the starting point for drawing. These drawings were then posted to a poet and novelist who re-captioned them. From here I discarded the drawings and wrote short video clips about a minute long which linked the pairs of captions. These were digitally filmed and edited postcard-size clips displayed on an iMac alongside the drawings in an exhibition with Southern Arts Touring Exhibition Service. The computer started to seem the most appropriate medium for showing my work. I could work like a painter with the freedom and control allowed and also incorporate aspects of live performance.

At around this time I was introduced to the work of Raymond Roussel who as a writer seemed to be working in a similar way [1]. Although writing in the early twentieth century I was impressed by how like a web page or computer game his work was. A contemporary and near neighbour of Proust, Roussel was an extraordinary person. He travelled the world but barely left his hotel room; he worked slavishly to produce self published books that sold only a few copies. His poetry leads the reader in tangents, twists and turns through the use of parentheses at the end of a line. Follow the author's path and we find not sub-plots but sub-thoughts which take us somewhere completely different from where we were in the original poem.

My work has inadvertently followed a similar path collecting other people's words and phrases and using them as inspiration for artwork of a completely different nature. For one of his poems, Roussel sent quotes to a detective agency which he commissioned to find an artist who in turn illustrated the individual lines with no knowledge of their original context; I sent my drawings to a writer who had no knowledge of their original starting point. As an artist, I would love to be as brilliant as Roussel but would not be happy to be as unreadable and inaccessible; therefore, although my work develops like a Roussel poem, I present each new piece or "parentheses" as a new piece of work. Links can be made and a pattern can be followed, but this is not the important thing about the work although this and Roussel's method is chiefly the source of all my current subject matter.

The advent of the computer puts us in a totally different position to Roussel. To read one of his poems, it requires turning the page backwards and forwards whereas with computer programming or hyper text we are able to allow the viewer to make shifts and connections very simply while leaving pieces of the work behind that might never be seen. Here, we have a totally new way of making art where the maker has to be concerned about what happens to a piece when something that is intrinsically linked to it, for example, a verse in a poem or sub-plot in a film, might never be seen.

From a long prose poem created from the original collection of phrases I wrote 31 new video clips to be placed in a computer program which would select the clips in different orders and a new duration each time used. In order to make this work I needed help in a writing a program and this was the start of my time with C&CRS. Previously most of the film, video and digital work I had done was in isolation using kitchen table techniques for sketch book type notes for my painting and performance. I had wanted to work with the computer more and more while being constantly aware of the certain paradoxes for artists working with any new technology.

Residencies

One thing that seems to worry a lot of artists is their lack of specialist knowledge in any area. While I do not advocate that artists need no technical skill, I believe that it is only when they are free from the constraints of a rigid technique that they start to produce interesting work.

How much does an artist need to know about the medium they are working in? Is the work diminished by being conceived by one person and executed by another? In relation to the latter, I often think of an artist who in the eighteenth century might have made a drawing which was carved on a wooden block for printing by someone far more technically capable in woodblock than the artist. In the case of the former an artist needs some humility and respect not only for the medium but the people they are working with. The most important thing is to be aware of how little you know, and to give credit and authorship to any specialist with whom you are working.

Figure 29.1 AndEnd, 2000, Video still, Broomhill Art Hotel © Ray Ward

I am not and do not want to be seen as a digital artist. I never really wanted to be painter: it was a means to an end. Inside my head there is this thing that I feel is really important and I want to find the most appropriate way to tell as many people about it as I can. I have a desire for external influence provided by collaboration and yet need control in the decision making which, through collaboration, is consequently better informed. When working with a computer scientist it is unimportant to me that I cannot read a programming language like Lingo or C++, but it is important that I become aware of the possibilities and limitations.

Working at C&CRS was good for me in that I collaborated with a programmer, Simon Nee, and that helped me to see what can and cannot be done. I have become aware of my strengths as an artist but also of my failings as a sometime digital artist. At times I expected too much from a computer program and started to realize why some programs are written how they are. They are working within the limitations of the technology. I was also not as ambitious as I first thought and while seeing the work of others realized that my concept was pretty mundane and possibly over stretching technically in the wrong areas. The most important things are concept and execution and I hope that despite all other limitations, my idea is strong and will work because of these being performed well.

The irony in most digital work is that while appearing to be super fast it takes longer than expected. My program is not finished and had I the knowledge which I claimed earlier I do not need, it probably would be. Is this problem with me or should artists really be expected to know everything? If so, then artists might expect everyone to know all about art. Suddenly there is no need for artists or any specialists at all and one of the benefits of digital technology being that it brings different people together to collaborate will surely be of no use at all?

Where does this take me? Half way through a project with ideas under development and a greater understanding of the process of making better work in the field. I continue to work digitally and despite it taking longer than expected my experience at C&CRS is now influencing directly how I approach future projects. Right now I am going through a good period creatively and the fact that ideas come to nothing does not bother me very much.

Figure 29.2 Yellow Man, 2000, Video Still, Broomhill Art Hotel © Ray Ward

Talking to artists who have a limited experience of working digitally I often here them saying "the work never gets finished" or "I could draw what has taken you two days in two hours". While sometimes true it is worth remembering how many drawings it takes to make a painting and how many drafts to write a sonnet. I can't help feeling as artists we are all building castles in the night air and while it is due to persistence and hard work that anything gets done, it is often due to chance which pieces of work ever see the light of day.

Reflections

Two years ago I worked at PVA in Bridport [2] on a week-long residential digital workshop with art practitioners (painters, video and sound artists, printmakers and curators). Although it only lasted a short time, I learnt so much from being with other artists in different specialized areas. Coming from such diverse backgrounds the work in digital technology became our common link, here collaboration was really starting to work and there was genuine cross over. Too often digital technology makes a claim to be collaborative or innovative when it is merely responding in word not deed to the requirements of sometimes not very knowledgeable funding bodies.

Too many artists feel a need to claim specialist knowledge in the digital field when they only know how to use a software application. This is a long way from being able to write a program. Artists have always used specialists to make brushes, paper, and for presentation. This does not make a bad artist but it sometimes leads to an artist sometimes being un-necessarily economical with the truth. Artists work in different ways and will use digital technology for different purposes this too has to be re-spected and is too often resented by computer specialists. True collabora-tion only comes when we all feel equal and consequently able to make a contribution.

An artist does not necessarily need to be a computer specialist only an art or communications specialist. However, what all artists must do is be aware of the debt they owe to others that have helped them and search out as many opportunities as possible for extending their work. The leg-acy of the recent past is that artists are individuals who work exclusively on their own. While this has probably never been true, the art world re-mains fixated on the individual. Compare this to scientific research where claims for individual ownership are less valid and there is acknowledge-ment of group effort.

In digital art I want to go somewhere I have never imagined going in painting or performance, I want to think in a different way and learn new and unexpected things about me and the world. There is plenty of good art around which may or may not use new technology but surely any artist who wants to communicate will try and work with the tools relevant to the time they are living in.

References

1. Roussel, R. New Impressions of Africa, Cantos I, II & IV: translated with an Introduction by Andrew Hugill, with Hypertext: see staff.dmu.ac.uk/~ahu/nia/preface.html

2. pva-org.demon.co.uk: PVA was set up in 1996 by a group of artists resident in the South West of England. The aim of the group is to devise artist-led exhibitions, collaborations and events in the south west of England and further afield. We also aim to devise work in the visual arts and digital media with local, regional and national significance.

30   New Directions for Art and Technology

George Whale

On the January 14th 2002, in a building no more than a stone's throw from Channel Four's futuristic, glass headquarters in the heart of London, a diverse group of artists, technologists and researchers associated with the Creativity and Cognition Research Studios (C&CRS) [1] gathered to consider the future of Art and Technology. Represented in this unique grouping were several nationalities and many points of view. Some of the participants were meeting each other for the first time. The day-long, round table workshop organized by C&CRS and sponsored by the Arts Council of England, was divided into three sessions, each devoted to considering new directions on three themes: practice, technology and collaboration.

Participants

Joan Ashworth (JA)
Linda Candy (LC)
Ernest Edmonds (EAE)
Dave Everitt (DE)
Mark Fell (MF)
Bronac Ferran (BF)
Ingrid Holt (IH)
Fré Ilgen (FI)
Jacqueline Ilgen (JI)
Michael Kidner (MK)

Lucy Kimbell (LK)
Colin Machin (CM)
Anthony Padgett (AP)
Sandra Pauletto (SP)
Mike Quantrill (MQ)
Esther Rolinson (ER)
Ray Ward (RW)
Alistair Weakley (AW)
George Whale (GW)

Practice

How are digital technologies made available to artists? How are creative ideas transmitted through technology? Where exactly is artistic "end-product" located? And what is its relationship to the audience and to the market? These essential questions relating to creative practice at the intersection of art and technology were addressed during the first session of the day in a vigorous and wide-ranging discussion.

Many kinds of digital technologies, from computer-controlled devices to visualization programs, can be integrated into art practice and issues of technology usage, configuration and design became central and recurring themes. It was evident that artists had taken distinctly different approaches to the deployment of these technologies. Whereas some had worked predominantly with ready-made, proprietary hardware and software, others had opted for custom-made solutions created with the support of C&CRS technologists. Much of the discussion revolved around the implications of these choices and, in particular, the ways in which interactive and programmed approaches to art making shape and influence practice.

Joan Ashworth admitted that she enjoys the sheer awkwardness of some interactive software ("What on *earth* were the designers thinking?"), because it gives her "something to work against". It is, perhaps, a paradoxical notion that technological limitations can serve as a stimulus, but one that was echoed by Fré Ilgen ("I think they *provoke* your creativity") and by Mike Quantrill:

> My work involves sensor systems, a space of 64 squares, to which the computer responds. It was awkward at first, but the constraints are now beneficial. Now, the question is: What am I trying to *do* with this space?

Mike observed that an artist with a strong, initial idea which turns out to be incompatible with the application, is much more likely to be frustrated than one who approaches it without preconceptions, receptive to whatever possibilities might be revealed or suggested. It appeared, in essence, to be a conflict between what Dave Everitt described as "constraints at a conceptual level" and the constraints of software, a conflict which some artists had resolved by producing their own software, alone or in collaboration with software programmers.

Colin Machin spoke of his experience of creating "configurable frameworks" for artists, his aim being to provide task-oriented software with enough built-in flexibility to accommodate project evolution: "When I write software to control something, I leave decisions as late as possible then say, Now, over to you." Artist Anthony Padgett recalled that in a collaboration with Mike Quantrill, "creativity went over to the program", raising the question of where, exactly, the "art" resides in computer-mediated projects: is it in the software, in the finished work or, as one participant suggested, somewhere on a "sliding scale, or continuum", between these two extremes?

Whichever approach is favoured, any artist working with digital technology will, as Dave Everitt put it, "hit a limit at some point", although it was acknowledged that it is not always easy to determine which limitations are real and which are illusory. For, in challenging recommended practice and conventional (i.e. expert) wisdom, some artists had found them to be illusory. Fré Ilgen recounted his experience with an expert in Virtual Reality (VR) systems:

> He tried to persuade me to use four walls. I said "Get rid of all that. Let's start with a black hole!" The expert thought that without walls, I would lose my sense of direction. You don't. Who cares about gravity in virtual reality?

Fré suggested that artists working within a digital medium can "push the limits beyond what is seen as acceptable with that medium", a view echoed by Dave: "artists ... may ask the kinds of questions specialists wouldn't raise" and open up "new lines of enquiry".

Communication was seen as a crucial element of any joint engagement with technology reflecting and shaping the human partnerships that are forged when "artists collide with other disciplines". Ernest Edmonds' observation, that dialogue can involve conceptual development, underlined the problem of describing difficult creative or technical concepts and the importance of developing mutual, or "problem-specific", languages to bridge the conceptual gap between domains. Interaction was identified as one aspect in particular need of a "natural language" of description. A good fifty percent of the work undertaken at C&CRS involves interaction between artist and audience or between artist and devices.

Digital technology, it was claimed, can bring other media together and encourage free movement between them, as well as have the potential to reach quite different (and larger) audiences and markets. Presentation was seen as a significant obstacle, since the use of conventional forms of presentation for digital work, for example, gallery projection of VR artworks, may "miss the point". All of the artists had experienced difficulty in selling digital artworks, finding that people tend to be far less keen to pay for something as intangible as electronic form than, say, a painting or a print. According to Linda Candy, this may be a result of the public becoming accustomed to obtaining music and visual work via the Web. Fré Ilgen reported that even in New York, where "every second gallery shows video or computer work", marketing is a struggle.

Most of the artists present took the view that, to survive, one must either find a supportive environment or think of other ways to make money, perhaps following the lead of artist Jack Ox, who has devised one possible solution which bypasses the usual gallery channels by marketing limited edition giclée prints online. The prints are of individual frames of VR artworks, visual interpretations of music, rendered at high resolution. Currently, she is developing a website making similar facilities available to other multimedia artists [2].

Linda Candy recounted a story of how Harold Cohen, creator of the computer art program, "AARON", had been approached by somebody wanting to obtain his software free from the World Wide Web. Apparently Cohen was more than a little dismayed at the thought of parting with his life's work so easily. Interestingly, a version of "AARON" is now being sold as a limited edition. Whether this will prove to be a money-spinner remains to be seen, but the marketing of original software may yet prove to be a viable option for some artists.

Linda's observation that "some of the best abstract digital art is in Las Vegas" triggered a lively discussion of commercial computer art and the new forms of presentation and interaction made possible by hefty R & D investment, especially in the games industry. A fiercely competitive market means that most games are transient, and few of them actually make much money. Nonetheless, it was generally accepted that the best of them could be "both beautiful and engaging". Mike Quantrill described his favourite game (evidently parenthood facilitates hands-on research in this rapidly changing field) called Counterstrike, a hugely popular game about terrorists which combines narrative, strategy, cooperation and interaction in an environment where players can communicate with others (and attack them?) "on a human level". It was pointed out that these same concerns are shared by many artists. Ernest thought it significant that many of the works by internationally renowned artists in London's Millennium Dome exhibition were located in the Play Zone.

Spin-offs from the games industry, including new, low-cost interaction and display devices and libraries of efficient software routines for real-time 3D rendering, animation and interaction were considered to be of great potential value, and ready to be exploited. Considering the speed at which these technologies are moving compared to the long-term nature of many fine art projects, Ernest believed that artists would be well advised to think ahead, because "what technology researchers are doing now may take five years to reach the market".

Technology

The theme for the second session was "Technology". Workshop participants were asked to speculate on future technology needs and to share their vision of possible new directions in digital art. The difficulty of making such predictions was underlined by Lucy Kimbell, whose work has exploited SMS (Short Message Service) technology:

> **LK:** Text messaging and the language of messaging evolved out of a human desire to communicate – nobody would have asked for it five years ago.
> **EAE:** That means that interpretation of this question needs to be considered. What are the important *areas* to which technology can contribute?

The ensuing discussion was dominated by considerations of input and output, as it was generally perceived that these aspects were "less resolved" than the intermediate, processing and manipulation stages. The prominence of interactive approaches at C&CRS was reflected in a concern with motion capture: specifically a desire for cheaper, more portable sensor systems which could be set up anywhere, new "haptic" interfaces and wireless, motion tracking technologies better able to pick up nuances of human movement and facilitating "action separate from the computer".

Converting visual material for input was seen as especially problematic, since most current input technologies are unable to capture much beyond the surface structure of drawings and paintings. Ernest reported that there is currently a lot of research into the capturing of drawn structure in the computer. However, the development of VR sketching tools of the kind envisaged by Fré Ilgen looked to be some way off. Joan Ashworth reported her difficulties with 3D input: the problem, she said, is that "everyone wants slightly different things" from technology. She gave the example of car designers and jewellery designers, and their differing expectations of 3D scanning technology in terms of scale.

> **EAE:** Apart from that, what do people find hardest at the moment?
> **MQ:** Output.
> **GW:** What is problematic about output, specifically? We have a range of output technologies - for example, technologies that enable us to make prints as big as a wall and rapid prototyping technologies to output 3D models directly, as sculptures.
>
> **MQ:** In drawing, the trace of activity is retained. I move a lot when drawing, which is as important as the trace and I would like to capture

that information – to find some way of using the movement information, to feed it back into the process.

AP: I did performances which tracked the movement and converted it
into a 3D model, which could have been rapid prototyped.

DE: We're looking at making *process* visible, getting away from working towards objects.

JA: If the technology was available to audiences, they could become familiar with the process.

The idea that we need new technologies for making transient process
concrete was not accepted by everyone. Ernest remarked that "People
do not think in these terms in traditional performance", and Colin Machin cited an example of a *pre*-digital record of process: the BBC's famous Potter's Wheel film which recorded (relentlessly) the process of a
pot being made. It was also suggested that computers might be used "to
explore ways of making artifacts that show process, like a Pollock
painting".

Other specific requirements included mobile networks, enhanced
home-working capabilities and faster rendering for high-resolution film
output. It was conceded that commercial development of such technologies would be demand led but, as Linda Candy indicated, there is
nothing to stop artists becoming more demanding, putting forward mar-
ketable ideas themselves:

> The people who might make interesting demands do not make them to the
> right people. More demanding people might give better demand-led devel-
> opment.

Reference was made to artists' engagement in technology development, notably in the specification of some graphics applications, and in
(indirectly) influencing usage in fields such as advertising. Lucy Kimbell
noted that artists had also been "very involved in solving conceptual
issues in Web projects", though under the rubric of "design". Linda recounted that the BBC's Imagineering department, were currently seeking ideas for designing sketching tools and tutorials to online users.
However, opportunities for experts to take charge of hardware and
software development within their own domains were considered especially significant, not only in art and design, but also in domains such as
architecture and medicine ("some of the best medical software is written
by medics").

Towards the end of this second session, attention turned to the so-
cial/political role of the artist in relation to digital technology. Anthony
Padgett opened by arguing that "part of the role of art is questioning,
political and self-reflecting, not just aesthetic", and wondered whether
artists weren't "riding on the back of" and therefore "implicated in the
whole structure" of technologies developed largely for "war or pornog-

raphy". Linda Candy took the view that an 'agitprop' versus aesthetic emphasis is the "artist's own choice", but that if artists want to take a political stance, then the technology can facilitate it. She cited the example of one artist who had used the World Wide Web to confront and challenge far-right political organizations.

Mike Quantrill's musing, that "maybe we have enough technology" received a surprisingly sympathetic response, and there was a general feeling that more effort should be put into promoting awareness of what is already "out there" (starting, perhaps, with more "intelligent" Internet searching and filtering capabilities), and facilitating more effective use and reuse of *existing* technology. As Anthony had commented earlier: "Often the strength of the artist is in combining existing technology in new ways".

Collaboration

The third and final workshop session was devoted to a discussion of collaboration, focusing on the human relationships at the heart of every creative partnership. Linda Candy began by presenting a classification of the many types of collaboration in art and technology (see Chapter 4: Collaboration and for more details an associated paper [3]). Asked whether collaborators needed to have shared goals, she replied that in the COSTART project [4], they "began with the notion of the assistant model of support, but moved closer to the partnership idea, although not necessarily with shared goals."

Fré Ilgen maintained that the purpose of collaboration is to solve a problem posed by the artist, but it was evident that even this fairly restrictive definition allowed for a number of different kinds of collaborative arrangements. "The key priority", said Lucy Kimbell, "is for both sides to agree the nature of the partnership". An artist's perspective on collaboration was offered by Michael Kidner:

> My experience of collaboration is that you learn from your collaborator. You see your own work through somebody else's eyes. It may be a shock or surprise, but it is always exciting. Neither partner knows what will come out of the collaboration.

It was generally agreed that any technologist taking on the role of assistant (as opposed to, say, full partner) had to be paid, because "You don't want them to feel that they're getting nothing" (Esther Rolinson). According to Mike Quantrill, who had worked with Esther, Anthony Padgett and Dave Everitt, the role of the technologist tends to vary from one project to another: "With Dave, we both worked on everything together instead of working on specialisms", although "there were points where the artist *had* to make a decision".

Ernest Edmonds expressed the view that collaboration offers "a different model of learning processes". All agreed that learning is a vital aspect of collaboration, especially the learning of new technologies by artists (which promotes self-sufficiency) and it was acknowledged that, in suggesting new uses of technology, artists may, in turn, contribute to the learning process. In addition, as Joan Ashworth pointed out, working alongside other artists in a *shared* environment promotes exchange of knowledge and cross-fertilization of ideas.

Many participants felt that judgements of success in collaborative projects ought to take account of the fact that significant outcomes may take time to accrue, that ideas may evolve over an extended, interrupted timescale. For Linda, this underlined the need to sustain successful, creative partnerships:

> Organisations should provide support for sustainable relationships ... partners need to be able to come back to half-resolved problems, to build skills, understanding, relationships...

Success in collaboration was seen to depend on the practices and personal attributes of the collaborators. Whilst it was recognized that collaborators need not necessarily spend a lot of time together, perhaps working alone for much of the time and meeting up only occasionally to resolve important issues, communication was considered paramount. Mike stressed the importance of talking, the need to "spend a lot of time talking, specifying the problem". Most felt that the technologist's communication skills must include not only a facility for elucidating complexity, but also a willingness to listen; conversely (and self-evidently) the artist must have something to say. Michael Kidner considered "a sense of curiosity" to be a desirable attribute in collaboration.

Issues of ownership and accreditation provoked some lively exchanges. Again, the need for continual communication and agreement was emphasized. The idea of the artist as "ultimate owner, director and developer of the work" was challenged by Dave Everitt, who took the view that "different kinds of ownership" of collaborative artwork may be negotiated, including co-ownership, wherein each partner is free to "promote it in their own way, without diminishing either". George Whale's suggestion that a written contract might be preferable to a verbal agreement was criticized on the grounds of unenforceability, with Fré Ilgen sensibly pointing out that there is "always a difference between the law and the pragmatics of everyday reality". The issue was left unresolved, mainly because many problems of protection for visual artists and their collaborators are still legally unresolved. Nevertheless, we were made aware of the need to become better informed. Bronac Ferran commented:

> Sometimes artists will want to give ideas away, other times protect them.
> In each case, they need to know their options.

C&CRS's approach is very much research-oriented, and the COSTART [4] project team were keen to hear the opinions of artists as to how the involvement of researchers had influenced their collaborative work. The response was wholly positive – the researcher's role in evaluating, contextualizing, developing the theoretical base and generating new knowledge from which others might benefit was regarded as invaluable. Interestingly, the researcher's role as observer was seen as equally important. Joan Ashworth remarked:

> The researcher helps ... you to be more reflective about the process ... and may identify problems in collaboration. I found it very valuable.

Linda Candy admitted that she had once experienced a situation in which an artist had been unhappy about having a third-party observer, and she appreciated that being exposed to scrutiny can be quite unnerving for those engaged in creative activity: "People need to be willing, and trust the situation". She elaborated on what she considered one of the most important aspects of the contribution of research, documentation:

> Published documentation provides a primary account of what people were doing... In art, there is not much process documentation; it is mostly product documentation, which people try to unpick. There is little about the evolution of thought *at the time*.

Directions for the Future

Finally, workshop participants were asked to think about what it is that is most important for the short-to-medium-term future in art and technology, either personally, or more generally. Here are the responses:

EAE: The most important thing is to build collaborations as full partnerships, through residencies, postgraduate study programmes or other forms of funding.

MQ: We need to build environments with supportive technologists, open to collaboration. If you have a good environment, good things can come out of it.

MK: Collaboration must be properly acknowledged.

SP: We should consider education for people on how to become an assistant, or how to collaborate. Credits should always acknowledge assistants and make clear their roles. (But they should also share the blame when things go wrong!)

CM: Aim to provide technology on a "semi-bespoke" basis - software you can configure to control your artwork. Facilitate artists to understand, use, ask questions and advance.

FI: Identify and target different kinds of artists who might be interested in the possibilities of digital technologies.

JI: The issue of time is crucial. Most artists have so little time to integrate technology into their practice.

AP: Art/religion/technology crossover. Apply technology more in the creation of spiritual happenings, developing common experience.

JA: Technologists must have artistic sensibility – otherwise they can't communicate.

IH: The social problems of collaboration can be very difficult and need to be considered, especially the issue of developing common goals.

GW: We need to step back occasionally and ask ourselves the question: What exactly are we gaining by using this technology?

MF: Move towards art that makes the artist/technician distinction unworkable.

LK: Start a public debate about the value of art led research.

DE: A stable, non-distracting, structured working spaces facilitating peer interaction is needed as well as a focal point for worldwide activity in this field, enabling networking and exchange of ideas.

AW: Go on collaborating, but ensure that the relationship between collaborators is equal.

BF: Promote opportunities to join up some of the funding bodies in shared work and encourage dissemination of process and collaboration. We need to substitute the word "problems" for "opportunities".

ER: Develop facilities for supporting an ongoing relationship and dialogue, so that I can pop in and out when I want.

LC: We need to understand what research is from different disciplinary standpoints. Science is based on the experimental method and this is not ap-

propriate for arts research. A methodology for practice-based research in
the arts needs to be explored and defined.

Conclusions

These final comments of the day reveal an overriding concern with
communication, an issue which figured prominently in all three workshop
sessions. Communication, in one form or another, has always been the
business of artists, but it is communication *between artists and machines*
that distinguishes creative activity at the boundary of art and technology,
for digital technologies are no mere extensions of hand and eye but provide new instruments through which ideas, understanding, and experience
might be conveyed from one person to another.

In this context, the constraints which have alternately frustrated and
stimulated artists (see Boden, [5]) can be seen as *communicative* constraints, and the dilemma of the artist engaging with technology has been
characterized as a choice between allowing the technology to dictate the
terms of the dialogue, or of bending or reinventing it to suit his/her accustomed language. Another possibility has been hinted at by Joan Ashworth:

> Digital technology has enabled me to work in a more contained and less
> physical way. The square footage of studio space required is less. It makes
> me feel restricted in some ways and my hands and body get bored with do-
> ing small movements. They need bigger gestures with more physical effort
> required to feel satisfied. [6]

Is this a case of an artist learning to function *despite* technological
constraints? Or rather, has the artist begun to discover new possibilities
for communication and expression *because* of them? Her use of the word
"enabled" suggests the latter.

Artists, if they have something to say, will have little interest in exploring technology for its own sake, in merely illustrating its capabilities,
as so much "computer art" seems to do. On the other hand, using technology in ways that fail to take account of its particularities may turn out
to be equally unrewarding. It was Ernst Gombrich who observed that, "Sitting in front of his motif, pencil in hand, the artist ... will tend to see his
motif in terms of lines, while, brush in hand, he sees it in terms of
masses"[7, p. 56]. Meaningful engagement with new media may equally
depend upon the artist's learning to conceptualize in terms of those media, which is not simply a matter of shaping the technology or being
shaped by it, but something much more interesting: the gradual emergence of a 'trialogue' between artist, machine and audience.

Extrapolation of current trends is a notoriously unreliable method of
prediction, since none of us knows what seismic technological shifts are

imminent. But what emerged from the day's discussions is that, whatever the technology employed, creative success will depend on effective communication. The artists, technologists and researchers at C&CRS are at the forefront in developing the languages that will facilitate this communication.

References

1. Creativity and Cognition Research Studios (C&CRS):
   www.creativityandcognition.com

2. Ox, J.: http://www.stillshot.net; http://www.bway.net/~jackox/

3. Candy, L. and Edmonds, E.A.: Modelling Creative Collaboration: Studies in Digital Art, In Computational and Cognitive Models of Creative Design V, J.S. Gero and M-L Maher (eds), Developing Ideas Sessions (2001) 3-12

4. Computer Support for Artists (COSTART) Project: creative.lboro.ac.uk/costart

5. Boden, Margaret A.: The Creative Mind: Myths and Mechanisms. Weidenfeld/Abacus and Basic Books (1990)

6. Ashworth, J.: Creating Graspable Water in Three-Dimensional Space, Chapter 17 in this book.

7. Gombrich, E.: Art and Illusion: A Study in the Psychology of Pictorial Representation. 5th edition, Phaidon (1995)

31   Defining Interaction

Linda Candy

Every medium, from paint to film, has its art and the digital medium is screaming out for uniquely digital content that can be called fine literature. I believe that the emergent order will be the inevitable result of efforts by artists rather than technocrats. [1]

Roy Stringer believed that it is the artist, rather than the engineer, who leads in the finding of new visions, or what he calls the "emergent order". Billy Kluver also remarked that "the artist widens the vision of the engineer" [2]. But is this just the railing of the artist against the power of the technocrat? What is the evidence from past experience that supports the idea that artists, as distinct from anyone else, have something special to offer innovative technology and the "emergent order"? The people who invented ARPANET (Advanced Research Projects Agency Network) on which the Internet was built, were not artists, nor were those who brought the portable music player and the mobile phone into everyday use. Many people from different walks of life and with different goals and expertize have contributed to the development of ideas, artifacts and new forms. If artists have a role to play in creating a new order, what kind of role is it and is it really distinctive from the role of designers, engineers and technologists?

If we take the artists represented in this book as a point of departure, one thing stands out. Every one of them embarked upon a journey of exploration into a new and mainly uncharted territory with few visible means of support. Those who have been on the journey for longer have found ways to pursue their art in tandem with teaching and research and have acquired the skills for an acceptable degree of self-sufficiency. To seek out collaborative opportunities with technologists, who can provide the right kind of knowledge support, also requires the determination and resilience of the innovator. And that is the key point: artists are innovators by their very nature and innovators are known to be risk takers.

The artist does not stand apart from the world. By virtue of unique inner visions, they transform the culture of the time. By creating 'works', they undertake an exploration of both their innermost selves and the cultural context in which we all live.

261

Changing Processes

This book has been an exploration of the creative process in art and technology as distinct from an analysis of the artworks and other outcomes of that creativity. Certain themes recur throughout: interaction, participation and collaboration. These notions are now firmly established in art and technology experiences.

Two particular things have happened in the world of art and technology. First, the significance of audience participation has been much advanced by digital technologies. Second, partnerships in art practice have grown significantly, so that the visual arts have developed some of the characteristics of film production, with teams of experts working together on projects. In one form or another, interaction between humans, and between humans and machines is a key characteristic. The computer is central to today's interactive art, where the artist and the audience play integral participant roles. Today, the scope for creating interactive art systems is manifestly attainable.

In the 1970s, when it was much harder to construct artworks that could transform viewers into participants, Cornock and Edmonds [3] put forward the idea that the computer could have an important role in defining the specification of the dynamic 'art system' and also managing the real-time result of that specification. This role is quite different to the computer as a means of producing graphic art images. By 'specifying" and 'managing', they meant that the computer controls the way an artwork performs in relation to its environment including its human audience, or, arguably the more appropriate term, its 'participants'. Because the role of the computer was envisaged to be so critical to the experience, they speculated that such work could transform the artist from an art specialist in creating artworks to a catalyst for creativity.

Interaction and Art Systems

We can envisage several situations that characterize the relationship between the artwork, artist, viewer and environment. The core categories devised by Cornock and Edmonds in the late 1960s are still relevant to the future of art. They were defined then as: static, dynamic-passive and dynamic-interactive. We can now elaborate on those descriptions and bring them up-to-date:

1. *Static*: in which the unchanging art object is viewed by a person. There is no interaction between the two that can be observed by someone else, although the viewer may be experiencing personal psychological or emotional reactions. The artwork itself does not respond to its context. This is familiar ground in art galleries and

museums where art consumers look at a painting or print, listen to tape recordings and talk to one another about the art on the walls and, generally speaking, obey the command not to touch.

2. *Dynamic-Passive*: the art object has an internal mechanism that enables it to change or it may be modified by an environmental factor such as temperature, sound or light. The internal mechanism is prescribed by the artist and the scope of the change is entirely predictable. Sculptures, such as George Rickey's kinetic picces [4], that move according to internal mechanisms and also in response to atmospheric changes in the environment fall into this category. The viewer is a passive observer of this activity performed by the artwork in response to the physical environment.

3. *Dynamic-Interactive:* all of the conditions of the dynamic passive category apply with the added factor that the human 'viewer' has an active role in influencing the changes in the art object. For example, by walking over a mat that contains sensors attached to lights operating in variable sequences, the viewer becomes a participant that influences the process of the work. Motion and sound capture techniques can be used to incorporate human activity into the way visual images and sounds are presented. The work 'performs' differently according to what the person does or says. There may be more than one participant and more than one art object.

When considering these categories, Cornock and Edmonds proposed that, rather than talk about "artworks", it was helpful to think in terms of "art systems" that embraced all of the participating entities, including the human viewer. It follows that the role of the artist is not so much to construct the artwork, but rather it is to specify and modify the constraints and rules used to govern the relationship between audience and artwork as it takes place in the world. Several examples of "art systems" have been seen earlier in Part 2 of this book, and form an important strand of the future development of approaches to making art. However, the way that we can interpret them is subtler than it was 30 years ago. They are also all examples of human collaboration and of interdisciplinary partnerships in practice.

Jack Ox makes variations on the *static* type of work. Music and images are closely related and in which the participant can move around in a three-dimensional visual space that is also a representation of a musical space. Although the viewer does not influence the state of the work, they choose a viewpoint and move around it in a very real and dynamic way. Thus it has something of the feel of a *dynamic-passive* piece to it [5].

Esther Rolinson's work is a direct example of the *dynamic-passive* variety in which the performance is influenced by the work's environment. She works with natural elements and architectural structures and creates installations in the physical world. She is using digital technology to control her light structures and to explore the way it affects the relationship between the object and the viewer [6].

Mike Quantrill works on interactive environments in which the visual work reacts to the movement of the participant in a physical space in front of the projected images. This work falls into the *dynamic-interactive* category but has a particular characteristic. Quantrill is more interested in his own interactions with the piece rather than in those of others. Although he sets up interactive situations, for a large part of the action he is the participant himself. It is through those levels of involvement that he feels he learns most [7].

The nature of "art systems" such as these is increasingly significant in modern technology-based art. Artists are putting considerable effort into the specification and construction of interactive situations of many kinds. As well as the interactions between the artworks and human participants, many other interactions have come to be important. For example, the ways in which the artist can interact with computers and digital media in general, in order to specify the works, is both complex and varied. The increasing degree of collaboration between technologists and artists both affects the necessary interactions between artist and computer and adds another dimension to be concerned with: interactions between technologists and artists.

Learning, Reflection and Research

The experiences of the twenty-five practitioners and researchers have been presented in this book. They are all working at the intersection between art and technology in innovative, mostly collaborative, projects that push the boundaries of art practice. From this, we furthered our understanding about the nature of interaction between people and computers. There is another benefit, however, from which we can also learn.

The process of being involved in *research* about their practice has proved both interesting and advantageous to many of the artists involved. As some of the comments in Chapter 30 reveal, the research provided both encouragement and help for the artist in reflecting on their practice.

Beyond the specific concerns of art and technology, the inevitable research related-activities that are introduced may influence the development of art practice in the future. Learning about technology was clearly important to the artists involved in these studies, but learning about their own art practice from the reflections that the research induced may have been equally or even more important. It is also very important that these reflections are part of a research activity that both documents the process and disseminates the outcomes. In this way, what has been learnt is shared with the world and all can benefit from the work. This sharing also encourages consideration and feedback by others. The research is leading to a social development process and so to an acceleration of the learning.

We know from experience that those countries of the world that invest in sport reap the benefits in terms of excellence in high performance events. This success has a spiraling effect in encouraging new generations to participate in sport and, in addition, strengthening spectator followings. When countries fail to make the grade at the Olympics, it matters enough to galvanize governments and businesses into generating funding for academies of sporting excellence to build the knowledge and skill so essential for success. The creative arts offer similar social and cultural benefits, but, in general, we are less conscious of this. There are differences, of course, but the common factors are interesting to note in the context of art and technology.

In sport, the differences between the high performers are so fine that there is strong motivation to draw upon leading research into new technologies that gives the crucial competitive edge over the opponents. Technology, such as motion capture systems, are used by athletes and coaches to study body action in order to identify faults in performance and put them right.

In the art world, the goals may be less overtly competitive than those in sport, but the intentions of the participants are not so different. Artists use digital technology to create artworks in ways they cannot achieve in any other way. To put it another way, they are seeking ways of enhancing their 'performance' as artists. And if it involves many years of struggle to take them on that unknown road, then that is what must be faced. For innovative people, this does not just mean becoming skilled in using a particular software application, rather it means developing strategies by which they can realize the challenges they have set themselves. Such strategies involve pushing the boundaries of what is technically possible, which means always needing to learn new methods, new knowledge and new ways of working.

When Michael Kidner says, "every time I start with a new material it seems I am getting involved in a new technology, so I am always an amateur", he is not being self-effacing [7]. That he remains an amateur is a measure of the importance he places on his artistic intentions. If he needs to acquire a technique to be able to realize a work, he will pursue it in whatever way seems appropriate. But once a work is finished, he moves on. He does not have the time or inclination to spend on becoming highly skilled as would be essential to produce quality craftwork. The artist who dedicates himself to becoming a skilled programmer, may become, in part, a professional technologist and may have to learn to think more like one. The technologist who creates attractive visual representations using software for image manipulation does not necessarily become a creative artist as a result. The artist's endeavour is concerned with something deeper than appearance and it is much harder to characterize. As many of the accounts by practitioners in this book show, work at the intersection of art and technology is concerned with organizing structures and principles, new art forms, new languages and the implications of technology for society. Few of these issues are tackled just by considering surface appearances.

Conclusions

It is not possible to predict how current artwork with digital technology will develop or where it might go. Nor is it desirable to do so. Even a satisfactory critical framework of new forms in art technology has yet to be developed, although books such as this may provide material that can help towards that work. In any case, the artists and technologists represented here have in common their desire for collaboration across the cultural gap and a willingness to open their creative practice to the scrutiny of the third eye of the researcher. This in itself is a very encouraging pointer to the future. Perhaps the emerging order will be defined neither by artists nor by technologists alone. Instead, we may look forward to new types of collaborations that embrace the intersections between technology and art. We have seen the beginnings of a re-defining of the intersections between fields where, in this shifting world, we might expect most change in the immediate future.

References

1. Stringer, R.: Quoted in the Web Wizards exhibition, the Design Museum, London. (2002)
2. Kluver, B.: Interview Chapter 1, 8-11 in this book
3. Cornock, S. and E. A. Edmonds, E.A.: The Creative Process where the Artist is Amplified or Superseded by the Computer. Leonardo, 16, 11-16 (1973)
4. Rickey, G.: A Retrospective. Guggenheim Museum, New York (1979)
5. Ox, J. The Color Organ and Collaboration. Chapter 24, 211 218 in this book
6. Rolinson, E.: Shifting Spaces. Chapter 28, 237 242 in this book
7. Quantrill, M.P. Integrating Computers as Explorers in Art Practice, Chapter 26, 225 230 in this book.
8. Michael Kidner from a private conversation with Ernest Edmonds (1996).

Biographical Notes

The Authors

Linda Candy

Linda Candy is Senior Research Fellow in the Department of Computer Science at Loughborough University, UK. She has a first degree in English and French, a Masters degree in computer-aided learning and a doctorate in Computer Science from Loughborough University. She is currently principal researcher for the COSTART project, Studies of Computer Support for Creative Work: Artists and Technologists in Collaboration. Her main research areas are creativity, interaction design and usability evaluation She has conducted studies of creative people including the designer of the Lotus bicycle and has published widely. She is a member of a number of international conference programme committees and has carried out a number of projects in collaboration with industry. She is co-chair of the international symposia on Creativity and Cognition and Strategic Knowledge and Concept Formation. She has been invited to present her work in Europe, Japan, Australia and the USA. For further details see: www.lindacandy.com.

Ernest Edmonds

Ernest Edmonds is Director of the Creativity and Cognition Research Studios, Loughborough University, UK. His research in human–computer interaction and creativity has led to more than 160 publications. The research included early advances in user interface architectures, virtual reality, intelligent user interfaces and user-centred design. In the area of creativity, he first published on the implications of computers for art practice in 1970. He has been using computers in art since 1968. His work has concentrated on logic-based generative digital videos, known as video constructs. He first exhibited a video construct in London in 1985 and has since shown these and other related works in Moscow, Sydney, Rotterdam, Liège, Vervier, Budapest and Koblenz. Recently he has been making interactive, participative work and investigating correspondences between visual art and music through the use of computers. He was chairman of the Access and Creativity task group for the UK's Technology Foresight programme and leader of its mission to Japan – The Interaction of Art and Technology. He is currently a member of the UK Arts and Humanity Research Board's Visual Arts and Media research panel. He is co-chair of the Creativity and Cognition conference series. For further details see: www.ernestedmonds.org.uk

The Contributors

The artists' work appears on the Website: www.creativityandcognition.com

Joan Ashworth

Joan Ashworth is an artist working in moving image with a background in stop-frame animation. While studying graphic design at Newport, Gwent, she was introduced to animation, both drawn and stop-frame. She immediately embraced animation as a means of expression and specialized in stop-frame animation for the majority of her degree, as it combined the study of many aspects of art, design and film. Later, studying film-making at the National Film and Television School, Beaconsfield, Buckinghamshire, Ashworth also explored live-action. She graduated in June 1987 with an 18-minute film The Web, based on Mervyn Peake's Titus Groan, the first book of the Gormenghast trilogy. This was made using stop-frame animation with puppets made of soft leather. The Web was shown at film festivals worldwide, winning the Mari Kuttna Prize for Best British Animation 1987 and broadcast on Channel 4. In September 1987, she set up a production company, 3 Peach Animation, with two partners, Martin Greaves (Producer, NFTS) and Andy Staveley (Director, Royal College of Art). The partners closed 3 Peach in 1997 and Ashworth and Greaves set up Seed Fold Films to pursue personal projects.

Bettina Brendel

Bettina Brendel, born and educated in Germany, arrived in Los Angeles in 1953, where she continued her studies at the University of Southern California. She was one of the pioneer abstract artists on the West Coast of the USA. Her interest in abstract thought and imagery led her to study the history and theories of modern physics at the New School for Social Research in New York City. She subsequently met and corresponded with Nobel physicist, Werner Heisenberg, in Munich, Germany. Her unusual ability of extra-sensory perception enabled her to envision unexplored areas of nuclear particle physics. She developed these ideas in many of her paintings over a period of 40 years. Brendel has been creating art on the computer since 1988. Her giclé prints have been exhibited and collected in the USA and in Europe. She is frequently invited to present her work at various international conferences on art and science and her work was exhibited at Creativity and Cognition 1996 in Loughborough, UK.

Harold Cohen

Harold Cohen, former director of the Centre for Research in Computing
and the Arts (CRCA), was an English painter with an established international reputation when he came to the University of California at San
Diego (UCSD) in 1968 for a one-year visiting professorship. His first
experience with computing followed almost immediately, and he never
returned to London. Cohen is the author of the celebrated AARON program, an ongoing research effort in autonomous machine (art making)
intelligence which began when he was a visiting scholar at Stanford University's Artificial Intelligence Laboratory in 1973. Together, Cohen and
AARON have exhibited at London's Tate Gallery, the Brooklyn Museum, the San Francisco Museum of Modern Art, Amsterdam's Stedelijk
Museum and many more of the world's major art spaces. They have also
been shown at science centres, including the Ontario Science Centre, the
Boston Science Museum and the Los Angeles Museum of Science and
Industry. Cohen represented the US in the World Fair in Tsukuba, Japan,
in 1985. He has a permanent exhibit in Boston's Computer Museum and
has given invited papers on his work at major international conferences
on artificial intelligence, computer graphics and art technologies. His
work is widely cited and it is the subject of Pamela McCorduck's
*AARON's CODE: Meta-Art, Artificial Intelligence and the Work of Harold
Cohen*. The painting machine with which AARON coloured real drawings
was premiered at the Computer Museum in Boston in 1995.

Dave Everitt

Dave Everitt's work is concerned with order and disorder in mathematical
pattern and biological input into art. His early work at Nottingham Trent
University involved music, visual images, photography, collaborative
work and installation. From 1986 to 1996 his main creative focus became writing. Musically, he is active in both experimental work and
venue-based music and has performed with members of the Royal Phil-
harmonic. He has spent a considerable time in the commercial media
world acquiring project management and computing skills, and in 1991
became a director of Ecomedia, publishing the magazine *Environment
Now*. In 1992 he travelled to Japan with the CBI Environment Unit,
working on environmental management software funded by Digital and
Mitsui. In 1997 he began to synthesize creative activities with computer
experience in information systems, psychology, cultural issues, history
and mathematics. In 1998, he began use digital technology to handle this
task, devising the bioMatrix exhibition at the School of Art and Design
gallery in October 1999. His two ongoing collaborative projects are the
emergency art lab and cubeLife. He has been a member of several steering
groups and arts advisory panels.

Thomas Hewett

Tom Hewett is professor of psychology and of computer science at Drexel University where he teaches courses on cognitive psychology, the psychology of human–computer interaction, and problem solving and creativity. He has been a visiting professorial researcher at the University of Vienna, Austria, Tampere University, Finland, Twente University, The Netherlands, Loughborough University, UK, the University of the Aegean, Greece, and the Battelle Pacific Northwest National Laboratory, USA. He is a member of the Association for Computing Machinery's Special Interest Group on Computer Human Interaction (SIGCHI). He is also a member of the Society for Applied Research in Cognition, the Human Factors and Ergonomics Society and the IEEE Computer Society. Hewett regularly offers a professional development tutorial on cognitive aspects of interactive computing system design to interface designers. He has made a number of invited conference presentations, is a published courseware author and has worked on the development of several interactive computing projects. He chaired the ACM SIGCHI Curriculum Development Group and was one of the general co-chairs for the CHI '94 conference held in Boston, USA. Recent research has focused on identifying areas in which computers can facilitate creative knowledge work, scientific problem solving environments and networked engineering design.

Beverley Hood

Beverley Hood was born in Darlington, England in 1970. She studied at Sheffield City Polytechnic, England, the Nova Scotia College of Art, Halifax, Canada and Duncan of Jordanstone College of Art, Dundee, Scotland where she was awarded an honours degree in Fine Art – Sculpture. She returned to Dundee in 1995, obtaining a post graduate diploma in electronic imaging. Hood is an artist working with a wide range of media, including digital technologies. Her practice focuses on hybrid approaches, such as combining traditional and non-traditional subject and media. Her work is diverse and has taken the form of interactive installation, web site, performance, multimedia, print, sculpture and 3D computer animation. In the year 2000, Hood was the John Florent Stone Fellow in the School of Drawing and Painting, at Edinburgh College of Art. She has developed projects with a wide range of organisations including VRC at Dundee Contemporary Arts, New Media Scotland, New Moves International, Akiyoshidai International Art Village, Japan and c3, Budapest, Hungary. Recently her work has been shown in the UK, Europe, North America, Japan and online, exhibitions include; Blue Skies, Stills Gallery, Edinburgh, Sum of Parts, Fruitmarket Gallery, Edinburgh, Infinitude, Gallery of Modern Art, Glasgow and Sukima Project, command N cube, Tokyo. She lives and works in Edinburgh, Scotland.

Jean-Pierre Husquinet

Jean-Pierre Husquinet was born in Ougrée, Belgium and studied art at the
Royal Academy for Arts in Liège between 1973 and 1979. He is a
painter, a musician, a sculptor, a printer and an editor. In 1979, he began
to specialize in silk screen-printing and in 1982 began to work in a geometric way. He is co-founder and co-editor of the magazine *Mesures Art
International*. His first works using rope as a material date from 1993
with an installation in the woods of Horion-Hozémont in Belgium. In
1995, he began teaching at the art school of Valenciennes in France. He
exhibits regularly, mainly making installations in different sites, natural
and industrial, throughout Europe, and in Korea, Russia, Estonia, Senegal,
where he also takes part in musical performances. In 1998, he realized his
first audio CD with four musicians and is preparing another one which
includes musical and visual correspondence work. He participated in the
making of two books with the poets Julien Blaine and Dominique
Sampiero and created many portfolios with various artists. He is now
working on a new kind of catalogue which is concerned with a subject
between anthropology and modernity.

Fré Ilgen

Fré Ilgen is an artist and theorist who exhibits regularly and widely in
Europe, USA and Asia. He was born in 1956 in the Netherlands and currently lives and works in the countryside near Engwierum in the north of
that country. He has a masters degree and worked previously for some
years at the European Design Centre, Eindhoven. He was the founder of
the PRO Foundation from which he organized four international conferences, seven international symposia and many international exhibitions.
His aim is to stimulate an international, multi-disciplinary dialogue on the
thme of art and society. Recently he has become interested in the relationship between art, philosophy and science and is frequently invited as
guest speaker and guest curator on this subject: for example, a Budapest
exhibition for UNESCO, international conferences in Japan and Europe
and a panel-discussion in New York. He also has received public and corporate commissions in Europe, USA and Asia. In 2001 a major book on
his artistic development of the last 20 years was published by the Foundation for New Arts in the Netherlands He is represented by Art Front Gallery, Tokyo, Japan; Gallery Artline, Amsterdam, NL; Maxwell Davidson
Gallery, New York, USA; Gallery Hüsstege, Den Bosch, NL; Nexus Fine
Art, The Hague, NL; Park Ryu Sook Gallery, Seoul, Korea; Theo Waddington Fine Art, London, UK; Waddington and Tribby Fine Art, Boca
Raton and Palm Beach, FL, USA.

Michael Kidner

Michael Kidner was born in 1917 in the UK. He received an honours degree in history and anthropology at Cambridge University in 1939 and from 1940 to 1946 served in the Canadian Army. He studied art in London and Paris between 1947 and 1953. In 1957, his work was included in Metavisual, Tachiste and Abstract Art in England, the first post-war exhibition of British abstract art. From 1957, he began his search for the objective use of colour leading to stripe and wave paintings emphasizing colour interaction. From 1966, he began to use colour as a code in conjunction with shape and his Columns work reflected the relationship between two and three dimensions. In the 1970s and 1980s, he explored wavy grid lines in which the area in between the lines become the structural elements of a space expressing infinity and the use of elastic cloth and fiberglass rods express spatial tension where the rods define the contour. From 1996 until the present day his imagery incorporates pentagon shapes and tulle material where the purpose is to undermine the gestalt. Kidner has had a number of one-person exhibitions and group exhibitions including the Museum of Modern Art, New York and the Tate Gallery, London.

Colin Machin

Having graduated from Hatfield Polytechnic in 1971 with a first class honours degree in computer science, Colin Machin went on to study for a PhD in computer science. His work investigated the relationship between the design of computer hardware and that of the operating system, culminating in the design and implementation of a novel variable microcode computer system and accompanying operating system. He was awarded a PhD in 1976. From 1974 to 1976, Machin remained at Hatfield Polytechnic as a lecturer before moving to Loughborough University, where he took up a post as lecturer in the Department of Computer Studies (now Computer Science), an appointment held to the present. A sometime member of the British Computer Society's Computer Art Special Interest Group, his contribution to the current debate stems from his expertise in real-time, microprocessor-based control systems. This is just the kind of technology that is required to power digital artworks. One of Machin's particular interests outside work is photography. Rather than simply taking photographs for posterity, he participates in the activities of a local photographic society and enters local, regional and national photographic competitions and exhibitions. A relatively new venture in this area of activity is into the realms of digital imaging – another application of computers to art.

Manfred Mohr

Manfred Mohr was born on 8 June, 1938 in Pforzheim, Germany. He worked in Paris from 1963 to 1983 and has lived and worked in New York since 1981. In 1960, he was making Action paintings and in 1961 received the school prize for art of the city of Pforzheim. In 1962, he began the exclusive use of black and white as a means of visual and aesthetic expression. In 1965 he studied lithography at the Ecole des Beaux Arts, Paris and his geometric experiments led to hard edge painting. In 1968, his first one-man exhibition took place at the Daniel Templon Gallery, Paris. In 1972, sequential computer drawings were introduced and he began to work on fixed structures. He received awards at the World Print Competition, 1973, San Francisco, and the 10th Biennial in Ljubljana. In 1977 he began to work with the 4D hypercube and graph-theory and in 1987 renewed the work on the 4D hypercube and extended the work to the 5D and 6D hypercube rotation and their projection as generators of signs. In 1990 he received the Golden Nica at Prix Ars Electronica in Linz and the Camille Graeser Prize in Zürich. In 1994, the first comprehensive monograph on Mohr was published by Waser-Verlag, Zürich and in 1997 he was elected a member of the group, American Abstract Artists. In 1998, he started to use colour, after using black and white for more than three decades to show the complexity of the work through differentiation.

Marlena Novak

Marlena Novak divides her time between her Amsterdam and Chicago studios creating work for exhibits in Europe and the United States. Her most recent digital video animation, Dancing Cranes, was premiered in England in 2001. The Mary and Leigh Block Museum (US) premiered the multimedia performance, Thresholds, consisting of Novak's computer-generated video installation, with live components of music and text. In addition, she has worked with the encaustic technique since the late 1970s. Her encaustic work is the subject of the documentary film, Marlena Novak: Surfaces in Transition. Since 1986, Novak has taught a variety of studio art and theory courses at DePaul University, North Western University, the University of New Mexico, and the Amsterdam's Instituut voor Schilderkunst. Her work has an international audience and is represented by collections and galleries throughout Europe and the United States, including exhibits in Berlin, Cologne, Stuttgart, Amsterdam, Kobe, New York and Atlanta. For more information: www.royboydgallery.com. See also: Surfaces in Transition, a documentary film featuring the encaustic technique of Marlena Novak, Ground Zero Productions, directed by Michael Hoffman, Hawaii.

Jack Ox

Jack Ox was born in Denver Colorado in 1948 and is currently living in New York City. She has been working on the visualization of music for over 20 years, including studies and research in musicology and phonetics. She lived in Cologne, Germany, whilst researching her 800 square ft visualization of Kurt Schwitters' Ursonate, a 41 ft sound poem in sonata form. The complete hand painted and collaged Ursonate will be shown in the Muzeum Sztuki, Lodz, Poland in 2002. Ox was in Vom Klang der Bilder, Staatsgalerie, Stuttgart in 1985, made an Ursonate presentation at the Centre Georges Pompidou during the 1994 Schwitters retrospective, and exhibited the 12 painting series of Anton Bruckner's Eighth Symphony in 1996 at the Neue Galerie der Stadt, Linz, Austria. Parts of her Ursonate installation have been exhibited at (among others) SoundCulture '96, San Francisco, California and at the Podewil, Berlin in 1998. The electronic version of the Ursonate can be seen at www.art.uiuc.edu@art/main.html and was created in collaboration with students and staff. Ox has been on the editorial board of *Leonardo* for over ten years, and is guest editor with Jacques Mandelbroijt of a special section, Synaesthesia and Intersense. Her project with David Britton, the 21st Century Color Organ, has received support from the National Centre for Supercomputing Applications, Silicon Graphics, Ars Electronica and Boston University.

Anthony Padgett

Anthony Padgett was born in Burnley in 1969. He is an artist with a degree in philosophy. He taught comparative religion in schools and then worked restoring monuments in the Holy Land with the Israelis, Palestinians and British. Padgett worked as a computer illustrator for Lancaster University's Archaeological Unit and as an intern with the International Council of Monuments and Sites. One of his 30 centimetre high sculptures was scanned and manufactured by computer lasers at two metres high. After a mystical experience he began to explore the link between mystical non-dualism (experiencing everything as One) and moral dualism (conflict between Good and Evil). His work breaks the boundary between art and spirituality, history and modernity. His art events include a millennium eve work, created at the Golden Gate, Jerusalem. His three solo millennium exhibitions were called Theism. These were held in galleries in Lancaster and London. Padgett exhibits his work in group shows and at computer manufacturing shows: for example, the Theism exhibition was held in the Quaker Gallery, London. www.theism.co.uk and www.millennium.co.uk

Michael Quantrill

Michael Quantrill is an artist whose work traverses scientific research and fine art. From 1987 to 1992, he worked as a programmer after which, he left the computing industry and began to formalize his interest in art practice. After studying art and design at Riley College, Hull in 1994, he studied fine art at Loughborough College of Art and Design in 1995. In 1997 he began an ongoing association with the Creativity and Cognition Research Studios at Loughborough University where he began to integrate his drawing practice with advanced computing technology. In 1998 he worked with Manu Uniyal on the ArtParty98 project. This involved a collaborative drawing tool that allowed a number of individuals from international locations to draw on a virtual whiteboard simultaneously. In 2000 he received funding under the Year of the Artist scheme to continue his work. Also in 2000 he formed the Emergency Art Lab with Dave Everitt, culminating in a commission to present work at the Wired and Dangerous Conference in Leicester, UK. In 2001, the Emergency Art Lab was commissioned to perform Club Confessional in the UK and Holland. Quantrill has written a number of papers and presented his work and ideas at various international conferences. He is currently studying for a PhD in computer science at Loughborough University, UK.

Juliet Robson

Juliet Robson is an artist who uses installation, live art, film and video to explore and deconstruct the idea of the 'norm', how the boundaries of what is perceived as the norm are fluid within varying contexts. She is also questioning her own assumptions often through dialogue with her audiences. Recently, she has been commissioned to create a permanent public artwork for the Arboretum, Nottingham, for the Year of the Artist. Robson has worked as a disability consultant for arts venues, organizations and events since 1996. She is an advisor to East Midlands Regional Arts Board having previously been a director. She is co-curator of VITAL SIGNS, a season of contemporary art in major venues across Nottingham profiling new commissions by international artists. Recent conferences include: Access Denied, Saddler Wells, London and Wired and Dangerous at The Richard Attenborough Centre, Leicester. Both were part of the Eastern Touring Agencies series of Get Wired conferences. She also participated in the Women's International ICT Conference, Kuala Lumpur, Malaysia. Robson graduated from Nottingham Trent University with a contemporary arts degree in 1994.

Esther Rolinson

Esther Rolinson has been based in the south east region of England since 1993. She studied for her degree in visual and performing arts at Brighton University, UK and since that time has worked solely as a visual artist working with three-dimensional design, gallery installations, digital imaging and architectural lighting. Presently, she is exploring the architectural applications of three-dimensional structures, light designs and digital technologies. In 1999, she completed a major permanent work, Light Decks for the Aquarium Terraces, Brighton, England. As part of Artsway's national touring exhibition Get Real, Rolinson is exhibiting work which investigates the feasibility of Folly, a digital sculpture. Esther has recently premiered a second collaboration with choreographer Carol Brown, Machine 4 Living at the Brighton Corn Exchange. She has also been awarded a major new public art commission, Stream – Hastings Lighting Project and a Royal Society of the Arts award to collaborate with Freemont Landscape Architects on the landscaping of the town centre of Redhill in England. For more information see Get Real: www.artsway.demon.co.uk/forth.html and the Millennium Seafront Lighting Project: www.hastings.gov.uk/hbc/prwk061299.htm

André Schappo

André Schappo is an IT systems manager who has engaged in diverse aspects of technology and human support functions. His working life started at the age of 16 as a farm worker followed by numerous jobs, including agricultural mechanic and barman. His first experience of computing was attending a course on Cobol programming as a mature student. This was followed by a Higher National Diploma and then a Degree Course at Leicester Polytechnic (now De Montfort University). Since then he has been involved in research in various areas, including, graphics languages, image processing, colour perception and management and computer supported co-operative work. In 1985, he joined Loughborough University as a member of the computer science technical team. Later, he took on a dual role in the support services for the department and the computing services function. He had responsibility for Apple Macintosh systems across the campus. This enabled him to extend an already strong network of contacts throughout the university which proved to be very important when he joined the COSTART project in 1998 as a technology coordinator. He fervently believes in the superiority of the Macintosh platform for both end users and systems people. He has found that most artists he has met also prefer the Macintosh and so, apart from his interest in art, it is also a common ground between him and the artists.

Stelarc

Stelarc is an Australian artist who has performed extensively in Japan, Europe and the USA, including new music, dance festivals and experimental theatre. He has made presentations and performances and participated in exhibitions in Australia, the UK, Italy, Austria, Germany, the Netherlands, Switzerland, the Czech Republic and Japan. He was a keynote speaker at Creativity and Cognition 1996 and CHI2002. He has used medical imaging, prosthetics, robotics, virtual reality systems and the Internet to explore and extend the parameters of the body. He is known for the internal filming of his body, the 27 suspension events using insertions into the skin, and constructing an electronic sculpture inserted inside the stomach cavity. In 1995 he received a three-year Fellowship from the Visual Arts/ Craft Board, The Australia Council. In 1997 he was appointed honorary professor of art and robotics at Carnegie Mellon University. As artist-in-residence for Hamburg City in 1998 he completed his Exoskeleton Walking Machine project. In 2000 he was awarded an honorary degree in law by Monash University, Victoria. He is now principal research fellow in the Performance Arts Digital Research Unit at Nottingham Trent University in the UK. His art is represented by the Sherman Galleries in Sydney. His work may be seen at: http://www.stelarc.va.com.au

Joan Truckenbrod

Joan Truckenbrod has exhibited her artwork internationally, including the IBM Gallery in New York City, the Smithsonian Institution in Washington DC, Museu de Arte Moderna in Rio de Janeiro, Musee d'Art Modern de la ville de Paris. Her work has been shown in one person exhibits in Chicago, Berlin, and London. In 2000 and 2001 she had one person exhibition in Paris and Wiesbaden, Germany. Collections such as Parade Publications in New York and ISA Holding in London include her work. Ms. Truckenbrod is a professor in the Art and Technology Department at the School of the Art Institute of Chicago. Her artwork is represented by FLATFILE Gallery in Chicago, Galerie de Gegenwart in Wiesbaden, Germany, Colville Place Gallery in London, and the Williams Gallery in Princeton, New Jersey. She has received a Scandinavian American Foundation Fellowship and a Fulbright Fellowship, research scholar's award. Her work has been featured recently in an article, Instantanés sur l'art électronique à Chicago, Computer Art@Chicago in artpress #246, May 1999, as well as in Computers in the Visual Arts (1998), Art in the Electronic Age (1993), Photographic Possibilities (1991), and Digital Visions (1987). Truckenbrod published her book *Creative Computer Imaging* in 1988.

Manumaya Uniyal

Manumaya Uniyal is a doctoral student in the department of computer science at Loughborough University. His areas of study involve economics, computer graphics, computer animation and virtual reality. In 1996 he completed his Masters degree in computer visualization and animation at Bournemouth University, UK. From 1996 to 1997 he worked at the National Institute of Design (NID), Ahemdabad, Gujarat in India. At NID he was involved in planning and setting up a computer animation laboratory. In 1997, he received a post graduate scholarship and joined the LUTCHI Research Centre, Loughborough University where he worked on a number of projects covering a wide range of areas. In 1998 with Michael Quantrill, he developed the ArtParty98 project. The project involved a collaborative drawing tool that allowed a number of individuals from international locations to draw on a virtual whiteboard simultaneously. The live artworks were project on a wall in the nightclub of Loughborough university student's union. He also worked on the Gallery of Future project at Loughborough University. During his research, he has conducted workshops and projects in the UK, India and Sweden and has written papers examining the application of virtual reality in the areas of law, health and tourism.

Roman Verostko

Roman Verostko, Professor Emeritus at Minneapolis College of Art and Design, trained as a painter and art historian and exhibited his first use of electronics in 1967, the Psalms in Sound and Image. With the advent of the personal computer, he gradually developed a personal expert system that includes his own software driving tech pens and paint brushes mounted on pen plotters. Recipient of the Golden Plotter First Prize (1994, Gladbeck, Germany) and an Ars Electronica honourable mention (1993), his work has been shown in art and technology exhibitions on four continents including Genetic Art – Artificial Life in Linz, 1993 and the ARTEC '95 Biennial in Nagoya, Japan. A past board member of the Inter-Society for Electronic Art (ISEA) and Programme Director for the 4th International Symposium on Electronic Art, Verostko has published articles and lectured internationally on the subject of Art and Algorithm. Recent works include an illuminated binary version of a universal Turing machine and a pen-plotted mural spanning 40 ft in the Frey Science and Engineering Centre at the University of St Thomas, St Paul, Minneapolis. Examples of his work may be seen at www. verostko.com.

Ray Ward

Ray Ward studied fine art at Trent Polytechnic where his work included painting, performance, bookwork and video. He has continued to use all of these media in his subsequent career as an artist, exhibiting regularly over the past 16 years. His current touring exhibition, The King Who Played Violin, (with Sates.org), shows how the use of different media influences his working process and vice versa. It is a show inspired by the words and thoughts of others including professional writers and the general public, which is realized through drawing and digital video. It is important to Ward that his art is about something more than technique or aesthetics and for this reason he would not claim to practice art but to do it. He leaves the issue of judging quality to the audience because for him the idea of such a thing gets in the way and it is something he cannot determine on the behalf of others. He feels as if he could draw all day and do nothing else but questions what this would say about him as an artist. He believes that you have to do different things and go different places to realise that it is all very much the same.

George Whale

George Whale is an artist and software engineer with special interests in drawing, print and computer-mediated creative collaboration. He obtained an honours degree in fine art from Portsmouth Polytechnic in 1983 and a Masters degree in computing in design from Middlesex Polytechnic in 1989. Currently a research associate at Loughborough University School of Art and Design, he has previously worked as a community artist, as a commercial designer and printer and as a graphics software developer. One of the original team members of the London Institute research project, The Integration of Computers, Print Technology and Printmaking (1994-1998), he has been involved in a number of digital collaborations, has exhibited prints internationally and is co-author of *Digital Printmaking* (A & C Black, London). His current research is directed towards modelling some of the cognitive processes underlying observational drawing activity. To the extent that this approach enables drawing strategies to be made explicit and their pictorial consequences to be understood, he believes that this research will have specific relevance to the future teaching and learning of observational drawing. For further information: www.lboro.ac.uk/departments/ac/ad/htmlpages/staff/gwhale.html

Bibliography

1. Ascott, R.: (ed) Reframing Consciousness, Intellect Books, Exeter (1999)
2. Benthall, J.: Science and Technology in Art Today, Thames and Hudson, London (1972)
3. Biederman, C.: Art as the Evolution of Visual Knowledge. Red Wing, Minnesota (1948)
4. Boden, M.A.: The Creative Mind: Myths and Mechanisms. Weidenfeld and Nicolson, London (1990)
5. Candy, L. and Edmonds, E. A.: (eds) Proceedings 3rd International Symposium Creativity and Cognition, ACM Press: New York (1999)
6. Ede, S: (ed) Strange and Charmed: Science and the Contemporary Visual Arts. Calousle Gulbenkian Foundation, London (2000)
7. Goodman, C.: Digital Visions: Computers and Art, Harry A. Abrams, Inc., New York (1987)
8. Harris, C.: (ed) Art and Innovation: The Xerox PARC Artist-in-Residence Program, MIT Press: Cambridge, MA (1999)
9. Holtzman, Steven, H.: Digital Mantras: The Languages of Abstract and Virtual Worlds, MIT Press, Cambridge, MA and London (1994)
10. Druckney, T. and Ars Electronica editors: Ars Electronica: Facing the Future, MIT Press, Cambridge, MA (1999)
11. Maeda, J. Maeda and Media. Thames and Hudson, London (2000)
12. Malina, F.J.: (ed) Visual Art, Mathematics and Computers: Selections from the Journal Leonardo. Pergamin Press, Oxford (1979)
13. Moser, M.A. and MacLeod, D.: (eds) Immersed in Technology: Art and Virtual Environments, The MIT Press, Cambridge MA and London (1996)
14. Mulder, A. and Post, M.: Book for the Electronic Arts, de Balie Amsterdam and V2 Rotterdam (2000)
15. New Ideas in Science and Art: Project on New Technologies: Cultural Cooperation and Communication, published by Council of Europe (1997)
16. Noll, A.M: The Beginnings of Computer Art in the United States: A Memoir, Leonardo, 27 (1) (1994) 39-44
17. Pontus Hultén, K.G.: The Machine, as Seen at the End of the Mechanical Age. The Museum of Modern Art, New York (1968)
18. Popper, F.: Electra. Musée d'Art Moderne de la Ville de Paris. Paris (1983)
19. Railing, P.: From Science to Systems of Art. Artists' Bookworks. Forest Row, East Sussex, England (1989)

20. Reichardt, J.: (ed) Cybernetic serendipity: the computer and the arts. Studio International. London (1968)

21. Reichardt, J.: The Computer in Art. Studio Vista. London (1971)

22. Reichardt, J.: Robots, Fact, Fiction and Prediction, Thames and Hudson Ltd, London (1978)

23. Rickey, G.: Constructivism: Origins and Evolution, George Braziller, New York (1967)

24. Rush, M.: New Media in Late 20th Century Art, Thames and Hudson, London (1999)

25. Scholder, A. (ed) with Crandall, J Interaction: Artistic Practice in the Network Eyebeam Atelier, published by D.A.P Distributed Art Publishers, New York (2001)

26. Schwarz, H-P.: Media-Art-History: Media Museum, ZKM Centre for Art and Media Karlsruhe, Prestel, Munch and New York (1997)

27. Sommerer, C. and Mignonneau, L (eds).: Art @ Science. Springer-Verlag, Wien and New York (1998)

Index

Colour Plates

Two Figures, 1999 Painting by AARON © Harold Cohen

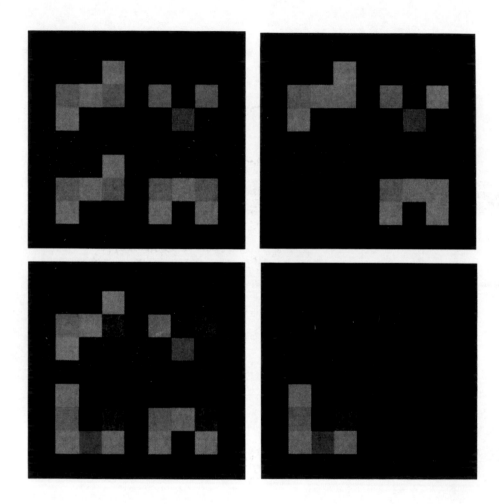

Sydney, 1995, stills from video construct © Ernest Edmonds

P-707/F, 2001 endura chrome/canvas/wood/vinyl elastomer © Manfred Mohr

EXOSKELETON, Cyborg Frictions, Dampfzentrale-Bern 1999 © stelarc. Photographer: Dominik Landwehr, Robot Contruction and Programming: F18, Hamburg. Exoskelton was funded by Kampnagel, Hamburg and SMC Pneumatics, Germany.

Contrapuntal, grasping blasts of light that warp the plane of experience, 1999, Roland Print on Capri Paper. 56"H × 40"W © Joan Truckenbrod

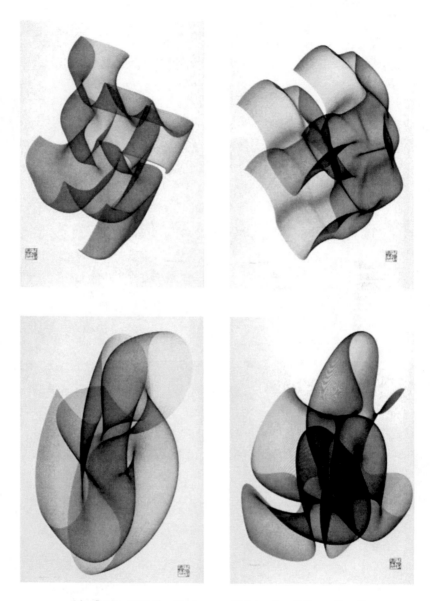

Cyberflowers, 2000, Algorithmic pen and ink drawings © Roman Verostko

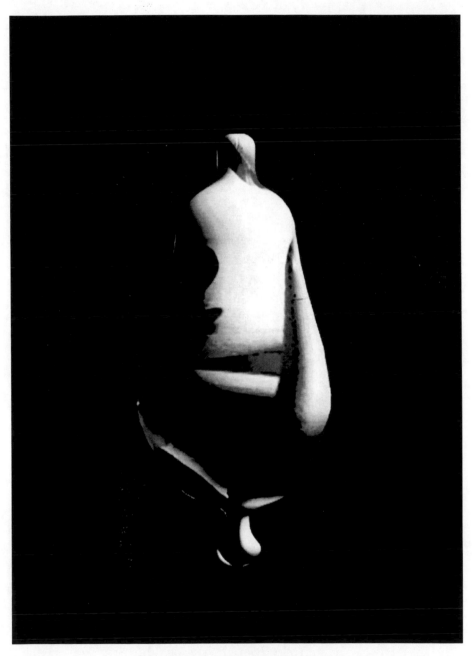

asex, 1999 3D Computer Model © Beverley Hood

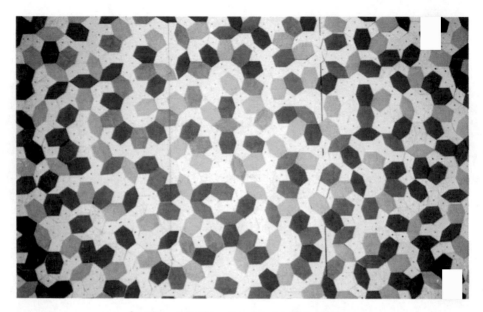

Dust Storm 1, 2000, acrylic on board © Michael Kidner

Windows to the Micro World, 2000, acrylic on canvas © Bettina Brendel

Digital Garden, 1998, Under Construction Exhibition, Gallery of the Future, Loughborough University © Esther Rolinson

Still from Stone Maiden, 2000 © Joan Ashworth

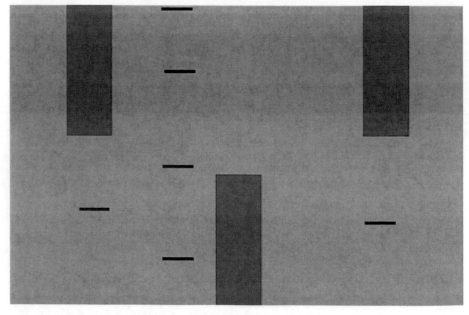

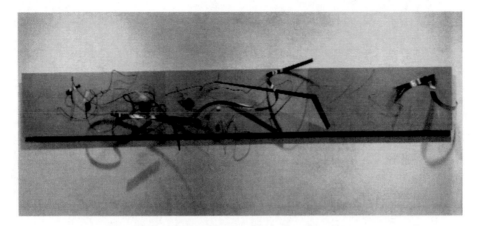

The Lemon Song, 2000 augmented relief MDF/wood/wire/stainless steel/acrylic paint 75 × 377 × 44 cm
© Fré Ilgen

Hey Joe, Virtual Painting 1997 © Fré Ilgen

CubeLife, 2000 screen shot © Dave Everitt

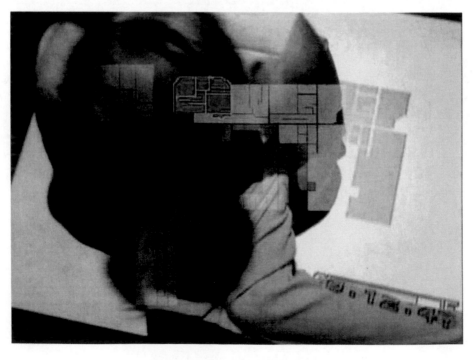

Norman Installation, 1999 © Juilet Robson

Rope Works, 1996, computer model © Jean-Pierre Husquinet

Roadway, 2001, digital video © Ray Ward

Visualization of "Im Januar am Nil" composed by Clarence Barlow, 1984 and realized in the Color Organ, 2001
© Jack Ox and David Britton

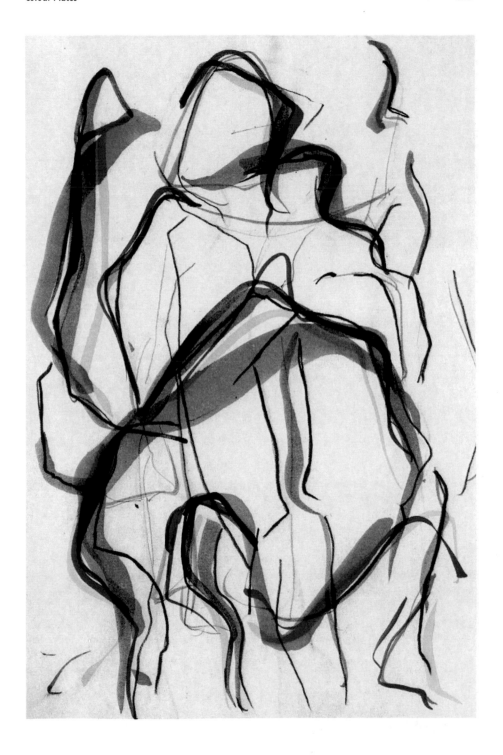

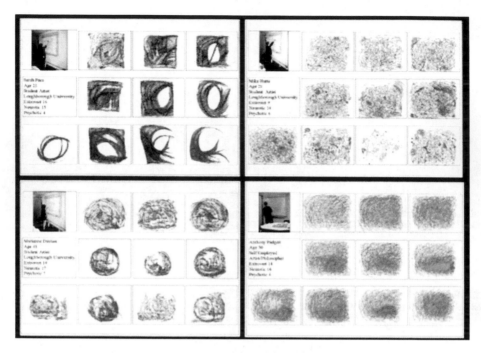

Four Softboard Drawing Experiments, 2000

Theism Sensor Conclusion, 2000 © Anthony Padgett